Adam Ferguson's Later Writings

Edinburgh Studies in Scottish Philosophy

Series Editor: James A. Harris, University of St Andrews

Scottish philosophy through the ages

This series covers the full range of Scottish philosophy over five centuries – from the medieval period through the Reformation and Enlightenment periods, to the nineteenth and early twentieth centuries.

The series publishes innovative studies on major figures and themes. It also aims to stimulate new work in less intensively studied areas, by a new generation of philosophers and intellectual historians. The books combine historical sensitivity and philosophical substance which serve to cast new light on the rich intellectual inheritance of Scottish philosophy.

Editorial Advisory Board
Angela Coventry, University of Portland, Oregon
Fonna Forman, University of California, San Diego
Alison McIntyre, Wellesley College
Alexander Broadie, University of Glasgow
Remy Debes, University of Memphis
John Haldane, University of St Andrews and Baylor University, Texas

Books available
Adam Smith and Rousseau: Ethics, Politics, Economics, edited by Maria Pia Paganelli, Dennis C. Rasmussen and Craig Smith
Thomas Reid and the Problem of Secondary Qualities, Christopher A. Shrock
Hume's Sceptical Enlightenment, Ryu Susato
Imagination in Hume's Philosophy: The Canvas of the Mind, Timothy M. Costelloe
Essays on Hume, Smith and the Scottish Enlightenment, Christopher J. Berry
Adam Ferguson and the Idea of Civil Society: Moral Science in the Scottish Enlightenment, Craig Smith
Hume's Scepticism: Pyrrhonian and Academic, Peter S. Fosl
Scottish Philosophy after the Enlightenment, Gordon Graham
Adam Ferguson's Later Writings: New Letters and an Essay on the French Revolution, edited by Ian Stewart and Max Skjönsberg

Books forthcoming
Eighteenth-Century Scottish Aesthetics: Not Just a Matter of Taste, Rachel Zuckert
Thomas Reid and the Defence of Duty, James Foster

edinburghuniversitypress.com/series/essp

Adam Ferguson's Later Writings

New Letters and an Essay on the French Revolution

Edited by Ian Stewart and Max Skjönsberg

Edinburgh University Press is one of the leading university presses in the UK.
We publish academic books and journals in our selected subject areas across the
humanities and social sciences, combining cutting-edge scholarship with high
editorial and production values to produce academic works of lasting importance.
For more information visit our website: edinburghuniversitypress.com

© editorial matter and organisation Ian Stewart and Max Skjönsberg, 2023,2025
© the text Edinburgh University Press, 2023,2025

Edinburgh University Press Ltd
13 Infirmary Street
Edinburgh EH1 1LT

First published in hardback by Edinburgh University Press 2023

Typeset in 11/13 Adobe Sabon by
IDSUK (DataConnection) Ltd

A CIP record for this book is available from the British Library

ISBN 978 1 4744 8021 5 (hardback)
ISBN 978 1 4744 8022 2 (paperback)
ISBN 978 1 4744 8024 6 (webready PDF)
ISBN 978 1 4744 8023 9 (epub)

The right of Ian Stewart and Max Skjönsberg to be identified as editors of this
work has been asserted in accordance with the Copyright, Designs and Patents
Act 1988 and the Copyright and Related Rights Regulations 2003 (SI No. 2498).

Contents

Preface and Acknowledgements	vii
Series Editor's Introduction	ix
Editorial Conventions	x

Part I: New Letters

Editorial Introduction	3
New Letters of Adam Ferguson	66

Part II: Essays

'Copy Dr Ferguson's opinions / Public affairs / <u>no Date French Revolution</u>'	133
Remarks on a Pamphlet Lately Published by Dr. Price, Intitled, Observations on the Nature of Civil Liberty, the Principles of Government, and the Justice and Policy of the War with America, &c. (1776)	137
Minutes of the Life and Character of Joseph Black, M.D. (1801)	173
Biographical Sketch: Or, Memoir of Lieutenant-Colonel Patrick Ferguson (1817)	190

Part III: Appendices

Appendix A: Further Correspondence in MSS EUR F/291/97	213
Appendix B: The Correspondence of Adam Ferguson and Sir John Macpherson	227

Appendix C: Further Miscellaneous Anecdotes about
Ferguson from Hugh Cleghorn   231

Bibliography   233
Index   243

Preface and Acknowledgements

This volume contains thirty-six previously unpublished letters and one new essay on the French Revolution written by Adam Ferguson. Penned during the last decades of his life, they were all addressed to his close friend Sir John Macpherson. We have also included several essays by Ferguson, some hitherto unavailable in a modern edition, as well as some supplementary material that will help to shed light on Ferguson's biography.

The book has been a joint project of ours for several years, and has inevitably been delayed by the COVID-19 pandemic. Throughout this time the staff of the Asian and African Studies Reading Room at the British Library have been unfailingly helpful. In particular, the archivist John O'Brien is due special thanks for helping us with the Macpherson papers. He organised, paginated, and made available for examination dozens of folders – easily several hundred letters and other documents – which had mostly not been consulted since their deposit two decades ago. John also put us in touch with Macpherson's descendant Mr N. W. Smith, who kindly granted his permission for the publication of this material.

Several people recognised the significance of the material contained here immediately and made the path to publication very easy. Chief among these are our initial editor at Edinburgh University Press, Carol Macdonald, and Professor James Harris at the University of St Andrews. The team at EUP have been helpful and prompt at every step, and Ersev Ersoy, Isobel Birks and Tom Dark have helped see this book through to publication.

We are also grateful to the four anonymous reviewers consulted by the Press at different stages, who all offered valuable criticism while enthusiastically recommending publication. Mark Philp gave useful advice on this kind of editorial work at a very early stage, while Joshua Ehrlich, Iain McDaniel, Jessica Patterson and

Mikko Tolonen have also offered helpful discussion on aspects of the project. Clare Loughlin helped us with material in Edinburgh at a late and crucial stage. Robin Mills read the entire manuscript and Johan Olsthoorn read parts of it. They both provided exceptional feedback and advice. There are undoubtedly others we have forgotten to mention equally deserving of thanks.

Most of this project was undertaken while Ian was a Leverhulme Early Career Fellow in the School of History at Queen Mary, University of London, and while Max was an AHRC Research Fellow on the 'Libraries, Reading Communities and Cultural Formation in the Eighteenth-Century Atlantic' project at the University of Liverpool, and a Leverhulme Early Career Research Fellow at the University of Cambridge. We owe thanks to all these institutions.

Finally, we are grateful to our friends and families, who have supported us in this project for several years. We first met as members of the same cohort of PhD students at the London School of Economics and Political Science, where we were both fortunate to benefit from the guidance of excellent supervisors, Heather Jones, John Hutchinson and Tim Hochstrasser. It seemed appropriate to dedicate this book to them.

Series Editor's Introduction

Philosophy has been taught and written in Scotland since the fifteenth century. The purpose of this series is to publish new scholarly work on any and every aspect of the history of Scottish philosophizing, from John Mair to John Macmurray. Scotland's most celebrated philosophical achievements remain those produced by Hume, Smith, Reid, and their contemporaries in the eighteenth century. It is, however, no longer possible to believe that the Scottish Enlightenment had no indigenous roots. Nor is it possible to believe that there was no significant philosophy produced in Scotland once the Enlightenment was over.

There is no single set of intellectual concerns distinctive of and unique to philosophy as it has been taught and written in Scotland. Historical study of Scottish philosophy must be, to a significant extent, study of the changing nature of philosophy itself. It should be open to the idea that the preoccupations and methods of philosophers today may not be those of philosophers in the past. It should also concern itself with philosophical connections and intellectual affinities between Scotland, England, Ireland, and the rest of Europe, and, where appropriate, between Scotland and America.

James Harris

Editorial Conventions

We have tried to reproduce the material as faithfully as possible. Although the papers in MSS EUR F291/97 are not ordered chronologically, we have chosen to organise the letters by date rather than as they appear seriatim in the folder. Dates and places are not standardised and instead appear as they do on the page. Occasionally, where full stops are omitted but a new sentence was clearly begun, we have indicated this in square brackets with '[.]', and then begun a new sentence with a silently changed capital letter. Pagination is indicated by '/'. Eighteenth-century spelling has been kept, as have inconsistencies in spelling and grammar. However, a small number of blatant typos and misprints have been corrected in the essays in the second part of this edition. [*sic*] has at times been inserted for clarity. All additions to the text have been marked by square brackets, including original pagination. In the essays contained in Part II, Ferguson's own footnotes are given in alphabetical numbering and editorial footnotes are in Arabic numerals.

To our PhD Supervisors:

Heather Jones and John Hutchinson
and
Tim Hochstrasser

Part I

New Letters

Editorial Introduction

1. Introduction

As scholarly interest in the Scottish Enlightenment continues to grow, so attention to the moral philosopher and historian Adam Ferguson (1723–1816) increases. Ferguson might be the greatest beneficiary of the cottage industrialisation of Scottish Enlightenment studies, for while his friends David Hume (1711–76) and Adam Smith (1723–90) have remained of perennial interest due to their pivotal contributions to history, philosophy and political economy, Ferguson's influence in Britain waned earlier, though his reputation remained more robust in America, Sweden and Germany, especially after Karl Marx's (1813–83) endorsement of his most famous work, *An Essay on the History of Civil Society* (1767), and the rise of sociology at the end of the nineteenth century.[1] Ferguson has been the subject of or featured prominently in many of the most important works on the Scottish Enlightenment over the last few decades,[2] and efforts have been made – above all by Vincenzo Merolle – to publish all of Ferguson's surviving manuscript materials.[3] The rediscovery of thirty-six new letters and a short essay on the French Revolution – all dating from the last several decades of his life and addressed to his close friend Sir John Macpherson (1745–1821) – in the British Library (MSS EUR F291/97) is therefore a significant development in Ferguson studies and in the historiography of the late Scottish Enlightenment.[4]

Adam Ferguson was born in Logierait – 'The Gateway to the Highlands' – on 20 June 1723, the youngest son of a Kirk minister. After attending Perth Grammar School, Ferguson studied first at St Andrews from 1738, and then from 1743 at the University of Edinburgh, where he fell in with a group now generally known as the 'Moderate literati'. Among the more famous members were William Robertson (1721–93), Hugh Blair (1718–1800), John Home (1722–1808) and Alexander Carlyle (1722–1805), who collectively went on to dominate civic and religious life in Edinburgh for the next half century.[5] Ferguson was the only prominent member of the literati who knew Gaelic, and preached in it during his nine years as an army chaplain to the 'Black Watch' Highland regiment from 1745 to 1754, during which time he served on the continent and in Ireland. After stints as a tutor and as Hume's successor as Keeper of the Advocates' Library for two years, Ferguson secured a chair in Natural Philosophy at the University of Edinburgh in 1759. In 1764 he transferred to the chair of Pneumatics and Moral Philosophy and then published his *Essay on the History of Civil Society* in 1767, the book for which he is now best remembered.

Ferguson occupied the moral philosophy chair until 1785, but his activities extended well beyond the academic. He tutored aristocratic students and toured Europe, wrote in defence of the North government's American policy in 1776, and then in 1778 sailed to America as the official secretary of the Carlisle Commission, which was sent to negotiate with George Washington (1732–99) and the Americans but failed. After his return to Edinburgh in 1779, Ferguson concentrated on his literary career and in 1783 published his three-volume *History of the Progress and Termination of the Roman Republic*. He published new editions of his *Institutes of Moral Philosophy* and wrote up his university lectures in the two-volume *Principles of Moral and Political Science, Being Chiefly a Retrospect of Lectures Delivered in the College of Edinburgh* (1792), before embarking on a trip to Italy in order to survey the ground on which the events of his Roman history took place. He published the second edition of this work in 1799, by which point he had retired to the country. In 1809 Ferguson moved to St Andrews where he died in 1816, having lived long enough to welcome the news of Napoleon's final defeat at Waterloo. He was buried in St Andrews Cathedral churchyard.[6]

As these well-known biographical details attest, while Ferguson might not have the popular name recognition of Hume or Smith – there is no Ferguson statue along the Royal Mile in Edinburgh – he lived one of the most interesting and active lives of the literati. He was, for example, the only one to cross the Atlantic, but the episode that best speaks to his adventurous character and liberal spirit is that, as war gripped the European continent in 1793, seventy-year-old Ferguson decided it was the opportune moment to undertake a European tour. He set off just as the Terror was taking hold in France, travelled through the war-torn Low Countries and Germany, down through Italy, and spent Christmas in Rome.⁷ There it turns out that Ferguson – assisted by an introduction arranged by John Macpherson – met the Pope, something that would have been unthinkable for many of his fellow ordained Presbyterian ministers in the Kirk.⁸ When he returned from the continent in summer 1794, Ferguson turned to analysing the French Revolution in his letters to Macpherson. He was the only member of the Scottish Enlightenment's golden generation to live through the entirety of the French Revolutionary and Napoleonic Wars, subjects which form the major topic of discussion in the letters and short manuscript essay printed in this book, which stretch from 1784 to 1811.⁹

2. The Significance of the New Letters and the Essays

The centrepiece of this volume is the thirty-six previously unpublished letters by Adam Ferguson to John Macpherson. He was Ferguson's most intimate correspondent, and their letters are perhaps the best source for Ferguson's thought after his published works; they are probably the best source for details of his life. Macpherson wrote to Ferguson's nephew, Robert 'Bob' Ferguson (?–1830), that he 'regularly preserved' his uncle's letters, which contained 'treasures of friendship, philosophy, and wisdom'.¹⁰ Vincenzo Merolle collected and published most of Ferguson's letters in 1995, but there were significant gaps where the Ferguson–Macpherson correspondence seemed to have dried up. In particular, the new letters here help to fill in the ten-year lacuna from 1780 to 1790 in the Merolle correspondence, which apart from a relatively short note sent in 1785 contains no letters from Ferguson to Macpherson.¹¹ We also add sixteen new letters from the Revolutionary and Napoleonic periods, including the (apparently) latest surviving letters Ferguson wrote to Macpherson, which trickled off as he aged and went blind in the 1800s.¹² Of considerable interest is a short manuscript essay on the French Revolution, which we suggest dates to 26 September 1797.¹³ We have also decided to include several of Ferguson's published essays hitherto unavailable in a modern edition, because they either pertain to revolution or were written during the period of the letters presented here. Finally, included in appendices are some accompanying reference documents, as well as anecdata about Ferguson preserved elsewhere in the Macpherson papers, and in the diary of William Erskine (1773–1852), who recorded some snippets related by Ferguson in his final years to Hugh Cleghorn (1752–1837), his neighbour at St Andrews, and the nephew of his one-time teacher at Edinburgh and friend William Cleghorn (1711–52).

The new letters are contained in Sir John Macpherson's large collection of papers at the British Library. They have been consulted by a few other scholars but have generally remained unknown to Ferguson specialists and scholars of the Scottish Enlightenment, having undergone an odyssey in the twentieth century.[14] In the course of researching and writing his abandoned work *The Invention of Scotland: Myth and History* (published posthumously in 2008), Hugh Trevor-Roper (1914–2003) tried to consult the Macpherson papers but was unable to do so. He wrote:

> Sir John Macpherson's papers were bequeathed by him to Hugh Macpherson . . . and they were still in the possession of his descendants in 1927, when they were lent to H. H. Dodwell for his publication *Warren Hastings' Letters to Sir John Macpherson* (London, 1927). Dodwell was director of the School of Oriental and African Studies in London.

His successor, Sir Cyril Philips (1912–2005), then took possession and 'evidently treats the papers as his private property'. He refused Trevor-Roper access to them.

> In 1981 Sir Cyril Philips, professor of Indian History, director of the School of Oriental and African Studies, vice chancellor of the University of London, was finally forced by mounting academic, family, and ultimately legal pressure, to disgorge what was left of the collection of Macpherson papers which he had guarded illegitimately, jealously, and incompetently for thirty-five years. For one more year the collection remained in purdah. Then, in 1982, four boxes of material, containing 218 items relating to Sir John Macpherson's career, by no means all that had been lent by the Macpherson family to Professor Dodwell in 1926, were passed to the India Office Library: their intended destination, following Dodwell's publication of the letters to Hastings. A long-running academic scandal, damaging to historical scholarship, had finally come to an end. Even so, access to the papers was severely restricted at first. The India Office Library collections were subsequently absorbed into the British Library, where the

Macpherson Collection (MSS EUR F291) is on permanent loan and now fully open to use by scholars.[15]

However, the collection remained restricted in the British Library's computer system – available only upon receiving permission from the archivist, who then had to organise and paginate every new folder of requested material. This probably explains why, despite the collection being technically available for consultation since 2002, scholars have gone through only a sliver of the papers – usually letters from major figures.[16] Most items seem to have remained untouched since their deposit. The Ferguson letters are no longer restricted, and the scholar who accesses them will find interesting discussions of subjects like domestic and international politics, the British Empire and the East India Company (EIC), and the French Revolution. In addition to an enlarged window into Ferguson's thoughts on these subjects, the letters also contain important specific findings that will help to deepen and even redraw our understanding of some key aspects of Ferguson's thought, as well as miscellanea of general interest to scholars of late-eighteenth-century Scotland and its Enlightenment.

The British Empire was omnipresent in the correspondence between Ferguson and Macpherson, but never itself the subject of direct discussion. Macpherson was a staunch supporter of empire, particularly for the financial security it could provide to Britain. Although Ferguson was wary of the dangers imperial overreach could pose to the state back home, he was mired in backdoor politicking in the EIC via Macpherson. Most of Ferguson's letters in the 1780s contained introductions for young Scots on the make in the East. It was common to seek preferment, however, and the only surviving letter from Adam Smith to Macpherson contains a letter of recommendation for William Burke (1728–98), arranged through Edmund Burke (1729–97) in 1787, shortly after the beginning of the Hastings trial.[17] Ferguson provided Macpherson with intellectual ballast for his idea that wealth transfer from India to Britain via private Company men was economically legitimate; in other words, it was not only acceptable but desirable for Company men to enrich themselves in India, perhaps nefariously, provided that their wealth stimulated Britain's economy.[18] As letter no. 6 shows, Ferguson was duly rewarded by Macpherson with a gift of £1100 – a large sum, equivalent to approximately £175,000 in 2020 – in 1786, £1000 of which was to be drawn upon the East

India Company.[19] Ferguson put the gift towards paying off the feu duties on his farm at Bankhead.

Yet, as is well known, Ferguson was wary both of empire and of the idea that commerce was a purely edifying force in international relations. Cryptic comments made by Ferguson on 1 and 7 October 1787 (letter nos 9 and 10), in which he expects the French to break their promises made in the form of the Eden-Rayneval commercial treaty between Britain and France, signals the beginning of a long-term exchange between Ferguson and Macpherson about international politics. Ferguson worried that the British had been lulled into a false sense of security by the treaty, and that the French would attack British imperial possessions around the world. The Eden Treaty was understood to have been based on Smithian principles of free trade, so it is possible that Ferguson saw himself as opposing Smith here. Unbeknownst to Ferguson, he was also opposing Macpherson, who had played an important early role in the origins of the treaty while acting governor general of Bengal in 1785–6;[20] as discussed below, Macpherson was strongly influenced by Smith's *An Inquiry into the Nature and Causes of the Wealth of Nations* (1776), a work Ferguson admired and used in his teaching. Yet Macpherson's correspondence with the other Moderates suggests that they were collectively drifting away from Smith over the decade due to political differences (see section 5 below). Irrefragable proof of Ferguson's break with aspects of what he understood as Smithian political economy is contained in letter no. 34, when he averred that 'Smith in pursuit of his general Principle of Free Trade would explode Universities as well as limitations of Commerce', but Ferguson disagreed on both counts. The state had to play a more active role if Britain was to survive as a modern state in the age of the French Revolutionary and Napoleonic Wars.

This criticism of Smith was voiced by Ferguson in 1801, after many of his predictions concerning the French Revolution had come true. The most significant contribution of the new sources in this volume is that they allow the most complete view of Ferguson's response to the Revolution now available.[21] As Anna Plassart has pointed out, it was long mistakenly assumed that Ferguson – likely because of his identification by J. G. A. Pocock as the most 'Machiavellian' of the literati, and interest in subjects associated with 'civic humanism', such as the militia – embraced the French Revolution, but it becomes absolutely clear in this collection of correspondence that even if he may have been ambivalent about it near the beginning, he became resolutely opposed to the Revolution not long afterward and remained so for the rest of his life.[22] As revealed more fully in the new sources, Ferguson identified the Revolution's moving force as the democratisation of the army and the spirit of ancient conquest newly unleashed, which was turned by the revolutionaries in Paris against neighbouring states so that the armies would not devour the civil government and subordinate it to a military government.[23] Incorporating the new letters with those in the Merolle collection reveals a 'negative' finding: there is little trace of the Revolution in Ferguson's letters between some short lines in 1790 and his letters to Macpherson in 1793. Partially this is because Macpherson was at this time on the move throughout the continent trailing Leopold II (1747–92), Holy Roman Emperor, and Ferguson himself noted that he did not know where to send his replies to the letters he received;[24] however, the lack of any surviving comments in 1791–2 is notable, and means that there is unlikely to be found evidence where Ferguson voiced outright support for the Revolution or its 'spirit'. This means that any interpretation holding that Ferguson was positively disposed toward the Revolution – as opposed to the effects it might have on French foreign policy – rests on extremely flimsy evidence.

When the French Revolution finally resurfaced in Ferguson's correspondence in 1793, it was not long until his first fully formulated account of the dangers of democracy and levelling, particularly in the army, in May 1794 (letter no. 24 below):

> to think there was such a ditch between those Infernals the French Democrats and this Country. Men innumerable not to be dismayed by defeats or urged by the Guilotine at their Backs to face any Ennemy in Front again & again after a death no less than after a Victory . . . For my part it is the most tremendous Ennemy that ever existed & not to be overcome till they go by the ears among themselves which they would soon do if they had no Other Ennemies. & to put them in this Situation is the difficulty: for their leaders know well how Ruinous it would be.

Until and *only if* there is more evidence discovered, it cannot be stated that Ferguson welcomed the Revolution, even in its early stages; almost all of his surviving commentary is negative.

The most significant of the new sources in relation to the French Revolution is the new essay, which contains Ferguson's most systematic analysis of the Revolution until his 'Of the

French Revolution with its Actual and Still Impending Consequences in Europe', Ferguson's last known extended analysis of the Revolution, dated by its editors to 1806–7.[25] The new essay, though short, is particularly interesting in that it elaborates in detail what Ferguson thought the Revolution's main dangers were and how they might be avoided. Ferguson feared that the 'levelling degradation of ranks, and violation of property' threatened 'the actual order of things in every state' of Europe, but he understood that this revolutionary ideology posed a new threat that could not be combatted with the traditional methods of war because it would only strengthen French cohesion and aggression.[26] Instead, he supported a concerted neutrality on the part of the European powers, so that the French army would turn in on the Revolution and the country would descend into civil war. To achieve this, Ferguson ventured the idea of a European convention or congress – along the lines of that proposed by Henri IV (1553–1610) – that would end hostilities and hammer out a settlement. Crucially, Ferguson proposed that such a congress might be maintained in the future and reduce war and jealousy of trade through negotiation and the removal of trade barriers. Ferguson then, very fleetingly, advocated a sort of 'European Union' (a term that Macpherson used directly). He did not return to what he acknowledged was a 'romantic' idea, but it is striking and perhaps speaks to the dire situation in which Britain found itself in 1797, seemingly isolated and facing invasion. Yet when the threat of invasion in 1797–8 subsided Ferguson returned to his position of agonistic patriotism.[27]

Beyond the major themes of empire and revolution that come out most clearly, the new letters contain a number of interesting new angles on Ferguson, the Moderate literati, and the late Scottish Enlightenment. As discussed below in section 5, relations among the Moderate literati remained warm for as long as they lived; the letters also reinforce that Smith, though close with and deeply admired by the Moderate literati, was nevertheless seen as somewhat apart politically and intellectually. He perhaps did not have the sense of fun that Ferguson, Carlyle and John Home seemed to possess in spades. However, none was as adventurous as Ferguson, and even though he had long been planning a trip to Italy, his departure in 1793 still seemed to surprise his contemporaries. Henry Cockburn (1779–1854) later recalled that 'one day in summer 1793' Ferguson set off in a strange sort of carriage, and with no companion except his servant James, to visit Italy for a new edition of his history. He was then about seventy-two, and had to pass through a good deal of war; but returned in about a year, younger than ever.[28]

Carlyle similarly wrote to Macpherson in February 1794 that Ferguson had 'Grown young again, and is out of our Reach, on the Grand Tour', joking that John Home 'has hardly forgiven Ferguson yet, for not telling him of his youthfull jaunt into Italy. Ferguson Durst not, for John would have surely fixed himself on him as a Companion, & that would never have Done.'[29]

We add four new letters from Ferguson over the course of this tour. Merolle gives a good summary of the trip, which Ferguson had been planning for at least decade, since the publication of his Roman history.[30] Though he had travelled widely by this point he had never been to Italy. He arrived at Ostend around 11 September (letter no. 21 below), then proceeded through Flanders into Germany, making stops (that we know of) at Frankfurt and Munich. His honorary membership of the Berlin Academy was apparently arranged along the way, as he was in touch with its secretary Johann Heinrich Samuel Formey (1711–97). From Munich Ferguson travelled down through the Tyrol to Venice, and then on to Rome. One cannot help but think of Gibbon on the steps of the Capitol, when Ferguson wrote to Macpherson from Rome that although he had not been able to meet all those to whom Macpherson gave him introductions, he could not 'be disappointed in the Object of my Journey so long as the Physical Face of the Country is open to me & the means of connecting it with its Antient State in my hands'.[31] Merolle points out that Ferguson almost certainly journeyed south to Naples at this point, and in letter no. 22 of 10 December 1793 Ferguson confirms that he intended to set out for Naples the next day. If his intentions in letter no. 20 are taken seriously, it is possible that Ferguson made it all the way to Sicily, but he spent Christmas in Rome. Ferguson made his way home via Florence (letter no. 23 below), where he was under the care of the first minister Marchese Manfredini (1743–1829), to whom Macpherson certainly arranged the introduction as he knew him well and had written a series of letters to him in 1792 that he then had published (see section 3 below). Ferguson was escorted around by Manfredini, introduced to the new Grand Duke of Tuscany Ferdinand III (1769–1824) as well as Pope Pius VI (1717–99). Letter no. 26 shows that once he was back in Scotland Ferguson sent a package to Pius (one of his published works?). He travelled back over the continent and landed in Dover on 6 May 1794, penning a letter (no. 24 below) that signals his increasing preoccupation with the dangers of the French Revolution.

Other smaller points of interest in the letters – some of which are discussed elsewhere in this introduction – include communication between Ferguson and the famous 'Orientalist' Sir William Jones (1746–94), through Macpherson (letter no. 4); some early mentions of the Scots poet Robert Burns (1759–96) (letter no. 6); and Ferguson's only references to the *Principles* in his known correspondence, on 6 February 1789 (letter no. 16) and 31 May (letter no. 19).

3. Sir John Macpherson

Almost certainly because the bulk of his papers remained inaccessible for so long, John Macpherson has not received the benefit of a full biographical study, which is a great shame considering he lived a remarkable life spanning Enlightenment Scotland, British India, and Revolutionary Europe. There is only one published secondary source – *Warren Hastings' Letters to Sir John Macpherson* (1927) – that discusses Macpherson in much detail, though there is a PhD thesis examining the early political careers of James and John Macpherson, which is useful for tracing the outline of John Macpherson's early life; however, it is now wildly outdated.[32] More recently, Joshua Ehrlich has published a short article reproducing letters between Macpherson and Sir William Jones that come from the same collection in the British Library as those in the present edition.[33] The entries in the *Oxford Dictionary of National Biography* and *History of Parliament* cobble some details together from published primary and secondary sources; however, by their nature, and their commitment to highlighting Macpherson's occasionally dubious morals, they fail to do justice to as multifaceted a man as he was. The short account here relies on Macpherson's personal papers as well as some of the material listed above.[34]

John Macpherson was born in Sleat on the Isle of Skye, probably in 1745. His family had 'followed the Macdonalds of Sleat and their fortunes' to Skye a few centuries earlier.[35] There were Jacobites in his extended family, but his father John Macpherson

(1713–65), who was a scholarly minister in the Kirk, supported the Hanoverians, though parts of his mother's (Janet Macleod, d. 1748) family, including his grandfather Donald 'The Old Trojan' Macleod (1692–1781), did not. Like many Highlanders and Islanders, Macpherson attended King's College Aberdeen where he matriculated in 1760 before moving to Edinburgh and studying at the Divinity School in 1765.[36] At this time Adam Ferguson had been hired to tutor the sons of Francis Greville (1719–73), Earl of Warwick: Charles Francis Greville (1749–1809) and Robert Fulke Greville (1751–1824). Ferguson in turn hired Macpherson as an assistant tutor – perhaps on the recommendation of Hugh Blair – and he moved into Ferguson's house. In his brief manuscript biography of Macpherson, Charles Greville wrote that during his idle hours in their Edinburgh years, Macpherson edited 'some Treatises on the Celtic Antiquities' written by his late father.[37] The controversy over Ossian was ongoing at this time and according to Greville it was Macpherson's knowledge of Celtic subjects which drew him into the circle of the Moderates:

> Professor Ferguson who admired & understood Celtic, & Dr Blair professor of Rhetoric & Belles Lettres a strong advocate for the Poems of Ossian, formed a lasting Friendship with [Macpherson], as did Dr Robertson & Many of the respectable Literary Men at Edin^r. in 1766.[38]

When he was offered the chance to go to Asia, these same men encouraged Macpherson 'for the sake of Information', because 'the History of [Robert] Orme [1728–1801] had pointed out the subject of India as interesting to ~~his~~ their Reflections as the Battle of Fingal.'[39] Macpherson apparently took a degree from Edinburgh in November 1768, but by this time any plans for a ministerial career were firmly behind him.

He was on the other side of the world when his father's book was published in 1768 – helped through the press by James Macpherson (1736–96), the 'translator' of the poems of *Ossian* – having in 1767 been invited by his uncle Alexander Macleod (?–1790), captain of the East Indiaman *Lord Mansfield*, to go with him on his next voyage to China. Macpherson never made it, instead disembarking in Madras, where he met Muhammad Ali Khan (1717–95), Nawab of Arcot and a British ally.[40] This was one of the settings of greatest corruption in eighteenth-century India, in which Europeans purchased the Nawab's considerable debts at extortionate rates of interest.[41] Essentially, the Nawab had become 'too big to fail' and he was allowed to continue *in situ* as long as payments to creditors, or promises for future revenues, were forthcoming. Macpherson, who had a lifelong talent for charming powerful men, quickly gained the Nawab's trust upon landing in Madras in August 1767 and participated on his behalf in the first Anglo-Mysore War – undertaken in part to service Nawabi debts. In late 1768 he returned to London with instructions to encourage the government, led by Lord Grafton (1735–1811) at the time, to intercede on the Nawab's behalf. He also enlisted James Macpherson in the case and together they led a press campaign in support of both the Grafton administration and the Nawab in 1769 and 1770. In gratitude for his service, Grafton helped John to a position as a 'Writer' for the EIC at Fort St George in Madras, for which he departed again in 1770.

Arriving in 1771, Macpherson entered the service of Governor Josias Dupré (1721–80). He held various positions during the 1770s, including paymaster of the army, but also continued to work with the Nawab. This and his restiveness (he desired a posting in Bengal), led the new Governor of Madras, George Pigot (1719–77), to dismiss him from the service for working against the Company. When he returned to London in July 1777, John joined James Macpherson in writing for Lord North's government and working informally on behalf of the Nawab and Warren Hastings (1732–1818), with whom Macpherson had become acquainted in Bengal in 1771–2.[42] In 1779 Macpherson entered the House of Commons for the borough of Cricklade, but after re-election in 1780 was accused, along with the electors of Cricklade, of corruption. His election was therefore declared void in 1782 but by this time he was back in India.

On his second major stint in India, Macpherson was stationed in Bengal, the heart of EIC government in Asia, where in 1781 he was appointed to the Supreme Council. At war against the Maratha Confederacy, the Mysore Kingdom and France, the Company was in dire straits. Its armies – European and Indian – had not been paid for months, and Macpherson feared particularly a revolt by sepoy troops. He drew up some financial measures, including issuing state-backed bonds to individuals in India and drawing bills on the Company in Europe, while Hastings was away suppressing a revolt at Benares. The situation eventually improved and to the end of his life Macpherson believed that in his role on the Council over this period he not only stabilised India but saved the British Empire in the wake of its American defeat. As he explained to Alexander Carlyle in 1783:

> I might have been a little too much of Ferguson's pupil . . . In such a situation with warm Ideas of the State of the Empire at Home, the prospect of losing America, and the accumulated load of our Debts to which there could be no relief but from India. I truly believed that on the success of our Administration depended the Purse, the Fate and the Fortune of the British Empire. If I was a Quixot in these opinions the Error was lucky I bit all my neighbours with them and hence the free Contribution & Public Credit that have borne us over the waves of the severest Storm or Monsoon that ever attacked the tenure of these mighty Colonies.[43]

The reference to Ferguson is an allusion to the potential dangers of overexposure to debt and how imperial overreach could threaten the metropole's security, but it is also an inside joke between his friends about Ferguson being cheap. The ideas here came to form the kernel of John Macpherson's intellectual system, discussed below.

On 1 February 1785, Warren Hastings officially handed over the reins of the governor generalship of Bengal to Macpherson, who during his tenure continued with the financial retrenchment that he had been advocating since 1781. It was during this period in India, when he was in positions of real power, that Macpherson began to apply the principles of politics and government that he had imbibed in his youth. As discussed in the following section, he wrote a heartfelt letter to Ferguson in January 1786 outlining how Ferguson's moral maxims had guided his life and led him to one of the most powerful positions in the empire.[44] In general, there is more research needed on this period of Macpherson's tenure in India, but there is reason to believe that it was not as disreputable (at least comparatively) as Cornwallis (1738–1805) – who superseded Macpherson in September 1786 – made it out to be.[45] He was given a peerage for his efforts – or to soften the blow of his supersession – but Macpherson remained angry with the Company, threatening to return to India of his own accord. Eventually he was bought off, apparently for a lump sum of £15,000.

Upon his return to Britain in 1787, Macpherson reinvented himself as a parliamentarian and political adviser. He cultivated a relationship with George, Prince of Wales (1762–1830), for whom he wrote a pamphlet during the Regency Crisis;[46] according to his friend Sir Nathaniel Wraxall (1751–1831), few were closer to the prince between 1788 and 1802.[47] The outbreak of the French Revolution fascinated Macpherson, who saw it as a testing ground for his ideas but also sensed an opportunity for advancement, and in December 1789 he set off for the Continent. He travelled around Europe for most of the next four years, reporting back to the prince – to whom he cast himself in the role of Mentor from *Telemachus* – and mostly following around the court of the new Holy Roman Emperor Leopold II.[48] Macpherson was introduced to Leopold in early 1790 by the former French finance minister, Étienne Loménie de Brienne (1727–94), who had related Macpherson's successful 'financial measures, adopted as governor-general, for sustaining the East India Company's credit in Bengal'. When Leopold became Holy Roman Emperor, 'Sir John accompanied or met him by his own desire wherever he moved; at Venice, Milan, Florence, and Vienna. Leopold confided in, and consulted him on points of the most important nature.'[49] Macpherson was also favourably received by Frederick William II (1744–97) of Prussia, and after the death of Leopold he sought to guide his son Archduke Charles Louis (1771–1847), the most successful Austrian general of the period. For example, in 1793 he wrote an essay to Charles and communicated it to him via the Genevan Jacques Mallet du Pan (1749–1800), who Macpherson came to know well in the 1790s. In fact, it was probably with the intellectual counter-revolutionary movement based in London that Macpherson had his greatest impact; he knew them all and occasionally wrote for the journals of Mallet du Pan and the Comte de Montlosier (1755–1838).

Macpherson returned to Britain in mid-1793 and resumed his correspondence with Ferguson and the other Moderates. From 1795 he made a more conscious effort to disseminate his 'intellectual system' (discussed below), and consulted Ferguson, Blair, and Home about his ideas. On 30 May 1796, Macpherson – with Ferguson's encouragement – was elected MP for Horsham.[50] The following year, he joined the 'Armed Neutrality' of 1797, led by the Scot Sir John Sinclair (1754–1835), which argued for the reconciliation of Pitt and Fox and the need to combat partisanship by forming a (short-lived) new faction; Macpherson wrote a pamphlet for the cause.[51] His talent for schmoozing came in handy again in 1801 when he acted as a mediator between the French plenipotentiary Louis Guillaume Otto (1754–1817) and other European diplomats in London and the Addington ministry, helping to organise the armistice of 1801 that was then formalised with the Treaty of Amiens in 1802. However, from this point Macpherson's influence seriously ebbed. He lost his parliamentary seat in 1802, lost favour with the Prince of Wales, possessed little clout in politics, and hounded governments and the EIC to enforce his claims on the Nawab of Arcot; eventually, a £1000 pension per annum convinced him to give up the fight in 1809. By this point, short of money and friends, he had retired to his farm at Ely near Tunbridge Wells where, apart from an attempt to join the fold again in 1814 as the Vienna Congress was anticipated, he was more subdued before his death in 1821.

4. Ferguson and Macpherson

Ferguson was revered as a teacher and cultivated a close relationship with several of his students. Like many of his academic contemporaries, Ferguson also occasionally worked as a personal tutor to aristocratic students, and travelled to the continent with them, but it was also common for richer students to attend the university and lodge with academics. At some point in 1765 Ferguson invited Macpherson to live with him and to oversee the education of the young Greville brothers, who had been placed under his care by their father the Earl of Warwick. Ferguson and Macpherson became close, especially after Macpherson's father passed away and Ferguson took on a paternal role while Macpherson was trying to decide which path to pursue in life. Apparently originally destined for the clergy, like his father, Macpherson later claimed that Ferguson was 'training him up' for an academic post, and as Ferguson turned his 'Treatise on Refinement' into the *Essay on the History of Civil Society* during these years, Macpherson edited his father's final work on the history of the ancient Celts.[52]

Macpherson did not maintain close contact with Ferguson and the Moderates in the late 1760s and early 1770s. Occasional letters were exchanged but he mostly asked James Macpherson to pass on his news. Yet Ferguson was clearly in his thoughts, and is mentioned often in the letters between John and James.[53] The pair anticipated Ferguson's appointment to a Commission on Indian Affairs mooted in 1772 and 1773, and John urged James, 'Pray assist Ferguson with all your soul as you would me', but it did not come to pass.[54] By 1773 Macpherson and Ferguson had been out of direct contact for a few years: on 29 September 1773 John wrote to James that he had not heard from Ferguson since he arrived in India, which had been in February 1771.[55] It usually took at least six months for an East Indiaman crossing around the Cape of Good Hope to make the journey to India, but Ferguson did not start writing until 3 November 1773, apologising to John for procrastinating.[56] Although letters trickled in, their correspondence resumed in earnest when Macpherson returned to Britain in 1777 and only became patchy once again (though only on Ferguson's side) between 1789 and 1793, when Macpherson was travelling around Europe, before tailing off finally in the few years before Ferguson's death in 1816.

A crucial letter (Merolle no. 241) penned by Macpherson on 12 January 1786 indicated a new development in their relationship. Nearly a year into his tenure as acting governor general of India, and therefore at the height of his powers, Macpherson felt it was time to announce his filial, intellectual, and moral debts to Ferguson. Macpherson stressed that he had 'followed your maxims in the practice of affairs' – maxims which he had first learned under Ferguson's tutelage in 1765 – and had 'amply experienced the truth of three of your favourite positions':

1*st*.   That the pursuits of an active mind are its greatest happiness, when they are directed to good objects, which unite our own happiness with that of our friends and the general advantage of society . . .
2*d*.   . . . that he who has not been in contact with his fellow creatures knows but half of the human heart . . .
3*d*.   That all that rests with us individually, is to act our own parts to the best of our ability, and to endeavour to do good for its own sake . . .[57]

Macpherson insisted that these principles had helped him to govern India – and as a supreme councillor to 'reduce the expenses of this colony about a million sterling per annum', of which he was especially proud – and to construct a philosophical system of principles for understanding and advancing a global society of commerce and knowledge. In thanks, Macpherson sent Ferguson the gift of £1000.

Ferguson had clearly seen potential in Macpherson, which is probably explained in part by David Kettler's suggestion that Ferguson, in his capacity as Professor of moral philosophy, envisioned himself as educating 'the statesman or warrior'.[58] John Macpherson became both of these things and – as governor general of Bengal, an occasional MP, and a favourite of the Prince of Wales – few of Ferguson's students achieved such high levels of influence (even if all of these stints were relatively short). This may be one factor why they remained close throughout their lives. Another is each's understanding of how best to get on in eighteenth-century society. Macpherson was well-connected and Ferguson was always on the lookout for potential governmental postings for himself, and opportunities for his four sons,[59] but Ferguson might also have hoped to exert a little indirect influence on British politics and foreign policy.[60] Macpherson told him as much when he declared that his governance in India – seen as a fiscal success if nothing else – was based upon following Ferguson's teachings.

When he began to devise his own theories on commercial society in the 1780s, Macpherson repeatedly cited Ferguson's teachings but also mentioned Adam Smith, whom he knew and considered a friend, and Ferguson's favourite author Montesquieu (1689–1755), whom he probably cited more than anyone else.[61] From these thinkers Macpherson learned not just about the origins and progress of civil society and the modern commercial system, but also the virtues of the British constitution. In a letter of 1804 he wrote that he was taught by Ferguson, 'the best Disciple of the Great Montesquieu', to understand the foundation of the 'The British Constitution and Empire . . . from the best the most exalted Principles'.[62] After Ferguson died in 1816, Macpherson wrote to his nephew Bob that he had

> invariably, as my letters to him progressively testify, attributed to his instruction the success of the public measures which I had the good Fortune to carry through in India. His ideas and those of the great Montesquieu were my constant guides.[63]

Ferguson clearly felt a paternal sense of duty towards Macpherson and adopted the position of a mentor throughout their correspondence. In addition to counselling Macpherson about proper moral conduct, he also offered opinions about Macpherson's ideas and actions. They seem to have agreed, for example, about the sensitive issues of empire and wealth. Because he was wary of the state's overextension in imperial affairs, Ferguson supported private enrichment in India to a surprising degree. He wrote to Macpherson he would be

> sorry if any thing be done [to] hinder The Companys Servants from acquiring fortunes in an Innocent way Abroad for after all that has been said this I believe to be the likeliest way of bringing wealth from India to Europe. The State I hope will leave the Company in all matters to Govern itself, & it will be wise in any Minister to leave them accountable for what happens there but it will be allowable likewise to squeeze them to the last farthing they can pay in consistence with that Interest they ought to have as trade to manage their aff[airs].[64]

Macpherson agreed and in his long letter of 1786, he wrote how his measures had strengthened the Company's finances while allowing individuals to make and send money back Britain, which ultimately increased its national resources.

> my system ... pours in upon Britain more streams of friendship and of aid, which every officer, civil and military, in these colonies wishes to send partially to his relations, and which, in the general remittance and receipt, give the British heart on this and your side of the ocean its most delightful exercises, and which gladden every village and place, from the cottages of the Isles of Skye to the palaces of London.[65]

When Macpherson was superseded by Cornwallis, Ferguson first urged him to take it in his stride, but then when he returned to Britain encouraged him to get back into parliament: 'Can you manage for your Fortune & your Liberality so as to be in Parliament without being straitned &c &c I may be wrong but that is the Situation I figure most likely to give your mind its Play'.[66]

One of the most fruitful periods of correspondence was that between Macpherson's return to Britain in 1793 and about 1801, when he was involved in the Amiens negotiations. The pair constantly discussed the French Revolution, its causes, and the best means of ending it. This is the context in which Ferguson wrote Macpherson the short manuscript essay (discussed in Section 8 below, on the French Revolution), as Macpherson was trying to hammer out and disseminate his own views on the subject.

5. Macpherson and the Moderates

In the early years of his Indian career, John relied on James Macpherson to keep the Moderate literati up to date on his activities, although he sometimes received recommendation letters requesting patronage for their family members and friends.[67] Upon returning to Britain in 1777, Macpherson re-established himself with the literati, with whom he remained in close contact for the next several decades. They seem to have adopted him as a younger member of the group. He wrote to Carlyle in 1783 of the pleasure 'that you will always consider me as the young man among you', and Carlyle showed the relationship was reciprocal a few years later when he wrote of the group's satisfaction at Macpherson's success, 'as you have been pleas'd in some sort to adopt yourself into a kind of Philosophical Filiation to us all'.[68] His correspondence with each Moderate was distinctive: Carlyle's letters were friendly and gossipy, Blair's warm and tutelary, Robertson's and Home's scantier and more direct, and Ferguson's frequent, intimate and expansive. The cohesiveness of the Moderates is underlined by the many overlapping anecdotes and the expectation that other members of the group were sharing information with Macpherson. To take one example, Home wrote to Macpherson at the end of 1785 that there was no need for him to relate details of current events because 'James [Macpherson] I presume takes care to inform you, in very good Gaelick of every thing he thinks material', and that in any case Carlyle had also just sent off several sheets to Calcutta.[69]

The very cohesion of the Moderates also helps to illustrate that Adam Smith – described by Blair at one point as 'a worth[y], ingenious, original odd man'[70] – though on friendly terms, was always slightly removed from the group, which viewed what they saw as Smith's political turn in the 1780s with wry amusement. In the same letter of 1785, Home wrote that

> Philosopher Smith is become so violent a Politician that is a little shy of your friends conjointly & severally, because they are not responsive to his key. He is become the humour[ous] Lieutenant (in Beaumonts play) & is desperately in love both with Charles Fox & Edmund Burke.[71]

Carlyle wrote to Macpherson several months later that 'the Parties in the State have Sour'd people a little at one another even in Edinb^r. – Blair & Home & Ferguson & I, are the only people you know, who are not Bitter Foxites', one of whom was Smith, who 'drinks hard with the landwaiters & Surveyors'.[72] Still, Macpherson was a great admirer of Smith and the Moderates kept him updated on Smith's state of happiness and health.[73] Just before Smith's death in 1790, Ferguson helped him burn most of his unpublished papers, and afterwards wrote to Macpherson that things had been 'a little awkward' between them. Merolle attributes this to Smith's accusation of plagiarism dating to the 1760s and related by Carlyle in his autobiography, but this explanation is unlikely since it raises the question about why Smith would have invited Ferguson in the first place. It is possible that it was what his friends saw as Smith's Foxite sympathies that generated the awkwardness to which Ferguson referred, or it may have been Smith's well-known social awkwardness. In any case, this political difference can be traced to the American Revolution, during which Ferguson wrote a pamphlet for Lord North's government (reproduced in this edition, see Part II), and Burke and Fox were leading members of the Rockingham Whig opposition.

Letters from the other Moderates to Macpherson also shed some new light on Ferguson and his work, particularly on the Roman History, which he wrote after his friends Hume and Robertson had become unusually wealthy from writing narrative history.[74] Carlyle wrote to Macpherson in early 1781 that the work was nearly finished – fortunately as Ferguson's health was very poor at this point – and provided a revealing comment about the reception of Ferguson's *Essay*:

> To My Great Delight I find his Book is as good as finishd, & is now in Smiths Hands, who speaks highly of it – This is so much the stronger testimony, That He & Some other <u>Sophs</u> here, were not so much pleas'd with his former book – For which I know no Reason, except that it was not wrote to the capacity of women & children.[75]

Carlyle later noted, perhaps with a twinge of envy, that Ferguson would be paid £2000 for the book.[76] Blair too had good things to say about the Roman History together with revealing comments on the *Essay*:

I have read a great deal of his Roman History. His Manuscripts (a very large work) is in my hands; and I have cheerfully taken a good deal of trouble in servicing the style, which is sometimes careless. It will be a very excellent History; profound and Political, & both instructive and entertaining; by much the best account we have of the Roman Affairs. His Style is what that of History should be, plain, manly & distinct; less ornamented . . . than that of Dr Robertson; but perhaps so much the better. It is a very different style from that of his former book on Civil Society; & much preferable, I think, in a Historical Composition. He has not yet concluded any bargain with the booksellers. But he ought to get a large sum of money from it; and is entitled I think to a great deal of Reputation by it. I hope he will live to enjoy it.[77]

Yet for whatever reason the book did not meet the immediate reception that his friends expected of it. In 1786 Carlyle wrote that

[Ferguson's History] is very slow in Rising into Fame – But by & bye, will be seen towring above our Head and Settling at last in the same Sphere with David Home's History. There are some Backbiters of it here, whom I hardly expected, and who take every opportunity to Disparage the work. It is not Blair, nor John Home, that I can assure you of – the First having always given it his Loud approbation, and the last his Enthusiastic Praise.[78]

Blair too lamented the following year that he was 'very sorry, and indeed much surprised that his Roman History has not succeeded with the Publick, as I always thought it deserved; which I am afraid hurt his Spirits a little.'[79]

Macpherson prided himself on his relationship with the Moderates and great thinkers more generally, especially Ferguson, which can be seen in the short intermedial role he played between Ferguson and Sir William Jones, the leading orientalist and founder of the Asiatick Society of Calcutta in 1784. Macpherson was among its founding members. In the summer of 1785, Macpherson lent Jones Ferguson's Roman History, and in May of the following year Jones wrote to Macpherson that he read for the second time the *Essay on the History of Civil Society*, and was 'extremely pleased with it, especially his chapter on the relaxation of national spirit.'[80] In the important letter to Ferguson of 12 January 1786, Macpherson mentioned 'the treasures in literature and the oblivious history of nations that are drawing upon us from the researches of Sir William Jones and others' as part of the global system of commerce he thought of himself as heading.[81] Macpherson also passed on Ferguson's praise of Jones in his letter of 16 February 1786 (letter no. 4 below), in which he recalled having met Jones once, and stated his hopes that Jones would get to the 'Bottom' of the 'Gentoo System'. Jones wrote to Macpherson with

> thanks for the pleasure which I have received from that of Mr. Adam Ferguson to you . . . One sentence of it is so wise, and so well expressed, that I read it till I had it by heart. 'Justice to the stranger,' &c . . . I am correcting proofs of our Transactions, which will, I hope, satisfy Mr. Ferguson as to the theology of the Hindus.[82]

As Joshua Ehrlich has shown, Macpherson prided himself on Jones's praise of him as 'the statesman and the scholar', whose 'mind can grasp the whole field of literature and criticism, as well as that of politics', a phrase he boasted about for the rest of his life and had engraved on his tombstone.[83]

Overall, the collective picture painted by the Moderates in their letters to Macpherson is one of warm friends ageing together goodhumouredly. A long description from Ferguson may be taken as representative:

> Your Friends here are all as well as can be expected. John Home stricken in years: but not afraid to tamper with the Tragic muse, his works may have their best Effect in pleasing himself, which is more than mine always do me, altho they keep me going in a morning when perhaps the day would hang heavy. Carlyle is struggling for his Clerkship, three antagonists have combined to unite their numbers against him & if they prove the Majority to divide the Spoil: but he bears the prospect manfully. Poor Blair is manly also, altho his Doctors say he has a confirmed stone in his Bladder. He has an appearance of Micrology on common occasions but at a push he gathers strength. Dr Robertson is complaining & obliged to use an Ear Tube to assist his hearing. I overheard Sir Robert Myrton a few years before he died muttering to himself, in his style, I am turned damned Auld now God Damn me by God and lo if it were not for the horrid Oaths; this is the Speech now accommodated to many of your Friends & to none more than your most affectionate & most humble servant.[84]

6. Ferguson on Human Nature and Moral Science

With the nature of the letters and the relationship between Ferguson, Macpherson, and the Moderates established in the previous five sections, the next three sections provide a brief outline of Ferguson's political thought. In the latter part, we shall see the ways we might better understand certain aspects of it through and alongside the new letters and the essay.

Ferguson's general method of studying humanity was the experimental one, pioneered by Francis Bacon (1561–1626) and Isaac Newton (1642–1727) in the seventeenth century, and applied to the study of human nature by philosophers from John Locke (1632–1704) to David Hume.[85] This approach involved observing the workings of the mind through introspection and studying human behaviour in history; it was known as the 'science of man' in the Scottish Enlightenment.[86] For the most part Ferguson used evidence from travel literature and historical sources when discussing past human experiences. When no evidence was available he invoked universal principles and known facts about human nature to bridge gaps, which is why Ferguson has come to be known as a 'conjectural historian'. We must remember, however, that this term was *not* his but rather his successor Dugald Stewart's, and that Ferguson was indeed often scathing of speculation independent of evidence.[87] Other terms, including progressive or developmental history, might be more appropriate, but that is a separate discussion.[88]

'Law' is a key term in Ferguson's writings, and its different meanings in various contexts need clarification. *Physical law* refers to universal facts and uniform patterns in nature. *Moral law* is that conduct which should be universally observed towards each other. The observance of *political law* can be compelled by force, but this is not necessarily the case of moral law. Moral science deals with what *ought* to be, and what human beings should strive for. It has its basis, however, in physical law. According to Ferguson, human beings are bound by three physical laws and principles: (1) self-preservation; (2) society; (3) progression.[89] The constitution of human beings impels them to preserve and defend themselves, like other animals. But unlike some animals, they also desire to be members of societies, and unlike all animals, they seek to improve themselves and their environments. Temporal happiness and misery are thus the natural punishments of moral law.[90] In terms of virtue, human beings cannot achieve perfection, only improvement.[91] They can and should, however, aim for perfection, and it is the office of the moral philosopher to illuminate what kind of perfection they should attempt to approximate.[92] As an example, the greatest good human beings should aim for is the love of mankind.[93] While humans can enforce the demands of jurisprudence, the compulsion of the moral law is the internal one of conscience. Morality and virtue cannot be compelled by force. They are either voluntary or they do not exist.[94]

Ferguson's most famous text, *An Essay on the History of Civil Society* (1767), was originally entitled *A Treatise on Refinement*. Given the nature of humans, they were destined to progress from rudeness to refinement and civilisation. Ferguson's outline of this development is considered at greater length in the following section in the context of the origin of authority and government. But we must now emphasise that the human inclination for society meant that people will always be found in groups rather than as solitary individuals. They should hence be studied as groups.[95] Against the *Second Discourse* by Jean-Jacques Rousseau (1712–88), Ferguson wrote: 'a wild man . . . caught in the woods . . . is a singular instance, not a specimen of any general character'.[96] The starting point of Ferguson's history of civil society was the denial of both the existence of the state of nature and its usefulness as an analytical device. 'We speak of art as distinguished from nature; but art is itself natural to man', he wrote in opposition to state of nature theorists from Hobbes to Rousseau.[97] 'If we are asked therefore, where the state of nature is to be found?' – he continued – 'we may answer, It is here; and it matters not whether we are understood to speak in the island of Great Britain, at the Cape of Good Hope, or the Straits of Magellan.'[98]

As already stated, Ferguson believed that human beings are naturally social, citing Montesquieu's remark that 'man is born in society'.[99] This does not, however, mean that they are *sociable* in the sense of being indiscriminately benevolent. In this way, Ferguson disagreed with Francis Hutcheson's moral sense theory, even though he agreed that benevolence was a moral ideal worthy of pursuit. For Ferguson, the sociality of human beings to a large degree stems from antagonism towards other groups. In letter no. 34, he applied this principle to Franco-British relations.[100] The principles of 'union' and 'dissension' are mutually supportive, according to Ferguson.[101] This has become one of the most discussed aspects of Ferguson's writings on human nature and social development. In politics, this meant that he accepted party politics, even though as a moralist he disliked many aspects of it, and as a political observer he was often troubled by it. As he wrote in one of the new letters (letter no. 18) addressing the prelude to the Regency Crisis: '[I]n forming our hopes we must not forget that we live in Faece Romuli not in Republica Platonis; We are a land of Party & when we cease to have Parties we shall scarce be alive.'[102] It was Ferguson's emphasis rather than his argument which was original. Hume was also convinced that human beings were inclined to gregarious as well as conflictual dispositions, and he had argued that government had probably originated as a result of quarrels between different peoples.[103] Like Ferguson, Hume accepted but disliked party politics, and viewed it as especially inevitable in mixed constitutions such as the British.[104]

Virtue, religion, and the quest for human excellence pertain to the moral sphere, according to Ferguson. By contrast, the main purpose of government is to defend the community from external attacks and secure individual rights through a system of justice. As he wrote in one of the new letters in this edition (letter no. 4): 'Justice to the Stranger who has no advocate to plead for Favour is the Soul of Government.' Whilst politics is first and foremost about the security of individual rights through a system of justice, it does serve a moral purpose in the process by providing a framework for sociality and progress, as well as for the performance of duty and virtuous acts, notably in defence of the community. Political institutions can improve as well as corrupt manners.[105] Since human beings are active and progressive animals, politics thus affords ample opportunities for active assertions:

> The trials of ability, which men mutually afford to one another in the collisions of free society, are the lessons of a school which Providence has opened for mankind, and are well known to forward, instead of impeding their progress in any valuable art.[106]

The next section turns to Ferguson's political science.

7. Ferguson on Political Science[107]

Three major events contributed to the polarisation of politics in Britain in the last three decades of the eighteenth century: 'Wilkes and Liberty', the American Revolution, and the French Revolution. These events inspired a movement for political reform in Britain.

Ferguson was alarmed by all three events, and sceptical about political reform even before it was supressed in the final years of the century as the French Revolution took a violent turn. On the question of 'Wilkes and Liberty', he wrote a series of letters to his friend the Scottish member of parliament William (Johnstone) Pulteney (1729–1805).[108] On the American crisis, he penned a pamphlet for the North administration. His response to the French Revolution was expressed in scattered letters and unpublished essays.[109] The newly discovered evidence collected in this volume includes sixteen letters as well as a new unpublished essay on the topic. In order to grasp his response to this event, however, we must begin by seeking to understand his other writings on political science. Ferguson wrote about politics in three personae: (1) as a man of letters, in the *Essay*; (2) as a university Professor of moral philosophy in the *Institutes* and *Principles*; and (3) as an occasional pamphleteer. This section argues that there was a large degree of unity across the various genres in which Ferguson articulated his political principles, even if the style and emphases differed. We begin by briefly sketching the wider intellectual context before returning to Ferguson.

7.1 *The Origin of Government*

In the early eighteenth century, Gershom Carmichael (1672–1729), the first Professor of moral philosophy at the University of Glasgow, incorporated seventeenth-century natural law theory into his teaching, in particular the writings of Samuel Pufendorf (1632–94) and Locke.[110] A cornerstone of the political component of seventeenth-century natural jurisprudence was the notion that political authority was not natural but established through individual consent of the governed – an argument with roots in Hugo Grotius (1583–1645) and Thomas Hobbes (1588–1679). In this tradition, political obligation was contractual. Carmichael's successor at Glasgow, Francis Hutcheson (1694–1746) – a Presbyterian Irishman sometimes called the father of the Scottish Enlightenment – agreed with Locke that consent was the *usual* method for establishing political authority. However, Hutcheson argued that it was possible to establish government 'upon a rude and unexperienced people' on the basis of 'justice or right', without any explicit consent. In other words, implied consent was sufficient for Hutcheson in certain 'extraordinary circumstances'.[111] Reacting to an earlier formulation of this argument in Latin in

Philosophiae Moralis Institutio Compendiaria (1742), Hume commented in a letter to Hutcheson: 'You imply a Condemnation of Locke's Opinion, which being the receiv'd one, I cou'd have wisht the Condemnation had been more express.'[112] Hume himself criticised Locke's theory of consent more openly in book three of his *Treatise of Human Nature* (1739–40) and in 'Of the Original Contract' (1748). According to Hume, political authority emerged gradually as part of a historical process.

This is the context in which Ferguson's attempt to explain the origin of government must be understood.[113] Even though Ferguson and Hume disagreed on many subjects, Hume's demolition of Locke's social contract theory paved the way for a historical understanding of the emergence of political authority. Ferguson's own arguments against social contract theory – although primarily aimed at Hobbes, Rousseau and Cesare Beccaria (1738–94) rather than at Locke[114] – shared much common ground with Hume. In particular, he objected that grounding political obligation in mutual agreement fails to explain the origin of the prior convention of promise-keeping. Ferguson agreed with Hume that instincts and practices of continuous possession, rather than reason and speculation, first gave rise to the institution of private property, as well as to government for its protection.[115] Like Hume, Ferguson highlighted that political establishments often originated in force, and were sustained by habit.[116] In the most general sense, 'political union' was simply an extension of the natural 'propensity to herd with the species', discussed in the previous section.[117] All governments *de facto* could become governments *de jure* with time and practice when the governed accepted the protection provided and in turn paid allegiance to the protector.[118] Political obligation thus rested on implicit or tacit consent.

In the *Essay*, Ferguson sketched a three-stage theory of human progress in a section on 'History of political Establishments' – originally entitled 'The History of Subordination' – from savages, in a state of equality; to barbarians in tribes; onwards to civilised people who owned property and lived under civil government. In the *Institutes*, he made use of more familiar terms in his three-stage theory when discussing the stages of 'hunting and fishing', 'pasturage', and finally, 'agriculture'.[119] Ferguson was one of a number of thinkers who employed stadial history in the Scottish Enlightenment and in Europe; others included Henry Home, Lord Kames (1696–1782), in his *Historical Law Tracts* (1758), John Dalrymple (1726–1810) in *An Essay towards a General History of*

Feudal Property in Great Britain (1757), and Anne Robert Jacques Turgot (1727–81) among the French Physiocrats.[120] As with many other Scottish thinkers, Ferguson viewed the development of a system of rank as an essential part of the process of civilisation and economic growth. In rudimentary economic activity, unequal abilities resulted in economic inequalities, the differences of which gave rise to distinctions of rank and estimation, and consequently to 'the division and subdivision of tasks', spurring on more advanced economic growth.[121]

Ferguson stressed that none of this was intended or planned: 'He who first said, "I will appropriate this field: I will leave it to my heirs;" did not perceive, that he was laying the foundation of civil laws and political establishments.'[122] The emergence of society and political union was thus a result of what has been termed 'spontaneous order'.[123] Some of the strongest formulations in favour of the notion of unintended consequences are found in Ferguson's *Essay*. 'No constitution is formed by concert, no government is copied from a plan', he wrote.[124] Instead, 'nations stumble upon establishments, which are indeed the result of human action, but not the execution of any human design'.[125] As will be discussed below, this may go some way towards explaining Ferguson's scepticism of planned reforms in general and the French Revolution in particular.

7.2 *Jurisprudence*

A key difference between Hume and Ferguson was that the latter, like Smith,[126] used the language of natural rights of the natural jurists. Rights, for Ferguson, were integral to 'the mode of our being'.[127] 'Every peasant will tell us, that a man hath his rights', he wrote in the *Essay*, 'and that to trespass on those rights is injustice'.[128] In his later jurisprudential writings, Ferguson targeted Hume specifically: 'justice cannot be said to be an artificial virtue, any more than the person of a man to which it refers is artificial'.[129] Rights were *natural* in the sense of being social: '[men] cannot for a moment converse with one another, without feeling that the part they maintain may be just or unjust'.[130] In the *Principles*, Ferguson offered 'the self-evident proposition' that

> a person has a *right* to the use of his faculties and powers; he has a *right* to enjoy the light of the sun, and the air of the atmosphere; he has a *right* to the use of his property, and the fruits of his labour.[131]

Rights were either original or adventitious, personal or real. Before the establishment of property and the distinction of rank, 'men have a right to defend their persons, and to act with freedom; they have a right to maintain the apprehension of reason'.[132] This was the key reason why slavery could never be lawful: people will always retain the original right of defending themselves, and they are thus 'inspired by nature with a disposition to revolt, whenever [they are] galled with the sense of insufferable injury or wrong'.[133] According to Ferguson, a person can never become a thing, whatever Roman law supposed.[134] As he wrote:

> Although a person may have forfeited his possession, his property, or his labour, to any amount, yet no one can forfeit all his personal rights, or from a *person* become a *thing* or subject of property. Criminals, accordingly, in the policy of some nations, are condemned to labour, or to confinement for life. In this, however, it is not pretended that their nature is changed from a person to a thing, or to a subject of property. Capricious tendencies having no tendency to prevent or to redress a wrong, are unlawful even with respect to those who have trespassed the rules of justice.[135]

For Ferguson, 'the enjoyment of what, without injury to another, is fairly occupied' was one of the 'original rights of the person', which he believed that Hobbes had 'overlooked'.[136] He explained that every rightful act of compulsion was 'an act of defence': 'The sovereign employs force to defend his country against foreign enemies . . . The magistrate employs force to repress crimes; the citizen to defend his dwelling or his person.'[137] The principle of compulsory law was limited to the repulsion of wrongs. It was related to the moral precept which 'forbids one person to be the author of harm to another'. For the promotion of further moral goals, such as religion or virtue, Ferguson stressed that force is wholly 'inadequate' and even counterproductive since morality cannot be enforced.[138] Ferguson had, of course, much to say about morality and virtue, but when speaking strictly in jurisprudential terms, he agreed with Smith that 'We may often fulfil all the rules of justice by sitting still and doing nothing'.[139]

Adventitious rights could be divided into three categories: (1) *possession*, for as long as something is in use; (2) *property*, exclusive and independent of actual use; (3) *command*, respecting the services or the obedience due from one person to another.[140]

These rights could not originate in any wrongful act, according to Ferguson, which is why he, like Rousseau but unlike many seventeenth-century natural lawyers, did not recognise any rights of conquest.[141] Government *could* originate in force, because justice had to be enforced, but conquest implied stealing something belonging to someone else.[142] Human beings could acquire rights to *things* through either first occupation or labour, when they belonged to no one, or the conveyance from one person to another by convention or forfeiture.[143] A delicate subject was the custom among European imperial powers 'to claim the dominion of newly discovered lands or islands'.[144] Although the competing imperial powers may be understood to have entered into a fair convention, Ferguson emphasised that this only applied to those who had *agreed* to it, and it was not an argument 'sufficient to deprive the native, however rude or barbarous, of the inheritance or possession to which he is born'.[145] As we shall see below, Ferguson tended to view empire-building through conquest as not only unlawful but pernicious to the conquering and conquered nations alike. At the same time, he seemed to have viewed the American settler-colonies as a different and special case.

7.3 Civil Liberty and Forms of Government

According to Ferguson, civil and political liberty equated to the security of rights.[146] Since art is man's nature, and the civil state the only relevant natural state, Ferguson hammered home the point by arguing that 'Natural liberty is not impaired, as sometimes supposed, by political institutions, but owes its existence to political institutions'.[147] In other words, rather than the absence of restraint, freedom meant 'just restraint', which was the only condition under which 'every person is safe, and cannot be invaded, either in freedom of his person, his property, or innocent action'.[148] The main threat to liberty was not a strong government, which was necessary for its existence, but the abuse of power. Like Hume and Smith, then, Ferguson tended to treat freedom and security as synonyms.[149]

Security entailed that the law must apply to governors and governed alike.[150] But, emphatically, liberty did not imply equality of rank or fortune. 'The nations who contended most for the equality of citizens', he wrote, 'in admitting the institution of slavery, trespassed most egregiously on the equality of mankind.'[151] Importantly, people were 'destined to inequality from their birth', as differences in strength of body and mind testified. As we have already pointed out, differences in industry and courage produced wealth disparities, which had in turn established a system of rank. The only way in which it made sense to speak of continuous equality was in the sense of 'the equal right which every man has to defend himself'. However, since this meant that people also have a right to procure whatever is deemed necessary for defence and security, there could be no limit to the inequality between people in the process of upholding their equal right to self-defence. Since there is no way of preventing wealth from becoming hereditary, persistent inequality of fortunes cannot be prevented 'without violating the first and common principles of right in the most flagrant manner'.[152] Ferguson thus concluded that it would be impossible, unjust, and inexpedient to prevent inequalities from developing as well as becoming hereditary. He argued consistently that this subordination produced 'government so necessary to the safety of individuals and the peace of mankind'. It also worked as an incentive to labour.[153]

How, then, were civil liberty and rights best protected in institutional terms? Hume had notoriously argued that civil liberty might be successfully upheld in civilised monarchies such as France where persons and property were secure. In one place he even hinted that they had become superior in this regard compared with mixed governments.[154] Ferguson was more emphatic that different orders needed 'a share in the government as may enable them to defend themselves, or put a negative on any measure which might be prejudicial to their respective interests'.[155] In antiquity, this meant that liberty existed only in small democratic states. Ferguson was, however, far from sanguine about the democratic form of government, partly because of the institution of slavery in ancient city states, but also because of its societal turbulence. 'The violence of popular assemblies and their tumults need to be restrained, no less than the passions and usurpations of any other power whatever', he stressed, indicating that a corrupt democracy was the worst form of 'tyranny'.[156] Fortunately, the practice of representation in modernity meant that all people could take part in government 'by deputation'.[157]

Ferguson's being in favour of 'the people' having a share in the government to protect their interests – preferably through representation – did not mean that he thought that explicit consent was a necessary condition for the legitimacy of laws. If we would acknowledge an 'absolute right in every individual to be bound only by his own assent', then this would imply that, prior to conventions establishing principles of representation and majoritarianism, 'a people cannot be bound to any act in which they are not unanimous'.[158] Ferguson's natural history of political authority and government, as we have seen, had little time for what he regarded as such fictions. In the *Principles*, he simply argued that

> when a plea thus amounts to something that has never been realized in the history of mankind, still more, if its object be such as cannot be realized, there is reason not only to doubt its validity, but actually to consider it as altogether nugatory and absurd.[159]

He continued:

> Laws are every where acknowledged to be binding on persons who are never called upon to give their assent, either by themselves or their representatives ... One of the sexes, though by nature vested with every right; and a great part of the other sex, upon an arbitrary distinction of nonage, are excluded altogether; many are kept away by disability of health or decline of age; yet, it never was supposed, in any case whatever, that these are to have a dispensation from the law.[160]

All nations legitimately excluded some people from full political participation. Ancient states had distinguished between free and enslaved people, which Ferguson lamented. In his own day, states excluded women and children, which he accepted, even though he suggested that this exclusion was to a degree arbitrary since some teenagers were more intellectually mature than others would ever be. All states distinguished denizens from aliens. Even Revolutionary France, he pointed out, required property qualification for voters. Modern Britain also had property qualifications, both for office holders and voters, which varied in different constituencies. But despite these exclusions and irregularities – especially marked in borough elections – Ferguson was convinced that 'the liberty of the subject is more secure [in Britain] perhaps than it ever has been under any other human establishment'.[161] Even those excluded from the vote enjoyed the security of the laws, equally applying to all, and they had to obey these laws as long as they remained within the state.

Ferguson was consistently suspicious of political reform. This can be seen in his response to the Yorkshire Association movement in 1780 and his correspondence with its leader Christopher Wyvill.[162] In the *Principles*, he argued that 'the character of the representative' was more important than the 'form of proceeding'. Even if 'the fewest exclusions . . . consistent with reason and public safety' was in theory the most preferable, in practice '[t]oo much fluctuation, or frequent transition from one set of rules to another, is, of all circumstances, the least consistent with that sense of security in which the possession and enjoyment of liberty consists.'[163]

In addition to political representation, Ferguson argued that sufficient executive power was needed for the citizen to be 'secure of the right which law confers upon him'.[164] Weak and feeble government could not advance civil liberty rightly understood, since '[l]aw without force, is no more than a dead letter'.[165] The key was to 'establish such a relationship between the executive and legislative powers, as that neither shall . . . encroach upon the functions or rights of the other'. Ferguson was not here desiring complete separation of powers, along Montesquieuian lines. Rather, he stressed that some fusion was needed, and that the executive power should have a voice in the legislature in order to establish a working equilibrium.[166] Nevertheless, he certainly agreed with Montesquieu that a degree of separation was a prerequisite for liberty to exist.[167]

Liberty was better preserved in states 'of moderate extent' than in vast empires. Medium-sized states were better at finding the right balance between 'the precautions of freedom' and 'the energy of government'.[168] Accordingly, 'conquest is no advantage to those who make it, any more than to those over whom it is made'.[169] Moderate states with systems of representation were also superior to the smaller, democratic city-states of antiquity, which relied economically on slavery and whose assemblies were turbulent. The mixed monarchy that had developed historically in modern Britain was the most suitable form of government in relation to its size and political economy.[170] According to Hume's *History of England*, which Ferguson cited three times in the *Essay*, the British mixed monarchy was an unintended outcome of centuries of wrangling among monarch, lords and commons. In the *Essay*, Ferguson described in more theoretical terms how mixed governments had emerged historically and argued for the superiority of this form of government.[171] 'In governments properly mixed', he wrote, 'the popular interest, finding a counterpoise in that of the prince or of the nobles, a balance is actually established between them, in which public freedom and the public order are made to consist.'[172]

This is also where, for Ferguson, moral and political science converge.[173] '[F]orms of government may be estimated', he tells us,

> not only by the actual wisdom or goodness of their administration, but likewise by the numbers who are made to participate in the service of government of their country, and by the discussion of political deliberation and function to the greatest extent that is consistent with the wisdom of its administration.[174]

The last qualification is important; Ferguson was as fearful of the 'disorderly populace' as he was of 'despotic master[s]'.[175] It is clear, however, that he believed that 'members of a free state' were furnished with 'the most improving exercises of ability'. If properly organised politically, nations could thus become 'formed to the character of manhood and public virtue'.[176] Governments should certainly be conducted by the wise, and the safety of every citizen was paramount. But the perfection nations should aim for was the encouragement of 'every ingenuous or innocent effort of the human mind'.[177] In the end, the form of government Ferguson favoured was Britain's mixed and balanced government. This was typical of the Moderate literati of the Scottish Enlightenment, who were strong supporters of the parliamentary settlement of the Glorious Revolution and the Hanoverian monarchy. It brought him into disagreement with political reformers wanting more ambitious reforms, notably the Welsh nonconformist preacher Richard Price (1723–91).

7.4 Ferguson, Price and the American Revolution

Dario Castiglione has argued that social contract theory became less prominent in radical argument in the late eighteenth century. Moreover, he stresses that 'conservative' critics such as William Paley (1743–1805) failed to notice this shift, as they continued to criticise contract theory on Humean grounds.[178] Ferguson continued the onslaught on social contract theory, as we have seen above, but he also directed much of his intellectual energy on the idea of 'self-government'. His understanding of civil liberty and what he viewed as the absurdity of theories of political authority based on self-government figured centrally in his disagreement with Richard Price, against whose *Observation on Civil Liberty* (1776) he wrote his American pamphlet. In the *Observation*, Price avoided the language of the 'original contract', but he nevertheless regarded his politics to be derived from Locke's political theory.[179] Price understood civil liberty as the principle of self-government, even though he conceded that it must be realised in modernity via the principle of representation.[180] 'As far as, in any instance, the operation of any cause comes in to restrain the power of self-government, so far slavery is introduced', he wrote.

Whilst Ferguson agreed with Price about the benefits of representation to protect interests and individual rights, he was scathing about Price's appeal to self-government and his definition of liberty as the absence of restraint. According to Ferguson, any civil community would be incompatible with Price's definition of civil liberty. '[E]ven where the collective body are sovereigns', he wrote, 'they are seldom unanimous, and the minority must ever submit to a power that stands opposed to their own will.' But his objection went deeper: 'If Liberty be opposed to Restraint, I am afraid it is inconsistent with the great end of civil government itself, which is to give people security from the effect of crimes and disorders, and to preserve the peace of mankind.' Price quoted Montesquieu as saying: 'Sleep in a state ... is always followed by slavery', probably with reference to Montesquieu's *Considerations*.[181] In response, Ferguson quoted at length from the *Spirit of Laws*:

> I confess I am somewhat surprised that Dr. Price, who quotes Montesquieu with so much regard on other occasions, should have overlooked what he has said on this. Among the other mistaken notions of Liberty, this celebrated writer observes, *That some have confounded the Power of the people with the Liberty of the people. That in democracies the people seem to do what they please; but that Liberty does not consist in doing what we please. It consists in being free to do what we ought to incline, and in not being obliged to do what we ought not to incline. We ought to remember*, he continues, *that Independence is one thing, and Liberty another. That if any citizen were free to do what he pleased, this would be an extinction of Liberty, for every one else would have the same freedom.*[182]

Ferguson spent most of the remainder of the pamphlet illustrating why it was not a sustainable political doctrine to let people govern themselves. His key argument was the same as in his lectures on moral and political science: civil liberty did not consist in independence but in 'the security of our rights'. This security would be undermined by turbulent democracy.

7.5 The Militia Question

Even though Ferguson viewed peace as a virtuous aspiration, he thought that preparation for defence was the surest way of achieving it, as political societies must defend against foreign aggressors.[183] Moreover, providence indicated that war was sometimes inevitable, and in such cases, 'the virtues of human nature are its happiness, no less than they are so in reaping the fruits of peace'.[184] The strength of communities ultimately rests on the quality of their people, which is why corruption is a key theme for Ferguson. He feared that Britain of his day risked becoming exclusively preoccupied with acquiring wealth and neglecting the means of defending it.[185]

Ferguson's preoccupation with militias was not due to any nostalgia for ancient politics. Rather, he regarded it as crucial element in the transition from feudal to modern times. As he wrote in a footnote in the *Principles*:

> The present order of things in Europe originated in the ascendance of persons having arms in their hands ... in the constitution of our own country, members returnable from the counties to parliament, as appears from the remaining form of the writ addressed to sheriffs for this purpose, were to military; none being thought worthy of a place in the councils of state, but such as were armed for its defence.[186]

Ferguson believed that those of higher rank with a significant property stake in the country had a special obligation and interest in defending the community. His 1756 militia pamphlet recommended arming the nobility and gentry in the first instance; all cottagers, day labourers and servants would be excluded from consideration.[187] At this time he was one of several voices among the Moderates who argued for the inclusion of Scotland in any plan to establish a militia.[188] In the end, William Pitt the Elder's Militia Act of 1757 excluded Scotland over fears of Jacobitism. Ferguson stressed that such unequal treatment of Scotland would exacerbate factionalism.[189] For him, a Scottish militia would act as a bulwark against Highland Jacobitism. Without it, 'A few Banditti from the Mountains, trained by their Situation to a warlike Disposition, might over-run the Country, and, in a critical Time, give Law to this Nation'.[190] On the other hand, 'When the Lovers of Freedom and their Country have an equal Use of Arms, the Cause of the Pretender . . . is from that Moment desperate.'[191]

Ferguson's preoccupation with the militia was revived and intensified in the 1790s, especially in 1797 when a French invasion loomed.[192] The Militia Act 1797 empowered the lord lieutenants of Scotland to raise and command militia regiments in their jurisdictions. Ferguson wrote triumphantly to Macpherson in 1797 (letter no. 30): 'I contended then that we must become a Military or Warlike People to defend ourselves year after year & Century after Century. The Coldest heads in the Country are now Sensible of it.'[193] After the threat subsided, Ferguson continued to propagate the militia, which he put at the heart of his vision for what a modern British state should look like in commercial modernity. As he writes in letter no. 27: 'for men to become warlike they must have war', but in the absence of this they should be in constant state of preparation, an idea he tried to impress upon Henry Dundas in 1802 during the Amiens peace.[194] This was part of Ferguson's vision for modern Britain, and how a state should organise itself and operate in a modern commercial society, as discussed in the following section.

8. Adam Ferguson and Adam Smith

In the 1773 edition of the *Essay*, Adam Ferguson wrote in a section entitled 'Of Population and Wealth':

> I willingly quit a subject in which I am not much conversant . . . Speculations on commerce and wealth have been delivered by the ablest writers; and the public will probably soon be furnished with a theory of national œconomy, equal to what has ever appeared on any subject of since whatever.[195]

A footnote clarified that Ferguson was referring to his friend Adam Smith's forthcoming *Inquiry into the Nature and Causes of the Wealth of Nations*, which was eventually published three years later.[196] Upon its appearance, Ferguson was ecstatic, writing to the author:

> I have been for some time so busy reading you, and recommending you and quoting you, to my students, that I have not had leisure to trouble you with letters. I suppose, however, that of all the opinions on which you have any curiosity, mine is among the least doubtful. You may believe, that on further acquaintance with your work my esteem is not a little increased. You are surely to reign alone on these subjects, to form the opinions, and I hope to govern at least the coming generations.

However, Ferguson's approval of his friend's work was not unconditional. He continued: 'You have provoked, it is true, the church, the universities, and the merchants, against all of whom I am willing to take your part; but you have likewise provoked the militia, and there I must be against you.'[197] The statement referred to Smith's conviction that a militia 'must always be much inferior to a well disciplined and well exercised standing army'.[198] As discussed in the previous section, Ferguson's support for militias was longstanding and unequivocal.[199] This section will focus on his wider engagement with Smith's work and political economy generally. As we shall see below, the new letters demonstrate that Ferguson appears to have grown slightly more sceptical about Smith's work, as he came to disagree with Smith on educational policy as well.

Ferguson may have been modest when proclaiming himself 'not much conversant' in political economy in 1773. His commitment to free trade was longstanding and preceded the *Wealth of Nations*. His general economic principles set out in the first set of his published lectures, *Institutes of Moral Philosophy* (1769), were similar to those in his later *Principles of Moral and Political Science* (2 vols, 1792). Already in the *Institutes*, he stressed that

> the state of a nation's wealth is not to be estimated from the state of its coffers, granaries, or warehouses, at any particular time; but from the fertility of its lands, from the numbers, frugality, industry, and skill, of its people.[200]

One common source for Ferguson and Smith was their older mutual friend David Hume, who was undoubtedly among the 'ablest writers' Ferguson referred to in the 1773 edition of the *Essay*.[201] In the *Essay*, Ferguson argued that commercial and political progress were symmetrical, or more precisely that the former paved the way for the latter, in typical Scottish Enlightenment fashion:

> A people, possessed of wealth, and become jealous of their properties, have formed the project of emancipation, and have proceeded, under favour of an importance recently gained, still farther to enlarge their pretensions, and to dispute the prerogatives which their sovereign had been in use to employ.[202]

This general argument is more associated with Hume, whom Smith credited as 'the only writer who, so far as I know, has hitherto taken notice' of the fact that 'commerce and manufactures gradually introduced order and good government, and with them, the liberty and security of individuals'.[203] Despite their apparent differences in tone and emphasis, Hume and Smith were certainly Ferguson's main interlocutors on the subject of political economy, and they are useful for both comparison and contrast.

Ferguson is sometimes believed to have been more critical than Smith and Hume about commercial modernity.[204] In some ways, however, he was in fact more positive. Notably, his attitude towards public credit was much milder than that of Hume. In the *Institutes*, he had briefly stated that public credit could be either useful or pernicious: 'It is useful to an industrious and thriving people. It is pernicious to the spendthrift and prodigal.'[205] In the *Principles*, he elaborated that debt financing could be useful since the alternative measure of hoarding savings meant withdrawing capital from lucrative trade.[206] His general argument was that we should not

> rashly . . . conclude, that a nation is the poorer for every article of debt it has contracted, until we have considered to what effect the money so procured has been expended, and whether the public advantages gained by means of it are fully adequate to the risk and the cost.[207]

He further pointed out that the practice of public credit was most suitable in countries where people or their representatives had a share in the government, since it required 'that the good faith of the public should be known'.[208]

Ferguson was certainly aware of the less positive sides of the politics of credit. The monied men who lived on speculation rather than by industry were unlikely to impress him.[209] He was also concerned about the prospect of public debt growing indefinitely. Since no progress in human nature is infinite, 'a load that is continually growing must overwhelm them at last'.[210] Rather than abolishing the practice, however, he supported schemes to reduce the national debt and the interest rate. He never came close to saying as Hume did that 'either the nation must destroy public credit, or public credit will destroy the nation'.[211] Instead, Ferguson believed that it was beneficial for the nation to have a portion of the national wealth in a transferable form, and he supported its regulation via the sinking fund.

Economic policy for Ferguson had three overriding and related objectives: engage the people in productive labour, produce commodities 'to subsist and accommodate the greatest number of valuable citizens and useful hands', and provide revenue for the government.[212] In rudimentary economic activity, unequal abilities and capacities produced economic inequalities, the differences of which gave rise to differences of rank and estimation, and consequently to 'the division and subdivision of tasks'.[213] When explaining the development of the division of labour within commercial society, Ferguson used the example of a pin factory, made most famous by Smith, but drawn from an unnamed French source, probably the *Encyclopédie*.[214] Moreover, he underlined that trade was not a zero-sum game, but rather 'mutual convenience to all the parties concerned . . . [and] gain and profit to all'.[215]

Ferguson tended to be suspicious of government intervention in the economy, and in the *Principles* he cited Smith's *Wealth of Nations* as an authority on this theme.[216] He argued that government should not protect certain sectors or monopolies, but promote 'the freedom of trade' and give 'equal protection . . . to the people in every branch of commerce unrestrained and unforced'.[217] Instead, the key regulator of commerce for Ferguson was the private interest of the trader. This principle was as far removed as it could be from public spirit, but the wealth it produced for individuals benefited the state by enabling productive labour and providing commodities. Accordingly, Ferguson stressed that 'private interest in trade operates with the least erring direction for the public benefit, and is secure of its purpose, where public councils would mistake or miss of their aim'.[218]

Crucially, however, economic activity needed government protection. Like Smith, Ferguson believed that the state had a crucial function in providing security of property and industry through the rule of law. In some ways, the state could even encourage commerce, chiefly by 'facilitat[ing] communications by commodious highways, inland and sea navigations, and every other conveniency that tends to lessen the difficulty of removing commodities from the place in which they are produced to that in which they are wanted'.[219] Government was also necessary to coin money and control the money supply.[220] What is more, Ferguson highlighted that there was a single, but important, exception to the general principle of free trade: 'where in the course of trade advantages may arise, or inconveniences may be incurred, respecting the safety or defence of the commonwealth, in every such case, safety is to be preferred to profit'.[221] Ferguson thus highlighted that maritime nations needed to encourage seamanship and all states 'the manners of a brave and ingenuous people'.[222] Smith would have agreed wholeheartedly. Indeed, Smith supported the Acts of Navigation for this very reason, despite acknowledging that they disadvantaged foreign commerce: 'As defence . . . is of much more importance than opulence, the act of navigation is, perhaps, the wisest of all the commercial regulations of England.'[223]

In some circles, Ferguson, like Smith, has acquired a reputation as an extreme advocate of laissez faire on the basis of some sweeping statements in the *Essay*, such as 'The Statesman . . . can do little more than avoid doing mischief'.[224] But the new letters in this edition show clearly that Ferguson came to view himself as *more* favourable to government intervention than Smith. When expressing his support for a national board of education in 1801, he wrote to John Macpherson (letter no. 34):

> Smith in pursuit of his general Principle of Free Trade would explode universities as well as limitations of Commerce, leaving every age to fund Education as well as Trade suited to the exigency of its own affairs. But I apprehend the *Public* must take some charge of both at least to check fraud & folly, and give a beginning at least to what once experienced will make way for itself.

This late letter not only shows that Ferguson, at least by 1801, was opposed to Smith's specific proposal to reform university education, but that he also viewed this position as part and parcel of a systematic anti-regulatory and anti-interventionist position. This may be unfair as a careful perusal of book V of the *Wealth of Nations*, as well as much recent Smith scholarship, will inform us. It may be viewed as particularly unwarranted since Smith certainly realised the importance of widespread education. Yet it is noteworthy because it tells us a great deal about how Ferguson thought about Smith's legacy at the start of the nineteenth century, and how he positioned himself in relation to it. Accordingly, even though Craig Smith's recent and salutary attempt to situate Ferguson's views on political economy in close proximity to Smith's is correct as far as his published writings are concerned, we must note that he revised his positions later in life.[225] As we have seen, Ferguson was deeply impressed by the *Wealth of Nations*, and its influence can be traced in the *Principles*. When the new evidence is placed alongside Ferguson's writings, however, it becomes evident that he was continuously mulling over the subject. In the end there were other aspects of Smith's great work that troubled him besides the treatment of militias. The new letters suggest that Ferguson appreciated the economically expanded role of the state as a result of wars against Revolutionary France.

Ferguson's appreciation of the expanded state, largely as a defensive measure against the French, is also discernible in his support for an income tax, expressed in the same 1801 letter. William Pitt the Younger had imposed an income tax for the first time two years earlier. Ferguson wrote in the letter to Macpherson that he had 'long since declared to you' in favour of the measure (letter no. 34). Although income taxes are not explicitly mentioned in any of Ferguson's published writings, the *Principles* contain arguments that can be mustered in its favour. In the *Principles*, he had stressed the importance of the whole burden of taxation not falling entirely 'upon one class of the people'.[226] He further supported staggered taxes, such as the land tax, rather than flat tax rates, which he regarded as oppressive. As he put it: 'It were absurd to exact no more from the rich than the poor can pay. And it would be cruel to extort from the poor as much as the rich may without inconvenience afford.'[227]

9. Adam Ferguson and the French Revolution

One of the most significant features of the new letters and especially the new unpublished essay is that they allow us to reconstruct more completely Ferguson's views on the French

Revolution. This is a subject on which there has been considerable confusion, likely because of a onetime fixation on Ferguson as a 'civic humanist' with sympathies for ancient republicanism.[228] That picture has been redressed over the last decade or so.[229] Iain McDaniel and Anna Plassart have together emphasised that Ferguson did not welcome the Revolution out of some latent republican sympathy, and instead viewed it with morbid fascination as a disastrous event that nevertheless proved the truth of many of his reflections on moral philosophy and the study of history. The new letters help to confirm that Ferguson's reaction to the Revolution was emphatically not 'exceptionally favourable', and the new essay in particular contains the only time Ferguson seems to have ventured a prescriptive solution for ending it.[230] It was based firmly on his theories of commercial society developed over the previous decades (discussed above) and, notably, it also contained a fleeting endorsement for a European union based upon these ideas.

One problem that has been present in assessing Ferguson's reaction to the Revolution is the lack of evidence from its early years. Few letters to any correspondents survive from the period from summer 1789 to the summer of 1793, and those that do contain little of substance on the Revolution. Some have indeed argued that he was ambivalent and perhaps also cautiously optimistic in the beginning, like his star pupil (and successor at Edinburgh) Dugald Stewart (1753–1828) and his favourite philosopher Thomas Reid (1710–96).[231] As we have seen, however, Ferguson was consistently suspicious of political design and reform projects. We have also shown that Ferguson was committed to the principles of unintended consequences and gradual, spontaneous progress. He explicitly warned against sudden changes from monarchy to democracy.[232] Elsewhere, he wrote that democracy was only practicable in a small state and in the *Essay* he was clear about the 'absurdity' of democracy in a polished society in which the division of labour had taken place.[233] It also required inequality and was thus more suitable for earlier, more rudimentary societies – usually supported by slavery, an institution of which Ferguson unequivocally disapproved – than modern commercial societies. Finally, he was fearful of popular disorder, arguing for strong government action to contain the 'Wilkes and Liberty' frenzy in London in 1768–70. Taken together, it appears that Ferguson is more likely to have been sceptical about the French Revolution from intellectual and political principles at the start.

It has occasionally been assumed that Ferguson welcomed the Revolution in its early stages based on one statement from a letter of 1790 to an unknown correspondent.[234] At the end of a short passage describing the democratic levelling taking place and the fall of the French nobility, Ferguson predicted that the French would as a result be 'better neighbours both in Europe & Asia than they have been heretofore'.[235] Yet this is better understood placed in the context of Ferguson's pessimistic view of Franco-British relations in the years before the outbreak of the war. In two new letters (nos 9 and 10 below) to Macpherson written in October 1787, Ferguson railed against the Eden Commercial Treaty, thinking that France had tricked Britain into a sham commercial treaty, but was really preparing for war:

> Here in all appearance is War and the Loving Friends joined in the Eternal bands of the Commercial Treaty more inveterate Ennemies than ever. Half the Drunkards have not had time to lay in their Claret, when to it begins to be surmised that the French are ready to strike in the East & West Indies, have taken hold of the Cape of Good Hope, & have allowed us to amuse ourselves with a Commercial Treaty as the Whale is amused with a Tube.

This is particularly ironic because Macpherson had helped to organise the negotiations in their early stages while he was governor general of Bengal in 1786,[236] but the point is that in his letter of 1790, Ferguson might only have meant that France would be too internally distracted to pursue much on the international stage.

After a lull, the Ferguson–Macpherson correspondence picked back up in 1793, when Macpherson returned to Britain and Ferguson set off on his trip to Italy. We add nine new letters from the period 1793 to March 1795, where only three (all from September and October 1793) were previously known. Four of these are letters written while Ferguson was on his European tour; strikingly, while they include comments on the military situation during the Flemish campaigns and the Siege of Toulon during the War of the First Coalition, the Revolution and its political trappings only feature from 6 May 1794, when Ferguson expressed his relief crossing the English Channel:

to think there was such a ditch between those Infernals the French Democrats and this Country. Men innumerable not to be dismayed by defeats or urged by the Guilotine at their Backs to face any Ennemy in Front again & again after a death no less than after a Victory ... For my part it is the most tremendous Ennemy that ever existed & not to be overcome till they go by the ears among themselves which they would soon do if they had no Other Ennemies. & to put them in this Situation is the difficulty: for their leaders know well how Ruinous it would be.[237]

Fully formulated here is the crux of the argument that Ferguson would make for the rest of the Revolutionary and Napoleonic periods: that it was the mixture of democracy and military spirit that made the Revolution uniquely dangerous. As Plassart discusses in a crisp chapter, Ferguson identified the democratised army as the revolutionary centrifuge: the democratic levelling undertaken by the National Assembly had affected the army most profoundly, whose 'rank and file' had long been treated abysmally by the noble officer class.[238] Since soldiers had imbibed the revolutionary doctrine and could now advance by merit and ability, they could not be counted on by the monarch or nobility to suppress the National Assembly. The revolutionaries in Paris played up the international threat in order to consolidate their position, and it was a gift that the Duke of Brunswick (1735–1806) crossed the Rhine, making it easier to rally the people around the tricolour. After repelling the invading forces, the French armies were sent abroad to spread the revolution, and could therefore not be present to subvert the civil government in Paris, which Ferguson repeatedly predicted they eventually would. McDaniel shows that Ferguson was acutely aware that the French army – driven by ideology and conquest – posed a new threat to Europe, whose commercial society had enervated martial virtue and therefore rendered other states vulnerable to France's revived spirit of ancient conquest.

Yet Ferguson had a consistent plan for stemming the violence of the French armies: refusing to engage except for defensive purposes. The war kept the French republic alive, but peace would force the revolution in on itself by generating a power struggle between the civil and military government. The civil government was safe only so long as the armies were abroad. Ferguson had predicted this would happen since 1793, when the Levée en Masse revived the spirit of ancient conquest: the republic could exist only so long as it continued to conquer. Ferguson was frustrated because he had 'from the first' realised that the aggression by the 'Jacobin Club was meant by them to foster the Revolutionary Violence' and by producing a hostile foreign reaction 'unite all France in support of them'; however, 'almost nobody' saw this, failing to realise the novelty of the conflict and blundering on as they would have 'any former war with France'. Therefore, Ferguson's constant refrain was to cease engaging with the French, publicly renounce any intention to acquire territory, and to prepare 'a dignifyed & inconquerable state of Defence' in order to make the French think twice about invading.[239] His approach can thus be contrasted with Burke's view that the British needed to wage an offensive war against Jacobinism at home and abroad.

Ferguson often threw out thoughts along these lines to Macpherson; however, in the short essay contained with the new letters, he offered a more systematic treatment of the Revolution's causes and the best means of ending it until his 'Of the French Revolution' essay contained in the Merolle manuscripts and dated by him to c. 1806–7.[240] Macpherson had probably encouraged Ferguson to write about the Revolution at essay length, but Ferguson indicated in other letters that he thought it a bad idea because British public debate might give away too much and influence French policy.[241] He was irritated by the pamphlets of the Genevan François d'Ivernois (1757–1842), which bore some similarities to the ideas of Macpherson, partially for this reason. It may have been written only for Macpherson – who was harvesting Ferguson's ideas for his own pamphlets[242] – but also might have been circulated to other figures like Blair.

The new essay is a transcript in neither Ferguson's nor Macpherson's hand, but contains on the outside in Macpherson's hand, 'Copy / Dr Ferguson's opinion / Public affairs / <u>no Date French Revolution</u>'. We suggest that the new essay was included in Ferguson's often-quoted letter to Macpherson of 26 September 1797, in which amidst a long discussion of the war and events in France Ferguson notes that he included 'a full Sheet' of further discussion. Though this is as far as the extrinsic evidence goes, intrinsically the essay's contents are firmly in line with Ferguson's views at the time. It contains a broad contextual picture on the Revolution's causes and effects both in France and throughout Europe unavailable in his other contemporary writings.

The essay stretches to about 1,050 words and first describes the Revolution's current threat to Europe before moving on to analyse the best means of ending the war and ensuring another one does not break out. The essay opens with the arresting line, 'The French Revolution has formed the most dangerous Crisis that ever took place in Europe'. However, here Ferguson goes further than he went in his letters and explains that it is not merely the serious threat of the French armies that worries him, but a wider problem inherent to commercial society, viz. democratic levelling and the expropriation of property by the poor:

> By that example the needy are invited to supply their wants, not by industry and labour the source of prosperity to themselves and their country; but by levelling degradation of ranks, and violation of property. They are taught to look for liberty in the subversion of all former authority and in serving the Government of their Country. The majority of the People are needy and have the force of numbers to subvert the actual order of things in every state.

The division of labour in modern commercial society had created inequalities that rose to such heights that 'the needy' now numbered high enough to completely overturn civil society – by despoiling property – if they wanted to. This is why, *pace* Plassart, it cannot be said that Ferguson feared mostly the military threat of the revolutionary armies.[243] They were spreading their doctrine at the end of their bayonets:

> The existing war in Europe is an attack made by such Revolutionists & an attempt to spread their contagion, to devalue the blame of their own distresses on other nations and by the presence of external war to keep their People united at home, to Justify under the alarm of danger from abroad the violence which their Leaders are disposed to commit on the Persons and Properties of their Opponents and fellow Citizens ... In this war every advance is a triffle [*sic*] that does not ward off the danger of French contagion, and no particular loss merits consideration farther than it lends to keep up or to spread the contagion to be dreaded.

Ferguson had written as early as part IV in the *Essay on the History of Civil Society* that democracy was 'absurd' in a polished society where the division of labour had taken place, and the French Revolution arrived to bear out his warnings. Democratic levelling, or 'French contagion', threatened civil society across Europe. Therefore the central aim of the allies should be to stop it:

> France is a house on fire in the midst of a great Town, every neighbour ought to join in extinguishing the flame at once for his own sake, and for that of the unfortunate owner whose ruin alas is to be lamented and if possible prevented.

However, as he had observed many times, Ferguson wrote that the revolutionaries had so far managed to keep feeding the fire by provoking external aggression, thereby strengthening their own position.

> For this purpose their Leaders have provoked such hostilities, and continue to prosper under their effects. They are hastening to bring their People into the condition of a wild military force independent of the accommodations & luxuries which appear necessary to other nations.

In other words, as Plassart and McDaniel have outlined, the revolutionaries were reviving the spirit of ancient conquest in modern Europe, where luxury had enervated martial virtue and made modern states particularly vulnerable to this reanimated species of aggressor.

The rest of the essay addresses how this was to be combatted by a concerted effort on the part of the other European powers. First, the confederacy of nations engaged against France had to abandon any notion that the war might result in territorial gain or advantage to them, and instead had to collectively prioritise the 'defensive cause' of limiting French contagion by imposing a blockade. 'Declarations & manifestos' would inform the 'People of France and of all Europe' that the war's purpose was 'merely defensive' and in support of 'securing a Barrier . . . opposed to [the Influence of France]'. Every nation should issue a manifesto to this effect, after having them ratified by a 'Convention consisting of deputies entrusted to frame and issue their declarations from a Joint authority'. Importantly, 'all the nations of Europe' and 'the People of France more especially' would be invited to send deputies 'to consider the best measures to restore or preserve the good order of nations'. If the French government rejected this 'candid and beneficent overture' it would 'at least satisfy the subjects of the powers at war that their object is reasonable, and merely defensive'; it would also show the people of France that the confederacy acted in good faith, and it was conceivable that 'a Party may arise in that Country more likely to extinguish the fire which now rages there than any efforts that could be made from abroad.'

The final lines are intriguing, because in them Ferguson suggests that the famous plan of Henri IV for a European union might be followed. Macpherson had repeatedly cited Henri IV as an inspiration, which may have rubbed off on Ferguson. However, the present crisis was more acute because in the era of Henri IV 'every Sovereign had the hearty support of his own subjects', whereas now the danger was 'in the bosom of every state, and if not well guarded is ready to burst out from thence'. Commercial society had produced inequalities that weakened the bonds holding political communities together, a problem that would have to be addressed by European states collectively. After restoring peace to Europe and 'opening an Era of new liberty & happiness' to France, it was possible that Ferguson's proposed union might provide a new basis for European international relations:

> Such a Convention if we may at all indulge as romantic an idea if continued might save to Europe many articles of ruinous expence, & many a destructive war, by bringing differences under negotiation and friendly arbitration & enabling nations to concert together Proportional reductions of Troops & other expences by removing obstructions to commerce &ct. &ct. &ct.

Arrestingly, Ferguson tentatively suggested a European union. Here we might reach the limits of reading Ferguson's reactions out of his published works; for according to Plassart and McDaniel, Ferguson viewed the threat posed by France – the revival of ancient conquest within a modern commercial society – as *sui generis*. Ancient Rome offered no lessons here, so it seems that Ferguson might have entertained a distinctively modern solution: a union of mutual interests, made possible by commercial society.

The new essay is particularly valuable because it is a systematic composition and not just off-the-cuff remarks thrown out by Ferguson because he wanted to use Macpherson's franking privilege as an MP to send letters to his sons abroad. This is a key point to make because Ferguson's opinions on the French Revolution are derived largely from his correspondence with Macpherson, in which well-developed ideas are mixed in with flashes of emotion (he had a famous temper), often in reaction to specific events. Though quite coherent, these occasionally half-baked ideas cannot be equated with, for example, the *Essay on the History of Civil Society*.[244] But when the new essay and letters are considered alongside each other, it can no longer be entertained that Ferguson might have harboured 'republican' sympathy for the French Revolution.

Though Ferguson's letters often shed light on his political thought, they also reveal that he, like most human beings, often failed to live up to his own high standards of principle and moral rectitude. The most glaring example is that for all his lifelong support of militias, when one was finally being raised in Scotland Ferguson sought to buy his son out of it.[245] Another example disclosed more fully by the new letters is that, despite his misgivings about the corrosive characteristics of empire and luxury, Ferguson endorsed private gain in India and happily accepted a gift of over £1,100 from Macpherson, with which he paid off the feu-duties on his farm at Bankhead.[246] The point is not to expose Ferguson as a hypocrite, but to emphasise that we cannot deduce his conduct simply from studying his published works or vice versa. But even though political statements are made in different contexts and at different levels of debate and abstraction, for the historian the discovery of new sources and more data is always a boon. Accordingly, reading the new sources collected here, along with the Ferguson's other letters, unpublished essays, and published works, doubtlessly helps us come closer to a fuller understanding of one of the central thinkers of the Scottish Enlightenment and a key figure in the history of political thought.

Notes

1. Duncan Forbes, 'Introduction', in Adam Ferguson, *An Essay on the History of Civil Society* (Edinburgh, 1966 [1767]), xiii–xiv; Fania Oz-Salzberger, *Translating the Enlightenment: Scottish Civic Discourse in Eighteenth-Century Germany* (Oxford, 1995), 89–90.
2. For important works on the Scottish Enlightenment in which Ferguson features prominently see Gladys Bryson, *Man and Society:*

The Scottish Inquiry of the Eighteenth Century (Princeton, 1945); Ronald L. Meek, *Social Science and the Ignoble Savage* (Cambridge, 1976); Richard B. Sher, *Church and University in the Scottish Enlightenment: The Moderate Literati of Edinburgh* (Edinburgh, 1985); John Robertson, *The Scottish Enlightenment and the Militia Issue* (Edinburgh, 1985); Oz-Salzberger, *Translating the Enlightenment*; Silvia Sebastiani, *The Scottish Enlightenment: Race, Gender, and the Limits of Progress* (Basingstoke, 2013); Anna Plassart, *The Scottish Enlightenment and the French Revolution* (Cambridge, 2015). For books focusing directly on Ferguson see David Kettler, *The Social and Political Thought of Adam Ferguson* (Columbus, 1965); Lisa Hill, *The Passionate Society: The Social, Political, and Moral Thought of Adam Ferguson* (Dordrecht, 2006); David Allan, *Adam Ferguson* (Edinburgh, 2006); Eugene Heath and Vincenzo Merolle, ed., *Adam Ferguson: History, Progress and Human Nature* (London, 2008); Eugene Heath and Vincenzo Merolle, ed., *Adam Ferguson: Philosophy, Politics and Society* (London, 2009); Iain McDaniel, *Adam Ferguson in the Scottish Enlightenment: The Roman Past and Europe's Future* (Cambridge, MA, 2013); Craig Smith, *Adam Ferguson and the Idea of Civil Society: Moral Science in the Scottish Enlightenment* (Edinburgh, 2018).

3. For Ferguson's unpublished manuscripts and correspondence see Vincenzo Merolle, Robin Dix and Eugene Heath, ed., *The Manuscripts of Adam Ferguson* (London, 2006); Vincenzo Merolle, ed., *The Correspondence of Adam Ferguson* (2 vols, London, 1995).

4. The letters were hiding in plain sight in a semi-restricted collection in the British Library. We are not the first to have accessed them, yet they have remained largely unknown to Scottish Enlightenment scholarship. See Section 2 for more information.

5. The classic account is Sher, *Church and University*.

6. For details of Ferguson's death and his epitaph see letter no. 3 in Appendix A.

7. Just a few months previously Edward Gibbon (1737–94) had taken a similar route in the other direction, fleeing the Revolution and depressed because it seemed unstoppable.

8. See letters 23 and 26 in this chapter.

9. Present in the Macpherson collection and included in Appendix A are subsequent letters from Ferguson's family and friends written to John Macpherson after their father's death.

10. J. Ferguson and R. M. Fergusson, *Records of the Clan and Name of Fergusson, Ferguson, and Fergus* (Edinburgh, 1895), 150.

11. This is taken from Ferguson and Fergusson, *Records*, 162–3, rather than the Ferguson letters in the Edinburgh University Library, on which Merolle drew. We have the complete original here (letter no. 3).
12. The latest letter that was available to Merolle is dated 16 September 1808 (Merolle, *Correspondence*, II, 509–10); ours is dated 13 August 1811 (letter no. 36).
13. The letter in which we believe it was included is in Merolle, *Correspondence*, II, 420.
14. See Joshua Ehrlich, 'Empire and Enlightenment in Three Letters from Sir William Jones to governor general John Macpherson', *Historical Journal* 62 (2019): 541–51, for additional details.
15. Hugh Trevor-Roper, *The Invention of Scotland: Myth and History* (New Haven, 2008), 251 n. 43.
16. See, e.g., F. P. Lock, 'An Unpublished Letter from Adam Smith to Sir John Macpherson', *Scottish Historical Review* 85 (2006): 135–7.
17. Lock, 'Unpublished Letter'. See also E. C. Mossner and I. S. Ross, ed., *The Correspondence of Adam Smith* (Oxford, 1977): 236–7, 300.
18. Merolle, *Correspondence*, I, 98–100. Both Macpherson and Ferguson followed the Smithian logic that the main objective of each country's political economy was the increase of the 'riches and power' in that country. See Istvan Hont, *Jealousy of Trade: International Competition and the Nation-State in Historical Perspective* (Cambridge, MA, 2005), 53.
19. A gift is mentioned in a letter from Macpherson to Ferguson in Merolle (no. 241) (Merolle, *Correspondence*, II, 316), but Ferguson acknowledges it and mentions the sum in his letter of 31 March 1787 (letter no. 6).
20. G. C. Bolton and B. E. Kennedy, 'William Eden and the Treaty of Mauritius, 1786–7', *Historical Journal* 16 (1973): 681–96.
21. For a step in this direction see Ian Stewart, 'Adam Ferguson, Sir John Macpherson, and the French Revolution: New Evidence and Perspectives', *Scottish Historical Review* (forthcoming 2023).
22. Plassart, *Scottish Enlightenment*, 128. See J. G. A. Pocock, *The Machiavellian Moment: Florentine Political Thought and the Atlantic Republican Tradition* (Princeton, [1975] 2016), 499–505. For examples following this line see Oz-Salzberger, *Translating the Enlightenment*, 103–6; Hill, *The Passionate Society*, 31–2.
23. For discussion see Plassart, *Scottish Enlightenment*, 125–55; McDaniel, *Adam Ferguson*, esp. 183–212.
24. Letter no. 20.

25. The new essay is 'Copy Dr Ferguson's opinions' in the British Library (hereafter 'BL'), MSS EUR F291/97, ff. 42r–45v. 'Of the French Revolution with its Actual and Still Impending Consequences in Europe' is marked essay no. XIV in Merolle et al., *Manuscripts*, 133–41.
26. 'Copy Dr Ferguson's opinions', ff. 42r–v.
27. Iain McDaniel, 'Unsocial Sociability in the Scottish Enlightenment: Ferguson and Kames on War, Sociability and the Foundations of Patriotism', *History of European Ideas* 41 (2015): 662–82.
28. Henry Cockburn, *Memorials of His Time* (Edinburgh, 1856), 50.
29. Carlyle to Macpherson, 3 February 1794, BL, MSS EUR F291/87, ff. 22r–v.
30. See 'Appendix L', in Merolle, *Correspondence*, II, 578–82. See letters 19 and 20.
31. Letter no. 22.
32. On extremely flimsy evidence, for example, the author 'regrettably' levels the 'repugnant charge' of homosexuality against Macpherson (James Noel Mackenzie Maclean, 'The Early Political Careers of James "Fingal" Macpherson (1736–1796) and Sir John Macpherson, Bart. (1744–1821)' (PhD thesis, University of Edinburgh, 1967), 56–7.
33. Ehrlich, 'Empire and Enlightenment'; Macpherson is also discussed in Ehrlich, *The East India Company and the Politics of Knowledge* (Cambridge, 2023).
34. Macpherson discusses his family history in a letter to an unknown correspondent in BL/MSS EUR F291/172, and BL/MSS EUR F291/102 contains a short biography written by Charles Francis Greville and corrected by Macpherson himself. Biographical material is available in Paul J. deGategno, 'Macpherson, Sir John, first baronet', in *Oxford Dictionary of National Biography*, accessed 26 July 2021, https://o-www-oxforddnb-com.catalogue.libraries.london.ac.uk/view/10.1093/ref:odnb/9780198614128.001.0001/odnb-9780198614128-e-17730?rskey=APGIYT&result=5; M. H. Port and R. G. Thorne, 'Macpherson, Sir John, 1st Bt. (1774–1821), of Bromton Grove, Mdx', in R. G. Thorne, *The History of Parliament: The House of Commons 1790–1820* (Woodbridge, 1986), accessed 8 October 2021, https://www.historyofparliamentonline.org/volume/1790-1820/member/macpherson-sir-john-1744-1821.
35. Macpherson to [?], BL/MSS EUR F291/172, f. 1r.
36. It was common not to take a diploma and it is unclear whether he did take one from Aberdeen. However, he was awarded an honorary doctorate from the University of Aberdeen in 1781 (it is located in BL/MSS EUR F291/172).

37. Published as John Macpherson, *Critical Dissertation on the Origin, Antiquities, Language, Government, Manners, and Religion, of the Ancient Caledonians, Their Posterity the Picts, and the British and Irish Scots* (London, 1768).
38. BL MSS EUR F291/102, ff. 7r–v.
39. Draft of a letter from Macpherson to Ferguson, BL MSS EUR F291/172, f. 16r; BL MSS EUR F291/102, f. 7v. Robert Orme was the author of *A History of the Military Transactions of the British Nation in Indostan, From the Year MDCCXLV* (London, 1763).
40. This paragraph relies on Maclean, 'Early Political Careers', 113–88.
41. Nicholas B. Dirks, *The Scandal of Empire: India and the Creation of Imperial Britain* (Cambridge, MA, 2008), 61–80.
42. Macpherson remained friendly with the prime minister's sons, George Augustus North (1757–1802), third Earl of Guildford, and Francis North (1761–1817), later fourth Earl of Guildford, in the 1780s (see letters in BL MSS EUR F291/146).
43. Macpherson to Carlyle, 29 October 1783, BL MSS EUR F291/87, ff. 8r–v.
44. Merolle, *Correspondence*, II, 314–17.
45. In a 1788 Report of the East India Committee, Sir Grey Cooper (c. 1726–1801) and Henry Dundas (1742–1811) spoke laudably of Macpherson's tenure as governor general, emphasising his financial measures.
46. [John Macpherson], *The Present Question, in its Constitutional Point of View* [1788], in MSS EUR F291/176.
47. Sir N. W. Wraxall, *Posthumous Memoirs of His Own Time* (3 vols, London, 1836), II, 10–11.
48. See the letter book to the Prince of Wales in BL, MSS EUR F291/76/1.
49. Wraxall, *Memoirs*, II, 10–11.
50. Ferguson had long encouraged Macpherson to re-enter parliament after he returned from India. See letter no. 17; Merolle, *Correspondence*, II, 393.
51. [John Macpherson], *First and Second Letter to a Noble Earl* (London, 1797).
52. Charles Greville, Manuscript biography of Ferguson, BL MSS EUR F291/102, f. 7v.
53. Maclean 'Early Political Careers', 276, 297, 299, 306–9.
54. Maclean 'Early Political Careers', 281.
55. Maclean, 'Early Political Careers', 297.
56. Merolle, *Correspondence*, I, 98–9. The first letter listed in the Merolle correspondence is estimated by Merolle to have been written c.

1772, but this is based on the assumption that the endorsement was written by Macpherson in 1773. However, based on the contents of the letter and the lack of communication between Macpherson and Ferguson this seems unlikely. Macpherson went through his correspondence and commented on parts of it in later years; it is therefore possible it was mislabelled retroactively.

57. Merolle, *Correspondence*, II, 314.
58. David Kettler, 'Political Education for Empire and Revolution', in Heath and Merolle, *Adam Ferguson*, 87–114. The focus on Ferguson's moral philosophy as educating the 'Statesman and Warrior' has repeatedly been pointed out by Merolle and Iain McDaniel, among others.
59. On this see Jane B. Fagg, 'Biographical Introduction', in Merolle, *Correspondence*, I, lxxxvii–xciv. Ferguson was also on the lookout for opportunities and marriages for his three daughters, though here Macpherson was of less help (see, e.g., Carlyle to Macpherson, 13 April 1787, BL MSS EUR MSS 291/87, f. 3r).
60. See, e.g., Merolle, *Correspondence*, II, 105.
61. See, e.g., Macpherson to George Johnstone, 8 April 1783, BL EUR MSS 291/110, f. 6v.
62. Macpherson to Robert Greville, 24 September 1804, BL EUR MSS 291/103, f. 48v.
63. Ferguson and Fergusson, *Records*, 150.
64. Merolle, *Correspondence*, I, 99.
65. Merolle, *Correspondence*, II, 315.
66. Letter no. 17.
67. Maclean, 'Early Political Careers', 276.
68. Macpherson to Carlyle, 23 October 1783, BL MSS EUR F291/87, f. 4v; Carlyle to Macpherson, 13 April 1787, BL MSS EUR F291/87, f. 2v.
69. Home to Macpherson, 12 December 1785, BL MSS EUR F291/107, f. 8r.
70. Blair to Macpherson, 20 November 1781, BL MSS EUR F291/83, f. 25v.
71. Home to Macpherson, 12 December 1785, BL MSS EUR F291/107, f. 8v. Burke and Smith had corresponded since the publication of *The Theory of Moral Sentiments* in 1759. They met and became friends in the 1770s.
72. Carlyle to Macpherson, 3 March 1786, BL MSS EUR F291/87, ff. 27r–28r.
73. Lock, 'Unpublished Letter', 135–7.

74. For the popularity of history in the eighteenth century, see Mark Towsey, *Reading History in Britain and America, c. 1750–1840* (Cambridge, 2019).
75. Carlyle to Macpherson, 8 February 1781, BL MSS EUR F291/87, f. 37v.
76. Carlyle to Macpherson, 30 November 1782, BL MSS EUR F291/87, f. 12r.
77. Blair to Macpherson, 20 November 1781, BL, MSS EUR F291/83, f. 25v.
78. Carlyle to Macpherson, 3 March 1786, BL, MSS EUR F291/87, f. 27r.
79. Blair to Macpherson, 1 August 1787, BL MSS EUR F291/83, f. 23.
80. Garland Cannon, ed., *The Letters of Sir William Jones* (2 vols, Oxford, 1970), II, 679, 698.
81. Merolle, *Correspondence*, II, 316. This was just a few weeks before Jones delivered his important 'Third Discourse' to the Asiatick Society.
82. Cannon, *Letters*, II, 727. Ferguson's aphoristic line which Jones memorised was 'Justice to the Stranger who has no advocate to plead for Favour is the Soul of Government & wins the heart more than Millions bestowed on Favourites' (see letter no. 4).
83. Ehrlich, 'Empire and Enlightenment'; Cannon, *Letters*, II, 672; W. E. Hughes, ed., *Monumental Inscriptions and Extracts from Registers of Births, Marriages, and Deaths, at St. Anne's Church, Soho* (London, 1905), 17.
84. Letter no. 17.
85. Ferguson, *Essay on the History of Civil Society*, ed. Fania Oz-Salzberger (Cambridge, 1997), 8; David Hume, *A Treatise of Human Nature*, ed. L. A. Selby-Bigge and P. H. Nidditch (Oxford, 1978 [1739–40]), xvi–xvii.
86. See esp. Smith, *Adam Ferguson*; Kettler, *Adam Ferguson*; Bryson, *Man and Society*, ch. 2.
87. See, e.g., Ferguson, *Essay*, 12.
88. On 'conjectural history', and how it can be distinguished from speculation, see Christopher Berry, *Social Theory of the Scottish Enlightenment* (Edinburgh, 1997), 61–70, and Christopher Berry, *The Idea of Commercial Society in the Scottish Enlightenment* (Edinburgh, 2013), 32–8. For criticism of the concept of 'conjectural history' as applied to Adam Smith, see Paul Sagar, *Adam Smith Reconsidered: History, Liberty, and the Foundations of Modern Politics* (Princeton, 2022), esp. ch. 1.
89. *Essay*, 16–21; Ferguson, *Principles of Moral and Political Science* (2 vols, Edinburgh, 1792), I, 26–36, 204–9.

90. Ferguson, *Institutes of Moral Philosophy* (Edinburgh, 1769), 188.
91. *Institutes*, 162.
92. *Institutes*, 162–4.
93. *Institutes*, 171.
94. *Principles*, II, 180–2, 318.
95. *Essay*, 10.
96. *Essay*, 9.
97. *Essay*, 12.
98. *Essay*, 14.
99. *Essay*, 21. Ferguson probably alludes to Montesquieu, *The Spirit of the Laws* (Cambridge, 1989 [1748]), 5.
100. See also Iain McDaniel, 'Unsocial Sociability'.
101. *Essay*, 21–9.
102. On Ferguson on party, see Max Skjönsberg, 'Adam Ferguson on Partisanship, Party Conflict, and Popular Participation', *Modern Intellectual History* 16 (2019): 1–28; Max Skjönsberg, 'Adam Ferguson on the Perils of Popular Factions and Demagogues in a Roman Mirror', *History of European Ideas* 45 (2019): 842–65.
103. David Hume, *Enquiry Concerning the Principles of Morals* (Oxford, 1975 [1751]), 224; Hume, *Treatise*, 539–40.
104. Max Skjönsberg, *The Persistence of Party: Ideas of Harmonious Discord in Eighteenth-Century Britain* (Cambridge, 2021).
105. *Institutes*, 317–19.
106. *Principles*, II, 507–8.
107. This is Ferguson's own term, notably in the title of the *Principles*.
108. Around same time, Hume wrote similar letters to his publisher William Strahan, who was also a Scottish MP. For Hume, see J. G. A. Pocock, *Virtue, Commerce and History* (Cambridge, 1985), 125–42; Moritz Baumstark, 'The End of Empire and the Death of Religion', in *Philosophy and Religion in Enlightenment Britain*, ed. Ruth Savage (Oxford, 2012), 231–57. For Ferguson, see Skjönsberg, 'Adam Ferguson on Partisanship, Party Conflict, and Popular Participation'.
109. Merolle, *Manuscripts*, 133–41.
110. James Moore and Michael Silverthorne, 'Gershom Carmichael and the Natural Jurisprudence Tradition in Eighteenth-Century Scotland', in *Wealth and Virtue: The Shaping of Political Economy in the Scottish Enlightenment*, ed. Istvan Hont and Michael Ignatieff (Cambridge, 1983), 73–87. For the wider context, see Knud Haakonssen, *Natural Law and Moral Philosophy: From Grotius to the Scottish Enlightenment* (Cambridge, 1996), esp. chs 1–2; Duncan Forbes, *Hume's Philosophical Politics* (Cambridge, 1975), ch. 2.

111. Francis Hutcheson, *A System of Moral Philosophy* (2 vols, London, 1755), II, 231–3. On this see, Dario Castiglione, 'The Origin of Government', in *The Oxford Handbook of British Philosophy in the Eighteenth Century*, ed. James Harris (Oxford, 2013), 491–529.
112. Hume to Hutcheson, 10 January 1743, in *The Letters of David Hume*, ed. J. Y. T. Greig (2 vols, Oxford, 2011 [1932]), I, 48.
113. See Berry, *Social Theory of the Scottish Enlightenment*, ch. 2; Christopher Berry, *Hume, Smith and the Scottish Enlightenment* (Edinburgh, 2018), chs 5, 7, 8.
114. *Principles*, II, 214–25.
115. Castiglione, 'The Origin of Government', 517.
116. Ferguson, *Principles*, II, 232–4; Hume, 'Of the Origin of Government', *Essays, Moral, Political and Literary* (Indianapolis, 1985), 37–41.
117. *Essay*, 118.
118. *Principles*, II, 245.
119. *Institutes*, 28–9.
120. James Moore, 'Natural Rights in the Scottish Enlightenment', in *The Cambridge History of Eighteenth-Century Political Thought*, ed. Mark Goldie and Robert Wokler (Cambridge, 2006), 291–316; Meek, *Social Science*.
121. *Principles*, II, 423. This process had been discussed by both Rousseau in the *Discourse on Inequality* and Smith in *The Theory of Moral Sentiments*.
122. *Essay*, 119.
123. Craig Smith, 'The Scottish Enlightenment, Unintended Consequences and the Science of Man', *Journal of Scottish Philosophy* 7 (2009): 9–28; Ronald Hamowy, *The Scottish Enlightenment and the Theory of Spontaneous Order* (Carbondale, 1987).
124. *Essay*, 120.
125. *Essay*, 119.
126. See Haakonssen, *Natural Law and Moral Philosophy*, chs 3–4.
127. *Essay*, 37.
128. *Essay*, 37.
129. *Principles*, II, 192. Hume had notoriously called justice an 'artificial virtue' in *A Treatise of Human Nature*, 477–84.
130. *Essay*, 38.
131. *Principles*, II, 184–5.
132. *Essay*, 38.
133. *Principles*, II, 243.
134. *Principles*, II, 241–2, 253–6. For justifications of slavery in the seventeenth-century social contract tradition, see Johan Olsthoorn

and Laurens van Apeldoorn, '"This man is my property": Slavery and Political Absolutism in Locke and the Classical Social Contract Tradition', *European Journal of Political Theory* 21 (2022): 253–75.
135. *Principles*, II, 253–4.
136. *Principles*, II, 195, 197.
137. *Principles*, II, 180.
138. *Principles*, II, 180–2.
139. Adam Smith, *The Theory of Moral Sentiments* (Indianapolis, 1982 [1759]), 82.
140. *Principles*, II, 195, 198–9.
141. *Principles*, II, 200–1.
142. *Principles*, II, 234.
143. *Principles*, II, 201.
144. *Principles*, II, 212.
145. *Principles*, II, 212.
146. *Institutes*, 288. See also *Essay*, 150–1.
147. *Institutes*, 288–9.
148. *Principles*, II, 458.
149. See, e.g., *Principles*, II, 461.
150. *Principles*, II, 477.
151. *Principles*, II, 462.
152. *Principles*, II, 463.
153. *Principles*, II, 463.
154. Hume, 'Of Civil Liberty' (1741), in *Essays*, 94.
155. *Principles*, II, 464.
156. *Principles*, II, 464. See also Yiftah Elazar, 'Adam Ferguson on Modern Liberty and the Absurdity of Democracy', *History of Political Thought* 35 (2014): 768–87.
157. *Principles*, II, 467.
158. *Principles*, II, 469.
159. *Principles*, II, 469–70. See also *Principles*, I, 262–3. Ferguson advanced a similar argument against Hobbes in the context of property: 'universal consent' to establish property rights in the place of everyone's right to all things in the original state amounted to something 'altogether visionary' that 'never can be obtained' (*Principles*, II, 237–8).
160. *Principles*, II, 70.
161. *Principles*, II, 473.
162. Merolle, *Correspondence*, II, 289, 291–2.
163. *Principles*, II, 474–5.

164. *Principles*, II, 487.
165. *Principles*, II, 492.
166. This was the standard way of defending the British constitution, which was a 'balanced' one. See also William Selinger, *Parliamentarism: From Burke to Weber* (Cambridge, 2019); M. J. C. Vile, *Constitutionalism and the Separation of Powers* (Indianapolis, 1998 [1967]).
167. *Principles*, II, 491.
168. *Principles*, II, 494.
169. *Principles*, II, 501.
170. *Essay*, 159–60.
171. *Essay*, 125.
172. *Essay*, 158.
173. See also *Principles*, I, 256–70.
174. *Principles*, II, 509.
175. *Principles*, II, 510.
176. *Principles*, II, 509.
177. *Principles*, II, 512.
178. Castiglione, 'The Origin of Government', 524–5.
179. Richard Price, preface to the fifth edition of *Observations on the Nature of Civil Liberty, the Principles of Government, and the Justice and Policy of the War with America* (1776), in Price, *Political Writings*, ed. D. O. Thomas (Cambridge, 1992), 20.
180. Price, *Observations*, in *Political Writings*, 23.
181. Price, *Observations*, in *Political Writings*, 30. Price is probably alluding to Montesquieu, *Considerations on the Causes of the Greatness of the Romans and their Decline* (Indianapolis, 1999 [1734]), 93.
182. See Part II.
183. *Principles*, II, 501–2. See also letter no. 34, and the long letters to Dundas in Merolle, *Correspondence*, II, 476–7, 480–1.
184. *Principles*, II, 502.
185. Ferguson, *Reflections Previous to the Establishment of a Militia* (London, 1756), 12.
186. *Principles*, II, 493. See also *Reflections*, 7.
187. *Reflections*, 19, 30–5, 37–8, 50–1.
188. See Alexander Carlyle, *The Question Relating to the Scots Militia Considered* (Edinburgh, 1760).
189. *Reflections*, 21–2.
190. *Reflections*, 24–5.
191. *Reflections*, 25.

192. On the situation generally see Mark Philp, ed., *Resisting Napoleon: The British Response to the Threat of Invasion, 1797–1815* (London, 2006).
193. Letter no. 30.
194. Merolle, *Correspondence*, II, 476–7, 480–1.
195. Ferguson, *Essay* (London, 1773 [1767]), 241–2.
196. The literature comparing Ferguson and Smith is rather extensive. See, e.g., Anthony Brewer, 'Adam Ferguson, Adam Smith, and the Concept of Economic Growth', *History of Political Economy* 31 (1999): 237–54; Richard B. Sher, 'Adam Ferguson, Adam Smith, and the Problem of National Defense', *Journal of Modern History* 61 (1989): 240–68; Ronald Hamowy, 'Adam Smith, Adam Ferguson, and the Division of Labour', *Economica* 35 (1968): 249–59.
197. Merolle, *Correspondence*, I, 142–3.
198. Smith, *Inquiry into the Nature and Causes of the Wealth of Nations* (Indianapolis, 1982 [1776]), II, 699–700.
199. See especially Ferguson, *Reflections*. See also John Robertson, *The Scottish Enlightenment and the Militia Issue*.
200. *Institutes*, 276; *Principles*, II, 421.
201. Ferguson cited Hume's key work on political economy, the *Political Discourses* (1752), in other contexts, along with Hume's *History of England*.
202. *Essay*, 247.
203. Smith, *Wealth of Nations*, I, 412.
204. See, e.g., Allan, *Adam Ferguson*.
205. *Institutes*, 274.
206. *Principles*, II, 549.
207. *Principles*, II, 455.
208. *Principles*, II, 450.
209. McDaniel, *Adam Ferguson*, 176.
210. *Principles*, II, 452.
211. Hume, *Essays*, 360–1. See also Hont, *Jealousy of Trade*, 325–53.
212. *Principles*, II, 430, 431.
213. *Principles*, II, 423.
214. Hamowy, 'Adam Smith, Adam Ferguson, and the Division of Labour'. Ferguson had already discussed the division of labour at length in the *Essay*. This is probably the reason why Marx, who quoted Ferguson on the matter, referred to Ferguson as Smith's 'master'. See Marx, *Capital: A Critique of Political Economy. Vol I: The Process of Capitalist Production* (Chicago, 1909 [1867]), 389 n.
215. *Principles*, II, 425.

216. *Principles*, II, 427.
217. *Principles*, II, 430.
218. *Principles*, II, 425.
219. *Principles*, II, 426.
220. *Principles*, II, 428–9.
221. *Principles*, II, 430.
222. *Principles*, II, 430.
223. *Wealth of Nations*, I, 464–5.
224. *Essay*, 138.
225. Smith, *Adam Ferguson and the Idea of Civil Society*, 178–9.
226. *Principles*, II, 437–8.
227. *Principles*, II, 440–1.
228. For Ferguson as 'Machiavellian' civic humanist see Pocock, *Machiavellian Moment*, 499–501. This has been followed by Oz-Salzberger, *Translating the Enlightenment*, 103–6; Hill, *The Passionate Society*, 31–2.
229. Smith, *Adam Ferguson and the Idea of Civil Society*, esp. 11–13, 214–15, points out the distortive tendency to read Ferguson as a republican; Marco Guena, 'Republicanism and Commercial Society in the Scottish Enlightenment: The Case of Adam Ferguson', in *Republicanism: A Shared European Heritage*, ed. Martin van Gelderen and Quentin Skinner (2 vols, Cambridge, 2002), II, 189, also challenges Pocock's interpretation.
230. See Fania Oz-Salzberger, 'Ferguson, Adam, 1723–1816', in *Oxford Dictionary of National Biography*, accessed 6 October 2021, https://www.oxforddnb.com/view/10.1093/ref:odnb/9780198614128.001.0001/odnb-9780198614128-e-9315?rskey=rc4R7d&result=2.
231. Fania Oz-Salzberger, 'Adam Ferguson', *ODNB*.
232. *Principles*, II, 496.
233. *Institutes*, 293; *Essay*, 179.
234. Merolle, *Correspondence*, II, 336–7. Merolle assumes this letter was written to Macpherson because it was directed to a correspondent in India, but if the date is correct – as seems likely from internal evidence – then that is impossible because Macpherson had been back in Europe for several years by that point. For different readings suggesting that Ferguson saw the Revolution as constructive see, e.g., Sher, *Church and Society*, 305; Hill, *Passionate Society*, 31.
235. Merolle, *Correspondence*, II, 337.
236. For an account of the Eden Treaty with Macpherson's role in it see Bolton and Kennedy, 'William Eden'.

237. Ferguson to Macpherson, 6 May 1794, BL/MSS EUR F291/97, f. 54r–v.
238. Plassart, *Scottish Enlightenment*, 125–55; also McDaniel, *Adam Ferguson*, 208–10.
239. Letter no. 28.
240. Merolle, Dix and Heath, *Manuscripts*, 133–41.
241. Merolle, *Correspondence*, II, 390.
242. Cf. Macpherson, *Mémoire sur le projet de l'Empereur Léopold avec une analyse de l'histoire politique de l'Europe depuis 1756* (n.d., [July] 1797), 20–4, with Ferguson's letters to Macpherson of 2 June 1796 (Merolle, *Correspondence*, II, 393–4).
243. Plassart, *Scottish Enlightenment*, 135.
244. Merolle, *Correspondence*, II, 350.
245. Merolle, *Correspondence*, II, 423, 446, 448.
246. Letter no. 6.

New Letters of Adam Ferguson

1. Adam Ferguson to John Macpherson

Edinburgh 13th Septr
1784

My Dear Sir

 I write this Letter merely to request your attention & regard in behalf of Peter John Cullen[1] who by the last accounts was a Captain on your Establishment in Bengale. During some part of the War he was Aid-de-Camp to General Godart[2] & had his share in the services performed by that officer under the Presidency of Bombay; his merits when inquired into, I trust will recommend him sufficiently. I am concerned for him chiefly as the son of My Friend and Colleague Dr Cullen[3] who is pleased to think that a Letter, to you, from me, may be of use to him on occasion; & it will be exceedingly agreeable to me to have contributed in any way to his Advantage. I have ventured / to assure the Father that you have a very constant remembrance of those whom you used to respect here; And that his name alone would be sufficient to secure your Regard to the Son. This I make no doubt will appear when he is known to you & opportunity offers, And here my Letter naturally ends: but I must not conclude without mentioning such particulars as occur to me & you probably wish to know.
 I received about a year & half ago the Letter[4] with which you Favoured me from the Ganges. It was then of an Old Date. I wrote you about this time last year & sent my Letter[5] to be forwarded by Mr Greville.[6] Your Friends here & I among the rest saw your Letter[7] to Mr Dundas.[8] And afterwards your Letter[9] to Dr Carlyle.[10] Your Uncle Captain McLeod[11] has been here part of the Summer, Married a Daughter & been / bussy in pursuing the Object of his improvements particularly Fishery in Harris to which place he has been some time returned. I was sorry to learn from him that you

had returned from Calcutta on account of your health. Mr Greville[12] passed here this Summer with his Uncle Sir William Hamilton.[13] Their Object was to trace Vulcanos & collect Materials for the History of the Earth about which I think all Europe at Present is agogue. French men & Italians are trouping through here every Day to Visit Staffa & the mountains of Morven. Your Friends here are well, only turning damned Old as Sir Robert Moreton[14] used to say of himself. If I in particular go on I shall certainly have nothing to complain of by & by but Old Age.[15]

My Wife after some months of the most anxious Fears for her Life is safely delivered of a son whom we call John[.][16] I wrote to John Home[17] to find me a Minister with a Long enough memory / that I might add the Surnames of M{c}Pherson Fletcher Campbell & Home but this he has not done so I have you to settle the namesakeship among you, & will conclude my Letter Least in avoiding a long one I get into more trifles. I am My Dear Sir

Your most affectionate
& most humble servant
Adam Ferguson

Source: BL/MSS EUR F291/97, ff. 1r–2v.

2. Adam Ferguson to John Macpherson

Edinburgh 1st Febry 1785

My Dear Sir

Your last Letter to me was of an old Date & has been long received.[18] I have however since had communication of your Letters to Dr Carlyle & to Mr Dundas as you kindly desired I should have. I wrote to you a Letter which I sent to your Friend Mr Greville to be forwarded & another some~~what less than a Twelve month~~ months ago at the Request of Dr Cullen to introduce his son an Officer on your Establishment in Bengale.[19] I have heard of your being ill & returned from Calcutta on account of your health & of your being recovered & returned to your Station. This agreeable part of the account is recently confirmed to your Friends here by the Report of Major Staunton[20] communicated by Jas. McPherson[21] to John Home, for which I have within these very few days felt a most sincere joy. /

I have now very little to write that merits your attention but could not think of letting my Friend Cap^tn Cameron[22] go your way without carrying my Respects & earnest Good wishes. You will be made to know him probably by other channels better than mine. I had the good Fortune to be the means of procuring him his first Commission at the Recommendation of Bannachar & I never knew more ardour than he has shown in pushing forward in his Line Whether at the hazard of Ennemies or by the Aid of Friends. The Reduction if it brought full pay would be no bed of Roses for him. He offered to raise a Company of 100 highlanders for your service if he might have the command & being disappointed in that goes out a Cadet as you will be informed. In short I believe he will soon be very fit for such service as yours. As to my little flock they are grown to / seven by the addition of a namesake to you and a John or two more my most valuable Friends. We are all in pretty good health for Valitudinary People. There is an English Proverb which says that an Old woman never dies after she has got a crooked headed stick to walk with. I interpret this proverb in my own favour for tho not literally an Old woman I live like one exposed to no hazard by Cold, Fatigue, Eating or Drinking. I am a Gentoo[23] And a Musselman in my Diet eating no meat & drinking nothing but water.[24] I am perfectly convinced it is the best diet for health strength courage understanding & so forth. What Business I have with thoughts is easier to me than ever & I have nothing to trouble me but inability to sit long over any literary application, & susceptibility of Cold. If you could transport me to some dry airy spot / near the Tropics where Dates & Oranges and Figs are in Perfection I certainly should thrive like a Roc[25] on the Mountains. But this like the other objects of mortal man is afar off. In the meantime I should be happy to see you returned even to these sour & stormy Regions with all your good Conditions & reasonable wishes obtained. You see how clear I keep of Politicks. There was a time when you thought I could send you political news even from hence: but those times are past even in the utmost conceit of my own Vanity. The little we know here goes sooner to you round the Cape of good hope than it comes to us here. Many a Storm from hence has threatened to burst on your heads & the Danger is commonly over before you hear the Cracks. There is a sort of weather set in at last of which I do not see the tendency; But God grant it may not blast the harvest

Publick or Private. Let us have the credit of governing you but do the best you can for the state of your selves. The smallest must depend upon you.

A. Ferguson

Source: BL/MSS EUR F291/97, ff. 5r–6v.

3. Adam Ferguson to John Macpherson

Edinburgh 16 April
1785

My Dear Sir

Since your last to me I have ventured to give some Introductory Letters to oblige my Friends here, & I am sensible that I ought to spare you a trouble which your situation will draw upon you most abundantly:[26] but the bearer of this has too strong a claim upon me to be resisted. He is the son[27] of my Brother and of one of the honestest men that ever lived. He was born in America & I have never seen him: but I am persuaded will not disgrace your Protection. The Father & he are refugees from that lost continent & partake in the distress / which a rooted affection to this Country has brought upon many.[28] The Son by the unalterable kindness of G Johnstone[29] & his unsuppressable fervour in behalf of honest men has obtained Leave to go to India tho without any destination or appointment. I have reason to believe that he inherits part of his Fathers sense & Worthiness & is qualified for Business & hope you may find protection & good offices for him without interfering with Pupils of more Expectation. His name is Robert Ferguson & so I present him to you. We are here nearly in the same state as when you heard of us last. The Children all well; your namesake John particularly thriving tho he / is not yet apprised of his Relation to you[.] The Mother & I frail & useless with little Object but that of keeping ourselves alive till the others can do for themselves. In all this I hope you will not perceive any improper touches of melancholy: for my Spirits play very easily upon a Gentoo Diet: without being tied down to the formalities of any Cast or exposed to the caprice or Rapacity of any Master whither Christian or Moor. As to the Politicks I am as usual much weighted but unqualified to communicate with you. I am My Dear Sir

> Your most affectionate &
> Most humble servant
> Adam Ferguson

To John McPherson Esqr /
[A note on f. 10v reads:
1786
Edinburgh 16 April
Adam Ferguson
In favour
Mr Ferguson]

Source: BL/MSS EUR F291/97, ff. 9r–10v.

4. Adam Ferguson to John Macpherson

Edinburgh 16 February
1786

[A note on the left hand side reads: (received from) 'D^r. Ferguson | 16 July 86]

My Dear Sir

I trust that before this comes to hand you will have received four letters of thanks for your Madeira. I hear much of its merits: but as I am no more than a hearsay Evidence I have thought it reasonable to wait till the [illegible: 'polite'?] witnesses were examined. I flattered myself also that by waiting a little I might know more of what is projecting in this Country with relation to India but did not consider that at this distance & in my present secluded state no information was likely to reach me till it had doubled the Cape of Good hope or travelled the Desert two or three times. I therefore drop that Idea of sending you any opinion or intelligence Quid delirant Reges.[30]

M^{rs} F:[31] & I are much obliged to you for the terms in which you mention her Brother[32] & extremely happy ~~from~~ to know from yourself & from him that your health is improved. We were made to believe it suffered from your Hospitality, if so we hope that by this time you have found out that it is not a fair match between a

Person in publick Station who has company every day & his guests who are in such company occasionally. My Diet would perhaps be much too low for you to descend to at once: but something like it, or rather what you find agree with you is certainly in your Power. A Person in publick trust must be considered as a Guest at his own Table with liberty to do what he likes &c &c &c you see how difficult it is for me to write without some grains of Doctrine in my Letter. But you are well off that I do not set about telling you what you are to be & to do in your / present situation. I know you may perform Signal Service to this Country & if you put up with the consciousness of having done so this Country will amply reward.[33]
Romulus & Liber Pater & cum Castore
Pollux. Post ingenta facta-------
Ploaravere suus non respondere favorem
speratum meritis &c &c[34]

I pity the man whether Romulus or Remus who because he is well disposed thinks others are to applaud and reward. There are persons who will do so and these will help you to smile at the Rest. Mrs Fer: and I also join in thanks for your thoughts of Joseph[35] when I came to his name in your letter my poor nerves gave way & I burst into tears she was anxious to know the cause & when I showed her the passage she burst into tears also neither of us attempted to explain this Effect. The Boy is turned of Eleven is bussy at what we call Education here, that is, so much taken up in learning Latin that he has not time to learn any thing else except a little writing. I know that if ever he has the good fortune to join you the best part of his Education will then begin: but he must not be illiterate & two or three years are necessary to give him the Elements that will enable him to guess what others mean when they talk of Learning. There are some particulars relating to myself which I wish you to know although I am unwilling to make a long Letter of them. In the first place I have returned from College & left Dugald Stuart in my place.[36] The publick is exceedingly pleased with him & I bear the load of retirement & solicitude better than expectation. Tho' I live like a Gentoo I could keep company with Canibals: if I durst go about & expose myself to sit at any fire side but my own. catching cold is my Infirmity & the fear of it obliges me to stay at home except for a short walk in the middle of the day & obliges me to go to bed when Others go to supper. Your Friend Mr Dundas has within these few months laid me under infinite obligation. You remember my request of having part of my Pension transferred to Mrs Fer. / This is now done with the addition of my three daughters & the survivor of them. This addition came by surprise upon me & I did not fail to thank Mr Dundas & Mr Pitt[37] with a Proper mention of the King[38] which I hope may reach him.

The next Chapter of my History concerns the Roman History.[39] There was an ill judged conditional bargain with the Booksellers Strahan & Cadell[40] & they levied me so much that I or rather my Friends at London Gen'l Clerk[41] & Mr Pulteney[42] took it out of their hands & have dispersed it in Other shops with what effect I know not: but have little expectation from it, knowing that Booksellers who are interested can do more in the sale of a Book than either Authors or Readers, who mean to instruct or be instructed. I have written to you some short occasional letters which I hope you have Received & forgiven my pressing upon you with Recommendations &c &c I have at present by me a short list of persons who wish to be known to you my answer has been that I would mention them with my best wishes when I should write. One is M[r] J: Durham[43] in the 16 Regiment of Seapoys son to Mr Durham of Largo.[44] Another is Dr Nasmyth[45] a young Man well spoken of who went out some months ago in the Medical Line. In the same Line Alex[r] Russell[46] son to Mr John Russell[47] of this Place he had been an assistant Surgeon in the Hospital at Calcutta but discontinued with many Others upon some change of Arrangement. The Father is my particular Friend. With respect to these Gentlemen or any others I may mention all I hope for is an Inclination to favour when there is no call of Justice in the way: but Justice to the Stranger who has no advocate to plead for Favour is the Soul of Government & wins the heart more than Millions bestowed on Favourites.

I once had the good Fortune to see Sir William Jones[48] & am happy the Learned have got such an Agent in India. The great Effect of the Gentoo System on the manners of its votaries makes me wish extremely to know the Bottom of it. I suspect it operates more by associating honour with certain observances than by any System of Doctrines and that in / looking for any consistent System of Faith where possibly there is none we are apt to go wrong: but of this I trust we shall know more from Sir William Jones. I have heard it confidently said that Mr Holwell[49] had been imposed upon in the account he took of the Bramines Faith but never could learn what to think. The Mythology he states is certainly a powerfull one in the mind that is penetrated with it: But it is time I should have done interrupting you when the Transmigration of Souls comes in question. Mine is to transmigrate I expect for half the year into a Bankhead Slot very lean of course; but the safer from any danger of being eaten when I come back to this Town in Winter, which by the way when you return will astonish you as one of the best built most commodious Towns in Europe all upon the level. Other people are obliged to use Air Balloons, when they would fly;[50] we pass from hill to hill in the Air in our shoes and Boots. All the People of this House not forgetting your Namesake John for whom I am Proxy send their most affectionate compl[imen]ts & most earnest wishes for every thing good to you. If you favour us with a line if no more than what the Centry calls on his Post if it be <u>all is well</u> we shall be glad. I am My Dear Sir

Your most affectionate
& most humble servant
Adam Ferguson

Source: BL/MSS EUR F291/97, ff. 7r–8v.

5. Adam Ferguson to Sir John Macpherson[51]

Edinburgh 15 Jan^{ry}
1787

My Dear Sir

I give you this trouble by Captain Robertson of the Busbridge Indiaman[52] of whom I hope I may be allowed to say what Voltaire[53] said to Madam de Chatelet[54] in presenting Feld Marechal Lord Stair[55] – <u>Il est digne de vous connoitre</u>.[56] So I am told by one of my Oracles Mr Dougald Stuart, who next to yourself make me feel the most what it is to have the affection of Worthy Persons. If you hear by these conveyances from our Friend Fonish[57] at London he will have told you that I received all your Packets of Jan^{ry} / & Feb^{ry} last, and that he has accordingly bore the Brunt of what falls upon him. Such things ought not to pass but between Parent & Child and I have requested the above Chieftean to be taken into the Clan that I may pass without Scandal for what you make me. The Business of this Letter is finished in the first sentence but if I do not stop here no one can tell how far I may go. Here all is Well[.] John Home has drank all his Madeira of the Second Pipe[?] is reduced to Beggary as witness the Bottle which he sent for here yesterday: But Carlisle is busy Battling the Third, And we hope soon to have our Dividends of what can be diverted from his own Osophagus. You may judge what Zeal there is for the continuance of your Government. I have been flattering myself that I should write you fully when I knew of / your determination to stay or Come. The first is what I wish if there be not better reason against it than the mere Supercession.[58] I declined writing by Mr Russell Surgeon of the Busbridge from my uncertainty of your motions. Be so kind as resolve me by the first opportunity. Here all join in kind respects except your unworthy namesake who would not part with the Fig he is now eating to save you and me from the Gallows. I am My

>Dear Friend Yours Most Affectionately
>Adam Ferguson

Sir John McPherson Bar't
[A note on 12 verso reads:
Dr Ferguson 19th (damaged)
By the Busbridge, re-
Commending Capt
Robertson]

>Source: BL/MSS EUR F291/97, ff.11r–12v.

6. Adam Ferguson to Sir John Macpherson

>Sciennes Edinburgh
>31st March
>1787

My Dear Friend

I received your Letters & Duplicate of the months of Ja^{nry} & Feb^{ry} 1786 inclosing a first and second Draft on the India Company for £1000 as also in the form of postscript a first & second order on Ja^s McPherson[59] Esqr for £100.[60] I gave Ja^s McPherson intimation of these particulars soon after they came to hand & desired the favour he would mention their being received as his opportunities were likely to be more frequent than mine. The first Bill went to be presented and is accepted Payable the 1st of September next[.] The second will probably stand an Article of your First Accounts with Ja^s McPherson. And to the Purpose for which you have destined them they certainly must go.⁶¹ If I had ~~been~~ Verifyed the other alternative of your Letter, that is if I had been dead when I came to hand my Children would probably in tears have stood round the reading of your Letter. Whether they would have observed anything / extraordinary in the Conduct of a Man whose kind affection is not altered by time place of fortune otherwise than by tokens of increase I know not. This would have required more knowledge of what is common than they have. I should certainly have acquitted you, if new Objects & interesting scenes had long since erased me from your Memory. And must own that in surpassing my expectations you have also exceeded the pitch of my mind. I have opened a Negotiation with my Feudal Superior for the completion of your Will & make no doubt that before the year goes round I shall be able to effectuate the relief you propose, in the form of some Charter or writing which shall record the honour & satisfaction I reap from your Friendship. So far I should have written some Months ago if I had not been kept in some degree of suspence with respect to the consequence of a change about to take Place in your Situation & prospects, and in doubt where a Letter might find you.⁶² This stop is now done away by your Letter of the 22d August and the Postscript of the 18 Septr 1786.⁶³ The first / would have left me in some distress: but the other affords relief, which I hope you will find efficacious & Permanent. The appointment of Lord Cornwallis⁶⁴ was the sequel of overtures made two or three years ago & suspended by jumbles of Politics &c &c And I am told that if the report of what you was doing had come a little sooner, it would not have been thought necessary at all. So much are the Masters disposed to approve of your Conduct: But this is their affair. Yours is to persist in the wisest and the happiest part which circumstances present for your Choice, & above all to entrust none of your satisfaction to the return which others may make. You wonder why ~~persons~~ those who approve the conduct of one Person should neglect his Colleague: but Lide anece:⁶⁵ you will have other thoughts before this Letter come to hand. Since you were to be superseded, I take the choice that is made to be of a Piece with the fortunate emergences to which you allude in one of your Letters & of which you have ever made the happiest use, guided as I verily believe by the intrepid & unsuspecting benevolence of your heart more than by the superiority of your judgement. Which however true is not so firm & unerring a support & light as the other. I had the fortune / to pass the Atlantic twice on the same Bottom with Lord Cornwallis.[66] Saw so much propriety in common things without any effort to appear greater than the occasion & still an Ability & Elevation that kept pace with the more arduous occasion that I became wonderfully attached to him & felt in the variety of Events that followed the Interest of a Brother or a Child. I am persuaded that if no untoward circumstance happen you will be friends, & tug at the Oar, while he steers, with as much, tho a different kind of satisfaction from what you had at the helm yourself. This is Ascribing much good to you both but you have taught me to believe: so let it proceed. We have discovered a new Poet here lately at the Plough I think equal to any of the Old.[67] This Vein is both Humorous & Heroic. Of the latter kind there is a Poem called <u>Cottars Saturdays Night,</u> from which I shall for the future be disposed to take or correct my notions of Heroic Poetry.[68] Worthyness & greatness of mind are brought to view under a great Variety of aspects without the memory stop of a supposition that they could / break forth with more lustre produce more happiness or have a better effect in the Palace of a King at the head of an Army or in dispersing inexhaustible treasures than they have at a Cottars fire side. This to me is the true genius of Heroic Poetry & it is exerted by this Noble Peasant with a Correctness and a truth which is admirable. Most people & I among the rest were long before they could be persuaded to look at his compositions but their reception at last does some honour to the Country, they have subscribed him above a thousand Pounds in Crown pieces. All this I do not mention under a Notion that the good in question is any way more connected with the State of a Cottar than with that of a Warrior or a King. The Cottar bears a noble mind where he Labours or where he sits & so may you or I. But gane moralizing too much. You tell me that now I am well I might write to you more frequently & so I might: but what are the two years you mention to the multiplication of Letters from hence to India: before what I write is well on its way we shall begin / to calculate when you may be preparing to set out on your way home. This writing of Letters to the Antipodes is something new in the World. When I think for instance where my Friend Sir John Macpherson now is I look asque down to the Ground and as you walk see you kicking your heels this way. You used to be fond of Suburbane habitations I have got one, and already feed myself with the Idea that when you come here of a Summer, instead of going to any of our Lodging houses which in Imitation of Londoners we call Hottles, you will take the Keyes of this habitation from me & people it while we are plying among the Slots at Bankhead, as we did last Summer & purpose to do every Summer till better times come: that is to say till we change our mind. We have been led to this practice by one of the Doctors Prescriptions which required my keeping a Horse or two, to drive myself in an open Chaise, <u>Air Exercise</u> and a / <u>Suspension of Thought</u> not less conducive to health than either of the other two. To lessen the Expence we went to forrage at Bankhead But we still gain more I believe in point of health than Oeconomy. There is a pretence for driving & a Pretence for Sauntering while there & this I find to be the Expence of what is called my recovery. I lead the Life of a Carter and a – herd & am fit for nothing else. And this is my best excuse for not troubling you with more frequent Letters notwithstanding the Geographical Apology as above squeezed out of my knowledge of the Earths Figure. My three greatest Ennemys are Pen Ink & Paper, whose hostile confederacy however I should despise if the same Thing that make them my ennemies did not disable me from making the War with any Advantage against them. We are Obliged to Carlyle for the Particulars I understand from my nephew, he / has taken the trouble to mention in his letter to you. We are all in every respect as well or better than when I wrote last to you. Your namesake in particular is advancing apace with his Animal course & not behind the ordinary Race in his Intellectual course altho he has not come the length of Bashfullness the first sign of Understanding in perceiving its own defects.

 I have seen Dr Blair since he received your Letter. Jn° Home is at London. The Principal is well.[69] Carlyle not having received any letter from you when last this way was somewhat disposed to grumble. Mrs. Ferguson thanks you for much & in particular for remembering her Brother, as I do for my Nephew. Be so good as mention my having his Letter & having heard from his Father within these few days. This is all I can write at Present. Pardon my having given you the trouble of recommendations, when the System you were concerned to accomplish made it irksome to be solicited.

Yours most affect[ionate]ly
Adam Ferguson

Source: BL/MSS EUR F291/97, ff. 14r–17v.

7. Adam Ferguson to Sir John Macpherson

Bankhead 22^d August
1787

My Dear Friend

We heard of your being at the Cape but not to come any further unless your Health required it. We are doubly pleased to know you are come and have got well. I speak for myself & all the House Man Woman & Child who have learned to consider you with most sincere affection. I in particular am happy to see a sunshine of mind. Whether it will remain in the latitude of Scotland to which you point will depend more on yourself: for you may easily overate our Society: it was not worth keeping yourself poor for.[70] You have taken the Effectual / way to have me of your Club by taking from the height to throw into the hollow as I am just now breaking a Gully that leads to my door. Your Bill accepted and payable on the first of ~~February~~ Septr was indorsed and sent off for Payments a few days before I received your Letter But there is still time if you please to stop Thief.[71] If I had given way to the first impulse of my mind on recovering your Letter[72] of the 10th from Southampton I should have instantly written under cover to somebody at London & the burden of my Letter would have been a desire to see you & learn many things which writing cannot convey. This is rather of consequence / to my Anxiety than to your Concerns. If the Season were not so far gone & so ungracious in point of Weather I could attempt the whole passage in my Whiskie[73] to London. But it is likely I may hope to see you in a more easy way. John Home Carlyle, Blair, Robertson, have each a Rumvair of Madeira for you unless you chuse to <u>Knoll</u>[74] it with your humble servant. I dare not say we are all alive as John Home & I were this Summer at Westerhale to see the Remains of Our Friend Johnstone laid in the Grave. If you have not withdrawn for good & all from the World he would have been of more consequence to you than we all. But so the world goes & I am told he died with an easy / tone of mind & a pleased impression that he was not to cease being but passing merely into scenes more fit for him than the Present. If you have not written before this reaches you I trust you will soon that I may have some notion how you feel matters at London or in the Irish Mans words <u>How are you after that?</u> Of all things be not disappointed for what others do. Fear nothing you will find a line to pursue & I doubt not will pursue it with the same felicity as in every other Instance. Jn° Home has been in Lochaber all Summer, should be home about this time but I have not seen him. This House join in the most affectionate Respects with your most humble servant

Adam Ferguson

Source: BL/MSS EUR F291/97, ff. 18r–19v.

8. Adam Ferguson to Sir John Macpherson

Edinburgh. Sciennes.
27 Septr 1787

My Dear Friend

I have the pleasure of both your Letters from London but that of the 25 August tho first in Date has come last, by some Accident of the Post.[75] It is agreeable to ease the full bosom & I am glad you have had an opportunity to do so to Gracious Ears. I certainly had no particular reason to think it would be otherwise in your case either with the Supreme or Subordinate: but I repeated my Caution against disappointment from a notion that ardent exertions carry a proportional sensibility to neglect or unworthy return: I ought perhaps rather to have flattered myself that persons who are most willing to do good are likewise most indifferent to the other rewards. I have no distrust of your doing well in every respect. As for my Mutton / & Turnips the Child that claims me & them as a Property has not a letter right. If any expression in my Letter seemed to carry an offer of Aid from me or my Bill no wonder you was diverted. *Non tali auxilio nec defensoribus istis; Tempus eget.*[76] Such Jokes will do better when we meet. That Farm which seems to have been created for my Purgatory still keeps me in a State of Purification completely occupied and on foot from Morning to night. There is no sort of sedentary occupation that would not soon send me to the real purgatory if there be such a place. We are all come into Winter Quarters at the Siennes in the Suburbs of Edinburgh, our coming so soon is owing to Mrs Fergusons state of Health which has been alarming for some months & needs the neighbourhood of Professional Assistance. /

The rest of your Friends here are well. Jno Home has been some time returned from the Highlands & set out yesterday with Mrs Home to his Annual sea Bathing at Holy Island[77] where he purposed to remain about three Weeks, if your coming do not shorten his stay. I will not attempt to give you any certain Intelligence of Mr Dundas; but report is that he is on a Visit to Gordon Castle[78] at which Place & the Duke of Athols[79] be purposed to be three weeks of which the greater part is past. That he will pass all the spare time he has at his highland Place in Strathern & will be as long from London as he can: Perhaps he may pass some time in Midlothian in his Passage from the highlands to London. And if it be material for you to see him &c this Interval may favour your conference, & your coming here a very pleasant Incident to your Friends. We have no account of / Andrew Stewart[80] but suppose he may be this time be in Scotland <u>Galloway</u> tho not come here. My Affectionate Respects to the Honourable Brothers.[81] I sent Charles a Letter to be forwarded to you above six months ago it may come back before the Century is done; but it is little matter whether that or any other of the scraps I wrote ever return or no. Blair has been at a Country House all summer near Jocks Lodge but as the City of Edinburgh has been interposed between him & me we have never met. Your namesake John McPherson Ferguson is the most noisy ungovernable person in this house fearing neither God nor Man. The Remainder will receive you with a mild & Bashfull Welcome. I am glad to hear you look well tho less in Flesh than formerly. If I could command myself in that respect there should be skin some muscle & tendon & Bones but no more.

Your most affection humble serv[ant]
Adam Ferguson

Source: BL/MSS EUR F291/97, ff. 20r–21v.

9. Adam Ferguson to Sir John Macpherson

Sciennes Ed^r 1st Oct^r
1787

My Dear Friend

I send with this as you direct some letters which have layn for you here some days. I am glad you had such deliberate interview with Mr D-s⁸² I was putting myself in the way of seeing him if possible for a few minutes in case you had missed him & if that cold not be, had thoughts of letting him know by a Letter to London the reason of my wish to see him; but I am glad to repeat what I hope is true, <u>non tali Auxilio nec defensoribus istis &c</u>⁸³ Among the inclosed is a letter which I opened according to the intention of the writer. The Situation of things is strange. My / suspicion is that the French will not abide by their declarations when the opportunity of doing otherwise offers.⁸⁴ I have yet received no Packet from Mr Dundas & am made to believe he is gone but the Packet may be left & come at leisure. There may be reason for your hurrying to the South as our Friend Ch^{s85} writes: but Gordon Castle I think is a place of consequence to you. I have inquiries about you from different Persons particularly from Dr Robertson that he may write you I could not tell him where but will now as soon as I can. I am unwilling to think as Ch. G.⁸⁶ would that your coming here will be only in the way of a stage to London: If I should be at the Farm send express to me. Mrs Fer. has just received Acc[oun]ts of her Poor Fathers⁸⁷ Death & is much affected / with it. Others are well[.] I am My Dear Friend yours most affectionately

Adam Ferguson

Sciennes Ed^r
1st Oct 1787

[Verso is addressed 'To Sir John McPherson Bart']

Source: BL/MSS EUR F291/97, ff. 22r–23v.

10. Adam Ferguson to Sir John Macpherson

Sciennes Ed^r 7th Octr
1787

My Dear Friend

I sent some Packets according to your Direction under Cover to the Duke of Gordon,⁸⁸ & in a day or two after Received your papers No 1st & 2^d from the hands in which you left them. I have been over them once and am beginning again. In the mean time congratulate you on the felicity of having had opportunity to render such distinguished services. It is impossible I think they can be neglected, at last, if the due consideration is properly urged &c &c. Here in all appearance is War and the Loving Friends joined in the Eternal bands of the Commercial Treaty more inveterate Ennemies than ever.[89] / Half the Drunkards have not had time to lay in their Claret, when to it begins to be surmised that the French are ready to strike in the East & West Indies, have taken hold of the Cape of Good Hope, & have allowed us to amuse ourselves with a Commercial Treaty as the Whale is amused with a Tube. I was about to Congratulate Mr Eden[90] on the distinguished part he has been acting but shall defer now till these clouds are cleared up. They are not more I hope than Clouds: but the French Rescript notifyed at Brussells & our most uncommon haste in restoring the War Establishment is very alarming. I should not have written with so uncertain a prospect of my Letter finding you: but in compliance with John Johnstone[91] of Alva who wishes earnestly we should meet at / his House. He proposes sending his Son abroad & presses me under considerations which I cannot resist to be present at their parting. One of my difficulties was the wish of missing you here & Mr Johnstone has written by yesterdays Post under ~~the same~~ cover to the Duke of Gordon in hopes to bring you his way or to have such an account of your motions as may help us to regulate our own. I have a letter from Jn° Home demanding Peremptory information of the time of your return that he may do you seule[92] & service these are his words, and he is now told both by Mr Johnstone & me of the Alva Project so that if it be not inconvenient to you we may pass a day or two at Alva together. If you steer for that Place inquire at Dunblaine or Stirling I will not be quite ten miles / out of your way, And you may be time enough at London before the Candles are lighted as Archibald late Duke of Argyle[93] used to say on such occasions as the present. At any rate I am in hopes that you may have a week or two to pass here before it be necessary to proceed farther.

I am My Dear Friend,
Yours most affectionately,
Adam Ferguson

Source: BL/MSS EUR F291/97, ff. 24r–25v.

11. Adam Ferguson to Sir John Macpherson

Edinburgh 26 Nov
1787

My Dear Sir

You wonder at my silence as I have done at the silence of others concerned in the subject of my last letter. It is within these few days that I am told Ensign James should had proceeded on a project which he had been some time forming with some others of his own description of going to the West Indies. He wrote to me at the time of my last letter to you that this project was dropt and desiring my assistance to be admitted into Service elsewhere. We are somewhat out of countenance & have many Apologies to make: but hope you will be able to smooth matters over & that His Majesty will not suffer for / want of Ensigns. We are here much in statu quo very displeasing to some & favourable to Others of which the last apply ~~my~~ bodily to me: but Mrs Ferguson continues meekly & the sport of every blast that is felt at the Crevice of a Window or elsewhere. I was in hopes by this time of being able to tell you of a finished Transaction relating to the Feu Duty of Bankhead: But my Lord Superior seems to rise in new demands upon my acceding to those he had agreed to.[94] I should have said his man of Business for he has declined treating personally himself. I hear of your being housed at Brumpton according to your Passion for Suburbane Situations. Do the preparations to meet Parliament keep off your Arrangements. I am at a loss / to think whether the Prospects of peace and plenty will help or impede your operation on that subject. I have erected a Monument to George Johnstone in My Room consisting of a Writing Desk & Apparatus in Plate forming a Complete Commode for a Gentlemen Scribbler which I now no longer am.[95] His Crest is on every separate Piece & a shield on the front of the whole when open with the following Inscription

From
George Johnstone
To
A: Ferguson
a
Last Farewell
Obuit -&c Etat -&c
Hic Manus ob Patriam pugnando Vulnera passi
Quique I Memores alios facere merendo.[96]

This I understand to be fulfilling his Will & profiting by the honourable mention he has made of me.
I am My Dear Friend
Yours most affectionately
Adam Ferguson

[27r reads in Macpherson's hand: 'D\ufeffr Ferguson / Edin. 26 Nov. 87']

Source: BL/MSS EUR F291/97, ff. 26r–27v.

12. Adam Ferguson to Sir John Macpherson

Sciennes 13 April 1788

My Dear Friend

I received your letter last night upon my return from the Farm, & if every Beast had not been at the Harrows all the week should have sent as usual to enquire for letters & received it sooner. The worst I hope is past & we shall yet meet to talk of all matters. If you had gone to India that meeting must have been in some other world than this probably. It is no small pleasure to me that a Person who has shown much good Nature to me & to whom I am obliged may yet behave in this matter so as to make me like my Obligation to him, you will guess & not mistake whom I mean.

As to the Feu Duty Business on which you Harp I will require what can be done & proceed clearly in it without leaving you to grope in the Dark with remittances &c. / The Lord Insisted for a Reserve of £8.6.00 or £100 Scots,[97] this he seemed to think necessary to his Qualification as a Voter on this as a part of his Freehold & I suppose he will at any Rate persist in this. The Other £50 Scots or £4.3.4 he may be content to sell on the same terms as he did the other part, (that is) at 26 Years Purchase & if so the Accounts will stand as follows.

   26 years Purchase of 4.3.4----£108.6.8
   Interest from Martinmas last ---£2.14----
                    Total-----£111.0.8

That you may not tease yourself any longer with uncertainties, if the transaction proceed to this Amount I will without ceremonie draw for the sum in any manner you may direct.

Mrs Ferguson is now much better, is got into the Parlour and Partakes with me in the Satisfaction of knowing we shall yet see you. Every one shows gladness except / your Friend John who being asked if he will behave better next time you come, says he will not, so that the way is to neglect him & he will tease with Familiarity. Dr Blair made a Long visit to Mrs Ferguson in my Absence & had got some Intimation of your Respite from India Voyage from Mr Val McLeod[98] And so had many projects for you in this Island which I hope you will accomplish so far as they are good. I am My Dear Friend

Your most affectionate
Humble servant
Adam Ferguson

[33v in Macpherson's hand: 'Mr Ferguson / 13 april 88 / Feu']

Source: MSS EUR F291/97, ff. 32r–33v.

13. Adam Ferguson to Sir John Macpherson

Edinburgh 16 April
1788

My Dear Friend

This goes by my Friend & successor in the College Mr Dugald Stuart, he is to be a few days at London in his way to Paris, and I hope will have an opportunity to pay his respects & become known to you. It seems that the impetus of writing seized you and me about the same time as I had written to you a few days before your Letter came to hand. I had received the former Letter to which you allude & give full credit to the mildness & Liberality of your dispositions: but the Aspect of things as they then appeared is like a Dream & the Stamp of right & wrong is not given by contingencies altho many people in their way of talking seem to think so. In our notions here the P[rince] himself has gained & his Party have lost.[99] I am glad to find you confirm the better part of this Notion. It seems to be in the Fates that the H[eir] apparent shall be at variance with the Reigning Power at least with Administration.[100] He has / Pretensions to Sway, which they cannot admit without giving him much of the substance while they keep the Form & the Responsibility. He is therefore never like to be contented and will think himself in a common cause with opposition & these the more they are offensive to the present Reign the more they will direct their hopes to a succeeding one.[101]

I do not know what the best understanding & the best dispositions can effect in such a scene. We are a Land of Party & every one must show that a Party may rely upon him otherwise he will be left to carry the burden alone & Plough without his draught Cattle. A Philosopher may divert himself even if reduced to this pitch: but with the ordinary even the best Race of Politicians it is Death & destruction. It appears to me that Mr P[itt] saw you coming upon him with propositions of compromise & Composition &c of which the Idea broke his Phalanx & placed him at the Mercy of those who were more in favour with / the rising Power. I own that he ought to think himself the servant of the Publick independent of Party: & upon this Idea he could undoubtedly serve himself in the best manner: but I shall return to the Plough without Horses, which may be very fit for use yet lye unemployed. I mentioned your being in Parliament but if you do not see a clear line of Party before you I mean of Party measured consistent with Integrity & honour I retract. If you are at any rate to reside at London the additional expence of being in Parliament may be a fixed thing & your choice must depend entirely on the part you foresee to act. If you can be of service personal or Mental to HRH this alone is an object worthy of any British Man: be the consequence what if will. Indeed to pursue such an Object worthily there should be indifference to personal consequences or at least no reliance on what may be contingent. The Minister of our Land[102] as you term him is here: from his short stay & the hurry of local Politicks I am not likely to see him: if he be conscious of wrong to you, he may think me estranged: but I / shall do nothing to breed that Notion. The only service I can do is to remain a link unbroken in case any good Offices can be made to pass through. So much for Politicks in which I talk without caution because my Letter does not go by the Post. The Book which you mention like its Author is a heavier Job.[103] There was a translation attempted at Paris some years ago in 12mo.[104] The three first Vols were sent me but with so many mistakes as I doubt must have stifled the farther performance. I have marked some corrections & send the Corpus delicti to Paris by Dugald Stuart that he may inquire what is become of the work & furnish the Undertaker with my remarks in case they can be of any use.

[A new passage in darker ink starts here]

So far I had written some days ago to be ready when Dugald Stuart who was gone to the west country, should call to receive my letter. I have since received on your subject from Mr Pulteney one of the most friendly & publick spirited Letters possible. His object is to furnish me with materials on which to Ply Mr Dundas for justice to you. His Doors are strictly guarded here against Burrough Politicians & I had no chance to be let in. But I wrote expressing my wish to see him & in the mean time rammed much of the business into my Letter: but this is all I yet know of &c.

A.F.

Source: BL/MSS EUR F291/97, ff. 3r–4v.

14. Adam Ferguson to Sir John Macpherson

Sciennes Edr 18th May 1788

My Dear Friend

This is to let you know we are well here hoping to hear the same of you. Mrs Fergusons Health is still sometimes interrupted but not so often nor so long as it had been for months past. For myself I am about to be a freeman filius Terra Emancipatus,[105] having agreed to let my farm & have the care of it to persons better qualified. So many young Children makes it necessary to live near schools, & I had no choice but either to live away from my family or away from my Farm, neither of which is desireable or expedient, hence the resolution to lett it on ~~which~~ terms to which my Future Tennant has exchanged Letters of agreement with me. But to carry this Transaction into Effect it is necessary to be infeft[106] in my new Charter. The / absence of people of Business in Vacation time has prevented my moving in the feu Duty Business any farther & required my finishing the matter as it stood: so I beg of you to be contented with what you have done. There is no alteration occurs to me to be made in the Terms of the Inscription of which I sent you a copy in a former letter.[107] There is to be a new India Budget opened I see by news papers & am anxious to hear of the particulars. Will this be considered as an opportunity to supply former omissions, & even to give notice of Effectual intentions, Whatever it be I shall be happy to hear you are well & can give any hopes of being seen in the course of the season. Dr Blair has withdrawn to his Country house. Carlyle has started in a Race for the Clerkship to the General Assembly before the Drum beat: So that he and all the other horses and Riders and Riders Liveries are come back to the Starting Post & the Race put off sine Die. Your other Friends are well. I wish I knew / as much of you & yours. John Home I see is become as lazy as I used to be to which he has no title being born an Active Strenuous Correspondent: but there is no help for it, he is likely to be here soon when we shall have all his news viva voce.[108] I am My Dear Friend,

Your most affectionate & most humble servant
Adam Ferguson

[31v: To / Sir John McPherson Bar't / London]

Source: BL/MSS EUR F291/97, ff. 30r–31v

15. Adam Ferguson to Sir John Macpherson

Ed^r June 21st 1788

My Dear Friend

I trust you will not doubt the safe arrival of your packet although my acknowledgement has been so long delayed. There is indeed nothing I could do but regret the possibility of inconvenience to yourself from your kindness to me. Your man of Business Mr McDonald[109] whom I met in the street two or three days ago took me aside & began with telling me you seemed to be very desirous of what you thought might be of use to me. After signifying that I was pretty full in that secret we entered on the Subject of Superiority & Qualifications to vote for Members of Parliament.[110] I have good reason to believe that the whole Barony of Ravelrigg, of which my Farm is a part is but a scrimp Qualification and that if it were split there would / be no Vote left. This ends the Subject of Ravelrigg & my Vassalage.

Qualifications in general I believe are not to be got for money. Persons who have valued Rent enough to admit of splitting give life rent superiorities to their Friends of whose Political Conduct they are assured and the acceptance of such Qualification is considered as a favour done to the giver. I rejoiced the more at the Attonement of last India Budget,[111] that our miserable news Papers here had left the matter as deep in guilt as it appeared to be formerly. I hope the sequel will be proper. I read much about Generals & Military operations, of one General in Particular whose victories were always the more decisive that they appeared for some time to be doubtfull. The longer the Ennemy kept his genius on the Stretch the more they suffered & the more he gained. Here I trust there is nobody to suffer & that your gain will be such as honest men will applaud. /

I saw Dr Blair the day after receiving your Letter & we both rejoiced at what followed upon the Budget, because we wished well to the opener[112] as to you. He was highly the [sic] Delighted with the thanks <u>Du Roy</u>, & I find, he repeated afterwards that you had got a Letter written with the King of France's own hand.[113] He did not know how Kings write and that it is well when Ministers apply the Griffe by his Majesty's Command. However I shall be happy to see this part of your Correspondence when convenient. If you go to Paris and there is no breach with us or among themselves you will be worried with Politesse and real kindness for they have kindness when it coincides with their Vanity. A French Lady can Love a Man of Fashion tenderly but would not look at Adonis if he were not a Man of Family: But you know more of their Character than I can tell you & I shall be as well pleased to see you this way / as to hear of you at Paris, if it equally suit your purpose. I apprehend you may find occasion to remain at London for some time after Parliament is up for that is the best time for Private Arrangements with such Ministers as stay in Town. When you propose to pass the Alps let me know and I will meet you on the Po or Rubicon in my Whiskie. I have long dreamed or languished over a project of revising the Roman History in Sight of the Scene where some remarkable passages happened, that is to say, if the booksellers require a second Edition.[114] But many such projects have passed over in thinking of them, as this may do tho I am sometimes in earnest about it. John Home has been returned some weeks rather in better health than he went. Your other Friends are well as are the Indwellers of this

House with the most unfeigned concern in your wellfare. I am My Dear Friend

> Your most affectionate
> & most humble servant
> Adam Ferguson

Source: BL/MSS EUR F291/97, ff. 28r–29v.

16. Adam Ferguson to Sir John Macpherson

Edinburgh 6th Febry
1789

My Dear Friend

I have your Letter of the 31st ult:^{mo} & whatever is good news to you shall be also good news to me. It is not your temper to see matters under an Ill Aspect & I flatter my self it is not put to the trial on this occasion or at the worst that it is like every other transaction or Event in human life still leaving somewhat more to be done. I felt the preceeding delays with great pain but hope they proceeded most from want of tractability in the Court of ---- Woe be to the Minister who can plume himself in services performed abroad & yet suppress the servant, I have known it happen again and again & expressed my apprehensions / of it to you while yet in India but you either did not receive my Letter or thought too highly to regard the consideration. My wish was not to discourage you but to prepare you for emergence which is most displeasing when unexpected. It is a Weed of which the root perhaps is fixed in the noble soul of our constitution and I know not how to root it up unless it should become the Practice for King Lords & Commons to give every returning servant from abroad a day of Audience in which he himself should report his services and apologise if he could for his failures. Here would be something as allarming as the last day of Accounts & as rousing as the Prospect of a Roman Triumph: But who will think of an Institution to enable the servants of the state abroad to keep pace in point of consideration with the spouters of a / Political assembly at home. I shall be sorry, you may believe, if you & I pull different ways: but the noblest Revenge is <u>good for evil</u> & I am well convinced it will be found the best wherever personal honour permits indifference to neglects or wrongs. The sufferings already incurred, if you knew all, are already the most severe, and as for my feeble intromission into any ones situation I feel it is my time to press with assiduities & respects which were solicited from me before. Whether you will understand all this or any part of it I know not and as little whether it be of any consequences that we should meet; but I long earnestly for the time. Having changed my course of life from country affairs to news papers and Books, mere necessity has forced me to recollect the substance of my Late Lectures & try to put the matter into / / the form of a Book[.][115] It is now about a couple of hours Pastime every morning whether it ever will be more is in the womb of time which indeed begins to grew very lank and meagre with your humble servant altho as to Absolute dying I am no more threatned with it than other people of my Age. I heard last night for the first time that your Friend and Relation Cpt^n McLeod of Harris is here with complaints of Health.[116] I have not yet seen him & do not know Particulars. I hear also that Poor Blair is confined, not with his Gout, which was always trifling but some uneasiness about his Bladder. Other Friends are well and those of this house in particular sympathise enough with me to listen with avidity to ever[y?] Post for accounts of your welfare. I am

My Dear Friend
&c &c

Source: BL/MSS EUR F291/97, ff. 34r–35v.

17. Adam Ferguson to John Macpherson

Edr 7th April 1789

My Dear Friend

I am a Letter in your Debt & must consider this silence as a just Judgement upon me until I shall break it myself. It is now about time to be forming a plan for the approaching Campaign & I am anxious to know whether any of the operations point this way. Altho I hear you are ~~well~~ in health I shall never think I see the bottom of the Well till we meet. I am rather advancing than declining in health, and as I made Effort two or three years ago to get into a Whisky I feel bold enough this season to meditate getting on horse back for the Summer & this is the Sum of my history hoping to hear as good or much better of you. I have just now a Letter from / My Nephew[117] at <u>Ishera</u>[118] of which I need not tell you the Geography even if I knew it. His Letter to you, which you transmitted, made me uneasy for I know not a more woeful situation than that of a Person without support squabbling with his Principal, his accounts are better now. <u>I am well he says & doing well, my conduct here has procured me flattering approbation from my Principal & he is pleased to say that it will do me credit with Lord Cornwallis.</u> Both Burnett[119] & he are a sort of Jews in their hearts & look for the coming of a Messiah even fix his Arrival for February last: but they may long look over the shipless sea & they conclude even with saying that they scarcely wish you to come. Can you manage for your Fortune & your Liberality so as to be in Parliament without being straitned &c &c I may be wrong but that is the Situation I figure most likely / to give your mind its Play. The <u>fuga seculi</u>[120] & the retreat to Philosophy & tranquillity I do not much approve of unless it be forced upon us & then to endure it with cheerfulness & ease is noble.[121] The Late Lord Mortons Father[122] was confined in the Bastile & passed his time tolerably in scraping the bottom of his chamber pot with a French sous piece after which I dont think any body need fear the want of employment although it will scarcely satisfy his mind to take up with such employment if he has better. Your Friends here are all as well as can be expected. John Home stricken in years: but not affraid to tamper with the Tragic muse, his works may have their best Effect in pleasing himself,[123] which is more than mine always do me, altho they keep me going in a morning when perhaps the day would hang heavy. Carlyle is strugling for his Clerkship,[124] three antagonists have combined / to unite their numbers against him & if they prove the Majority to divide the Spoil: but he bears the prospect manfully. Poor Blair is manly also, altho his Doctors say he has a confirmed stone in his Bladder. He has an appearance of Micrology on common occasions but at a push he gathers strength. Dr Robertson is complaining & obliged to use an Ear Tube to assist his hearing. I overheard Sir Robert Myrton[125] a few years before he died muttering to himself, in his style, I am turned damned Auld now God Damn me by God and lo if it were not for the horrid Oaths; this is the Speech now accommodated to many of your Friends & to none more than your most

affectionate & most humble servant
Adam Ferguson

Source: BL/MSS EUR F291/97, ff. 36r–37v.

18. Adam Ferguson to Sir John Macpherson

Edinburgh 18th May 1789

My Dear Friend

I have received your Letter[126] of the 4th & in hopes of seeing you as you propose, shall not now go deep into Explanations. My Letter to Mr Dundas procured me an interview: but as it contained most of what I had to say, our conversation was desultory allusion to those contents. Mr Pulteney Interests himself warmly in a publick view, <u>that so much disinterestedness & successfull exertions as yours should not go without some mark of Public approbation</u>.[127] He furnished me with some strong points of view on the Subject both in his Letter & when he was in this country last summer. I quoted his conversation of that time to avoid seeming to be in concert with him now, and as an opinion more impartial and more weighty than my own. We apprehend mischief to you both from designed / communications from the East & from indiscreet reports of the part you took in the Late Interregnum.[128] These I endeavour to combat & met with so little contest on every point that I could not help thinking I had to do with a Friend. He acknowledged your merit & put, what to me at last was a disappointment, upon different considerations operating in the minds of the Directors and unfavourable time &c. I shall make my Report to Mr Pulteney by the time Mr Dundas returns to London, he told me he had been plying him & would return to the Charge: but thought it expedient he should hear the same thing from different Quarters. I conceived your connection to be merely Personal & Affection to H.R.H. & he owned that in a claim of merit for publick services Party should have no weight & I think that proper conduct in such instances is the more dignified, that it is held in the face of Party opposition.[129] He was sensible that Sloper[130] had a provision made for / him merely because he was superseded; so that with the proper line you have taken <u>above complaint</u> &c & the continued attention of persons who feel your claim as a publick concern; matters may yet come to a proper Ishue? Can you recollect whether the Report of Lord Cornwallis's marriage which got into the news papers about a twelvemonth ago, came to Europe through any correspondence of yours. M^r D[unda]^s imputes his Lordships disinclination to you to his believing you spread that report. Which I told him I could not by any means believe. In the end I repeated my vow of last year that I was willing to forfeit all the Effects of his kindness to me or mine if he ever had reason to repent of any act of confidence in you so you see how deeply we are committed. If there could be cordiality & affection where you mention--- What Halcyon Days: but in forming our hopes we must not forget that we live in Faece Romuli non in Republica Platonis,[131] We are a Land of / Party & when we cease to have Parties we shall scarce be alive. Our Parties somewhat marr the Executive Power but the Legislature not at all. How little the Grevilles or I knew when you joined us at Lauriston[132] what a Friend we were taking to our bosom. I understood that Charles had parted with one house is this another? Where is it? I should pray also but the Person you allude to as far as I could judge <u>alte spirat</u> not to Fortune nor even to Birth: but to some heroick and commanding Figure. As to the Book[133] I am afraid the persons you mention are now more likely to embroil Europe in a War than to raise its dropping head I mean the head of the Book. The translation set on foot by the Booksellers at Paris I suspect has given it a knock. D Stuart mentioned to me a young man of promising character whose name I have forgot who would be likely to repair the wound.[134] A word from your great men to him might decide & animate his Efforts otherwise I am afraid they know as little of translators as translators know of them. I should not dislike to make out the little bridge you mention: but with my Age and infirmities it must not be made essential condition to any Bargain. [no signature]

Source: BL/MSS EUR F291/97, ff. 38r–39v.

19. Adam Ferguson to Sir John Macpherson

Edr May 31st 1789

My Dear Friend

I have wished for a truce to politicks till I have the pleasure of seeing you & in this mind have kept silence since I received your letter of the 15th.[135] I feel the truth of what you say completely & make no doubt that soon or late matters will take the turn they ought. I write at present merely to put a question. How long do you think it will be before we can see you here? My head runs upon some little Solitary Tour on horseback either before or after you pass but should be vexed to be out of the way when you are here.¹³⁶ I have been working at a systematic <u>transcript Extract</u> or <u>Paraphrase</u> of my Lectures¹³⁷ & feel a Languour towards the Close of the Sketch / for it is yet no more from which I wish to rouse as I have experienced could be done in former times by getting on the Road with a servant, living in Inns & snatching the moments of Study between stages &c. &c. We have just fought the Battle of Carlyles Clerkship but are defeat.¹³⁸ Your Brother did not come up.¹³⁹ Captain McLeod of Harris kept the Field till he was carryd off in distress. Professor McLeod¹⁴⁰ of Aberdeen lost his Vote by informality in his return or Commission, Professor McLeod¹⁴¹ of Glasgow a fixed vote against us. The maneuvring was as keen as those of the Interregnum with you. God Bless you My Dear Friend

I may hear from you in less than ten days and am your most affectionate

humble servant
Adam Ferguson

[41v contains the address: 'To / Sir John McPherson Bar't/ at Brompton/ near/ London']

Source: BL/MSS EUR F291/97, ff. 40r–41v.

20. Adam Ferguson to Sir John Macpherson

Edr 12 August 1793

My Dear Friend

Having seen your name among the Presentations at Court I wait only for the arrival and redeparture of one Post, thus to sing your welcome to the British Shore. It is so long since you have heard from me, that if my conscience acquit me that is all, & you will require not only memory but monition to recollect that such a Person exists. But I trust, that as you always delayed giving me any instructions where to address you, my silence will appear rather my misfortune than my fault. Your being in the Low Countries made you expected home: but my hopes of seeing you did not rest altogether on that expectation. Having been long meditating, & being now verging towards the execution of a project of excursion without any determinate limits short of Brundisium,¹⁴² Rhegium¹⁴³ or even Lilybaeum,¹⁴⁴ for I despise your modern names, I had thoughts of seeing you wherever you should be.¹⁴⁵ This, you will say, is bold at my Age: But from sundrie / circumstances it has come to pass, that here Laborem in Senectutum seposui;[146] and last by neglecting it I should miss anything I can do towards bettering my Roman History I have determined to set about it now, having leisure money & clean shirts all of which Don Quixote neglected in his first expedition.[147] My first endeavour was to have been, to find you out, and I am happy to think this is to be so easy a matter. It will be about two weeks before I leave this place & if you have any commands for me shall be here at least ten days to receive them. I need not tell you of your Friend Dr Robertsons Death.[148] The Rest of us are nearly as you left us all to the natural progress or decline of human affairs. John Home is somewhere at his Travels in the North of England. All in this house join in rejoicings for your happy return &c &c

> I am My Dear Friend Your most affectionate
> & most humble servant
> Adam Ferguson

[47v: 'To / Sir / John McPherson Bar't']

> Source: BL/MSS EUR F291/97, ff. 46r–47v.

21. Adam Ferguson to Sir John Macpherson[149]

Ostend 11th Sept 93

My Dear Friend

Here I come wither at the beginning of a Feast now at the end of a Fray:[150] for the last was very hot the two or three last days & this Place is Crowded with wounded &c &c. but the Fray it is to be apprehended will continue & recommence.[151] All we know here is a vague report. The matter was once taken to have been a very serious defeat: but has turned out a Victory.[152] I ask again & again why the Devil the combined Armies stretched out their Front to more than a Hundred Miles. That some part is not cut off is miraculous, so appears to us who know nothing of the matter. We had a fine Passage of about 14 hours: but loathsome as usual to land men at sea yet bad as it was if my whole journey lay through such passes as this I should deem it impracticable & wish to go on board again. The whole Horses of the Place are pressed for the use

of the Army & I & my Lit Bo thing / remain sur la pavé.[153] I am told however I may have Horses tomorrow morning & so much for my progress. If I make any Voluntary stop I think it must be at Aix la chapelle[154] My Bankers name there is Robert Barclay:[155] if you direct a note to his care I may receive it, and you will be able to tell me the particulars and importance of the late action better than any one here. All we know is that the Army upon the whole has not lost Ground and the French still more than the Allies have suffered extremely.
I am My Dear Friend

        Your most affectionate
        Humble Servant
        Adam Ferguson

Ostend 11 Septr / 1793

[49v: For / Sir John McPherson Bar't / Care of Messrs Drummond & Co / Bankers Charing Cross / London]

    Source: BL/MSS EUR F291/97, ff. 48r–49v.

22. Adam Ferguson to Sir John Macpherson[156]

        Rome 10th Dec^r
        1793

My Dear Friend

I have received both your letters through the hands of Mr Jenkins[157] & have the greatest pleasure in every notice of your wellfare & remembrance however short & beg of you not to wait for matter but drop me a line when you are writing letters if it should contain no more than the Mariners Hail through a speaking Trumpet what Cheer Ho.[158] I have rode Quarantine here for about six weeks & propose setting out for Naples tomorrow, but as my stay there is uncertain on account of the Crouds of Strangers which I am told are there be so good as direct still under Jenkins' Care. As soon as the season invites to look northward I shall move towards Florence & make some stay to consider of my Route & motions homeward. You will by this time probably know that Sign^r Erskine[159] is at London & this compleats the series of my disappointments in looking for the Persons to / whom you favoured me with Letters: but I cannot be disappointed in the Object of my Journey so long as the Physical Face of the Country is open to me & the means of connecting it with its Antient State in my hands. I beg your Pardon for troubling you about news, extreme hunger has no delicacy in asking for food. I have since made a shift to find news papers to devour, & true or false, acquiesce in the Notion that I have what is going. We have pretty frequent & immediate communication with Toulon the Roman State is exceedingly cordial in all the supplys it can furnish to the Garrison:[160] but my notion is that unless the Combined Powers make offensive War on the Rhone & be masters of the Field the Example of Toulon has little chance of being followed in France & that our possession of it is a mere Snare for &c &c. I already mentioned my correspondence with Berlin.[161] The Notice to me from thence was at second hand from Count Herlsberg,[162] in a Letter from Monsr Formey[163] telling me that my formal thanks should be addressed to the Count. I accordingly wrote to him in English informing him that I did so from Respect as I should be sorry to incur any impropriety or Ambiguities in a letter to him. To Mr Formey I wrote in French a familiar letter respecting the particulars he mentioned to me. So in this matter I hope they will be satisfied that if [letter ripped]

Sensible of ~~this~~ my Respect ~~of~~ or make [ripped]
honour done me if should not be neglec[ripped]
berd by man I meet with here [ripped]
The Summer I hope will bri [ripped]
on the Thames or the Forth & [ripped]
forever after God Bless you [ripped]
Affectionate Friend
Adam Fe[ripped]

Source: MSS EUR F291/97, ff. 50r–51v.

23. Adam Ferguson to Sir John Macpherson

Florence 17 March 1794

My Dear Friend

The times do not permit the free writing of Letters and we must submit. Si Vales bene est, ego Valeo,[164] is still worth a Postage & so take it in return for the kind Notes with which in the course of the winter you have favoured me. The Date will tell you where I am & you will infer the rest. If you yourself were here to receive me you could not have exceeded the kindness of your Friend.[165] I am indeed out of Countenance at the trouble he takes but after some difficulty at first find it easiest to let him take his own way. He presented me to the Grand D.[166] the day after my Arrival & I am much Captivated. He carries me to the Museum The Gallery[167] & to Visits in his Carriage & I dont clearly see how I am to get away: but away I must be and take some road by which I may see you soon after midsummer. There are recent ~~you~~ accounts of your welfare in which I sincerely rejoice. Please to know that I have been presented to His Holyness the Pope[168] & have taken the most favourable impression of his Personal Character. My Blessing attend you &c &c

[54v: To / Sir John McPherson Bar't / To the Care of Messrs Drummond / & Co Charing Cross./ <u>London</u>]

Source: BL MSS EUR F291/97, ff. 52r–53v.

24. Adam Ferguson to Sir John Macpherson

Dover 6th May 1794

My Dear Friend

Old England I have you once more, so conclude the Learned Travels of Mr Walker.[169] And I shall have you also in a day or two which adds not a little to the Joy of touching the Dover Beach this morning after a night of sea sickness & solicitude occasioned by varying winds & other circumstances which threatened a tedious Passage. There is war in West Flanders[170] as you have heard as well as in Haynaut but I passed undisturbed as every Ploughman I saw did with his Plow, which I believe is the case in all countrys a little used to War. What would happen if the alarm were given of an Ennemy landed at Johny Groats[171] house I dont know: but sick as I was last night it gave me pleasure to think there was such a ditch between those Infernals the French Democrats and this Country.[172] Men innumerable not to be dismayed by defeats or urged by the Guilotine at their Backs to face any Ennemy in Front again & again after a death no less than after a Victory. Think of it / and till when we meet whether

this be not more tremendous, than an Ennemy however valiant who will fight well but be dismayed of the be [sic] defeat. For my part it is the most tremendous Ennemy that ever existed & not to be overcome till they go by the ears among themselves which they would soon do if they had no Other Ennemies. & to put them in this Situation is the difficulty: for their leaders know well how Ruinous it would be.[173] I have not got my things from the Boat which is not yet got into Harbour & write with Inn Ink and Paper so dont know if my letter will be legible when you receive it but we shall I hope meet in a day or two and so My Dear Friend
God Bless you

Your Most Affectionate
humble servant
Adam Ferguson

[55v: To / Sir John McPherson Bar't / The Care of Messrs Drummond/ & Co Charing Cross / London]

Source: MSS EUR F291/97, ff.54r–55v.

25. Adam Ferguson to Sir John Macpherson

Edinburgh 6th June
1794

My Dear Friend

The lost sheep is found and as much Joy as you can conceive, & here ends my history, with which I should not trouble you if it did not occur that I may not possibly hear from you till I write. We are not without our fear of French Politics as you know, nor is any Nation in Europe safe as long as that Ferment continues to work. The mere mob here has no serious Object but might be led to any mischief, when brought together, rather than want Fun & there are undoubtedly persons disposed to lead them.[174] The Kings Birthday[175] has been remarkably quiet owing to the Provosts[176] precaution in having four or five hundred Gentlemen sworn in Constables with new Batons made & painted for the occasion & what no less effectual a Band of Sailors ready to press whoever appeared to give any disturbance.[177] We have got into a new house the 2d time my family has removed since I left home so that Chaos itself was order compared to the State of my Books &c, my only consolation is that / I have got into a Room 36^{ft} by 25 x16 feet high when all my things ly about in the floor without stopping my march. I still hope to see you here as well as to hear from you. & remember that your letters are the only chance I have of knowing how the world goes. I am My Dear Sir

Your most affectionate
humble servant
Adam Ferguson

[57v: To / Sir John McPherson Bar't / at Brompton / London]

Source: BL MSS EUR F291/97, ff. 56r–57v.

26. Adam Ferguson to Sir John Macpherson

Ed^r July 4th 1794

My Dear Friend

I wrote to you of my arrival here & have not been without longing to hear from you. But the times are too serious for idle correspondencies as I can do nothing by day I wish them to give me next by night but in vain & I make no doubt you are equally affected. I trouble you merely that I may neglect nothing that may be required to procure a successful conveyance to the Packet destined for His Holyness the Pope which I formerly mentioned to you.[178] As Mr Hypsley[179] was the Primary spring in this matter I meant to direct the Package to his Disposal. But a doubt which must arise in these troublesome times about his place makes me wish you if you should see Mr Erskine[180] to ask him for a Direction to some proper agent at the Port in Italy for which the ship may be bound / to have this package forwarded to its destination. Samuel Burnet[181] No 26 Ironmonger lane cheapside has charge of it. He tells me it may go with a Convoy next month or this month & I have given him Mr Hypsleys direction: but have desired him at the same to give you the trouble of a Call & in consequence of this Letter to know your mind about it: And you will pardon so much trouble. The thing is of little consequence but I am anxious to keep my word & avail myself of an honour intended me. All here join in most Affectionate wishes & in hopes of seeing you before summer ends. I am My Dear

friend
your most affectionate
humble servant
Adam Ferguson

[59v: To / Sir John McPherson Bar't / at Brompton by / London]

Sources: BL MSS EUR F291/97, ff. 58r–59v.

27. Adam Ferguson to Sir John Macpherson

Ed^r Septr 8th 1794

My Dear Friend

I have received both your letters.[182] For that by the Post which came first that of the latest date, <u>gaudeo libenter</u>[183] & hope that H.M. will never more have occasion to ask. What did he resign for? So long as K & Government are legal & just neither he nor I have any other Party to follow.[184] The other letter also came in due time & I am glad to know what you are about; as to consequences so far as a person is well employed in his vocation I think he secures the main object. I never could consider this as a common War with France farther than it is Life & Love[.] Beyond this the Powers at work in that country should be left to settle their own affairs & the result would be more favourable to their neighbours than twenty Victories upon the Frontier.[185] But God forbid I should venture to censure those who see more of the matter than I do. I devoted myself as much as I could or they seemed to heed to Mr Wynch & his fair Daughter & it was a very pleasant task altho we quarrelled about Mont Blanc & the merit of his carriage of which I disapproved possitively & they have fortunately taken a different one to the Highlands, & had much need as the weather has been very bad. John Home happened to be in town for a day & I had / an opportunity to introduce him to Mr Wynch in the Street. Dr Blair we met at Sir William Forbes's[186] and I wished very much to have made a Party for them here. But Mrs Ferguson is & has been confined to bed for some weeks under a severe attack of her GoutoRheumatike affections in her stomach & Bowels. It is matter of extreme distress & Pity & but for the experience of her capricious case would thereafter be fatal almost every day.[187] Whatever you say I dare not flatter myself with the hopes of seeing you this season. It is more pleasant and perhaps more useful too to be stirring the grate at London. We talk much about enrolment and arming and exercising but dont do much, we may perhaps become the more ready to do more if occasion should press. My notion is that for men to become warlike they must have war & I am not so confident of our disposition to learn as to make me wish for the School opened in this country. I endeavour to go back upon the Wars &c of the Roman Republick as if we had no such things of our own to mind & in fact I have not. You may believe I did not fail to thank Mr Morison[188] for the Notes he made at your request on the two first Vols of the French Translation & promised to avail myself of them. Some of them bear upon the Translation more than the original, and in one, / the most material perhaps, that which relates to the reducing of Saturninus[189] & his accomplices in the Capitol by cutting the Water Pipes. I must continue to think myself right & supported by the express terms of Cicero as quoted in the Text & Plutarch who certainly knew more of the matter than we do. See Book 2d Chap. 6 or Vol 2nd page 252 of the French Translation. The words of Cicero are the last of what remains of his pleading for Rabirius. Since I was in Italy I am able to read Strabo[190] with pleasure which I could scarcely do before. So much from an Idle man who is

My Dear Friend Your most Affectionate
humble Servant
Adam Ferguson

[61v: To / Sir John McPherson Bar't / at Brompton / near / London]

Source: BL/MSS EUR F291/97, ff. 60r–61v.

28. Adam Ferguson to Sir John Macpherson

Edinburgh 9th Jan^{ry} 1795

My Dear Friend

I rejoice much in seeing your name at a letter; for the silence was beginning to be awefull, and I, in the language of this Country, to be Ury.[191] I accept of the Omen that the year of Slack Correspondence is past. That of the year 1793 I read with great Pleasure, having been from the first been convinced that the War declared on the heart of the Jacobin Club was meant by them to foster the Revolutionary Violence & that the conduct opposed to them ought to have been modified so as to disappoint their aim not so as to unite all France in support of them.[192] But the wire in this Idea I suspect must have been drawn too fine, as I found almost nobody disposed to distinguish between this & any former war with France or the conduct of it as any other than a vigorous endeavour to distress that hostile Nation / in all parts & respects. Nay some knew so little of human Nature broke loose from ordinary travails on some great object of hope, as to assert we had caught the French at a disadvantage and ought to dismember this Country or lay them so low as to ensure the future safety of Europe against them. I gave the <u>correspondence</u> to Dr Blair in a company where I could not tell him whence it came, & he has returned it with the enclosed Note, still ignorant of <u>the Voyageur</u>.[193] Neither he nor I can tell what is to be done now. After breaking our Teeth in an attempt to Bite, now to pretend that we meant only to kiss & be friends, would only raise a horse laugh in that <u>Sabot</u>[194] the Convention. If we can do any thing for the Continent so much the better: but the great Object of our Policy, surely, is a dignifyed & inconquerable state of Defence in which we may see with Indifference all the machinations of an Ennemy to Invade us. Such a Fleet as may meet that Ennemy when wind & weather permit & such Numbers of our People in Arms in the Island as may fight the Invader with fresh numbers every day until he is destroyed.[195] Such a defence will allow time / for the French to see the bottom of their hopeful project & do for them what all those efforts of Europe only suspended and delayed. I rejoice that you will still find occupation and so God Bless you which is all from your most

Affectionate Humble Servant
Adam Ferguson

[63v: To / Sir John McPherson Bar't / at Brompton near / London]

Source: BL/MSS EUR F291/97, ff. 62r–63v.

29. Adam Ferguson to Sir John Macpherson

[5 Jan'ry 1797]

My Dear Friend

I had applied for the enclosed[196] before your proposal came to hand of deferring the business till we met; This I am sorry is so distant a prospect that the delay here mentioned bears no proposition. By the report made to me the aggregate sum was very nearly what this paper bears & the matter being so far advanced will have had delay enough at the end of 40 Days. In my disuse of such business I had forgot to say when it should be payed & they fixed what they call the term of <u>Par</u> for me.[197] Excuse so much talk about it: better this subject than publick affairs at present. I never was less proud of Parliament than I am so far as I have yet read of what passed on January the 30th[.][198] We do the Ennemy too much honour in being affronted or intimidated with anything they can do or say. I would continue the Negotiation by Couriers as if nothing / had passed to interrupt. My Language of the House of Austria should be that we stand or fall with that House: but I doubt the Court of Vienna will not thank us for proposing to place them Defenceless in the Low Countries betwixt us & the French.[199] If the French propose to round their territories on the Side of Bavaria & Swabia they will be tempted to leave us in the Lurch. I therefore would listen to even such an accommodation as that leaving the Low Countries independent to look for a Coalition with Holland &c in one great Republick which in League with us might withstand even the impetus of France. As to the United Provinces my Language should be that we have no principle of Hostility to that People, that while independent we supported them: when become the Possession of a Nation with which we unfortunately were at War, we seized what we could to abridge the resources of an Ennemy.[200] When again left to themselves we shall attend to all / their concerns with the utmost candour. This is not a time to be thinking of new acquisitions. Every foot we have at present beyond great Britain I consider as Articles of weakness. I still pray to God I may hear the Drum beat to Arms on Sunday after Prayers as in Switzerland.[201] Talk not of the Malignant & disaffected these will never feel their own insignificance enough until the great mass of this People learn to have a Confidence in themselves. When you have read so far you will think there is enough and I am My Dear Friend

Your most affectionately
Adam Ferguson

Hallyards
5 Jan^{ry} 1797

Source: BL/MSS EUR F291/97, ff. 99r–100v.

30. Adam Ferguson to Sir John Macpherson

Hallyards 14th April
1797

My Dear Friend

If it were not for these inclosures[202] I dont know where I should find an excuse for troubling you with letters. I am come to the end of all my Speculations or rather come round to what occupied my thoughts four years ago, when France was becoming a dreaded Republican with all her millions of men & resources to be directed for Ages if we hold out so long and that Republick dont blow up of itself against this Island. I contended then that we must become a Military or Warlike People to defend ourselves year after year & Century after Century. The Coldest heads in the Country are now Sensible of it & till I see our publick councils directed to something effectual of that sort; to think of the Publick is a torment. Yours most affectionately

A.F.

Source: BL/MSS EUR F291/97, ff. 64r–v.

31. Adam Ferguson to Sir John Macpherson

Hallyards 17th April [1797]

My Dear Friend

I am truly much obliged to you for not leaving me in the hands of newswriters for an account of the Debate in which you took a part.²⁰³ If I had been in the Gallery I should have sweated. Although I am far from considering oratory as the Test of Wisdom or of Virtue. It is of Cataline²⁰⁴ himself I think that Salust says: 'Satis loquentia, sapientia parum'.²⁰⁵ And the utmost I wish for a Friend is with Horaces Verse Sapere & Fari quae sentiat.²⁰⁶ This I hope will be your Lot without aspiring to those talents of oratory which are supposed to constitute well nigh the whole of a Statesman in this Country & Age rather of Debate than of Deliberation or Council. Mr Pollens²⁰⁷ motion seemed calculated to turn away the imputation of ruinous ambition from this country & might have passed without encouraging the Ennemy to think that the Legislature had laid the Executive Power at their Feet. A Direct injunction / to make peace might have had this effect. And every motion to that amount must have been impolitic in any other view than that of Furnishing Administration with an opportunity to declare their regret of the origin and continuance of the War which was undertaken solely for the defence of this Country & the Rights of Nations which they hoped might be secured in the terms of a desireable Peace for the attainment of which all their means²⁰⁸ were directed: but which could not be hastened by any general injunction of Parliament. Of two or more Nations any one can make War: but all must concur in making Peace. Of this I have no immediate expectation: & if I am wrong I pray you to set me right. I agree with those who require security to qualify a Peace. If they mean the Demolition of Dunkirk & the Restitution of Flanders to a Powerful ally who will be always ready to make common cause with us on that Frontier, And if they hope to Obtain this, they know more of the matter ~~of the~~ than I do. The attainable security in my opinion is at home, some permanent Military arrangement / which pervading the respectable body of the People and all the middle & higher orders of the Community with a Spirit which no Ennemy will dare to insult in our own Quarters: I know you think promiscuous arming may be dangerous to the State but next to the most wise perfect and Fortunate Selection I think a general Arming is the best: for in this way if there be a tendency to dissease this vis medicatrix²⁰⁹ of the whole frame will correct it. With this security, altho matters may not be on the continent as we would have them, yet I think we may venture to lye upon our Oars & wait the Chapter of accidents from which I still think much may be expected if the French are left to themselves. It is now a long time since I wrote to my Friend Sir William,²¹⁰ And as I could not sleep last night for thoughts that arose on the Subject of the Security to be Armed at in Peace &c which on the whole is no more than that I now mentioned I address to him by this Post. Yours most affectionately

Adam Ferguson

Source: BL MSS EUR F291/97, ff. 65r–66r.

32. Adam Ferguson to Sir John Macpherson

30th June 1797

My Dear Friend

I have within these few days received the contents of three covers & partake in fancy the tranquillity of your Farm. Mrs Nugent[211] has given me a more particular account of it and without the spite that might be expected considering her own disappointment in wish to have purchased it. Your number of guests are is fully sufficient at a time. My family being more numerous my guests can scarcely be so many as yours: but the waters of Tweed or Manor are not so much run after as Tunbridge Wells. I have had but few Particulars of Clerks[212] exit I rejoice at his exemption from pain or strugle but could have wished that he had gone off knowingly & deliberately for the Sake of his humour / which was always exquisite to me, & which on occasion I should expect to be singular as I have known it to be when every body about him thought death at their door. He was about a month younger than me, and as you observe never omitted to do me all the good in his Power. And he was of the same mind respecting the world altho his manner especially in the later part of his Life was not generally agreeable to them. Remember me to Mr Grevile if with you. And I now pray you to give me as much of your Politics as possible. I have been for some time like few Physicians out of concert with my own prescription; the opiate is good for nothing, it does not prevent dreams sometimes worse than realities. If we should stumble upon a peace &c &c As the War ceases to press upon France the ferment seems to operate at home. All I wish is that our Politicians would do nothing to stimulate / or draw upon themselves the <u>Delenda est Carthago</u>,[213] which I have been long afraid might continue to unite the French even after all alarms from abroad of offensive war had ceased. Our little Seaman[214] whose accounts you have honoured with your Attention is off the Texel[215] or Dogger Bank[216] but without any hopes of touching on this Coast. If you see Sternutatorius a near relation as I guess of Paperius Curzor[217] <u>See the Monthly Magazine for May p. 339</u>,[218] please make my compliments & tell him I rejoice to hear is work is in the Press, having occasion for snuff papers I allways thought it was my duty like Gentlemen who kill their own Mutton to supply myself & accordingly have a Considerable Stock, but without any desire to exclude from the Market authors that deserve well of the Publick & make no doubt that a Peace will bring a growing demand from Snuff Shops & Grocers & Pasty Cooks &c &c Yours most affectionately Adam Ferguson

Source: MSS EUR F291/97, ff. 67r–68r.

33. Adam Ferguson to Sir John Macpherson

[27 January 1800][219]

My Dear Friend

It is full time that I return the inclosed according to desire. I am glad to find your correspondent returned to his former station & hope the Master is well; as the newspapers encourage us to think. The other letter also I shall put in a cover to you. In return for all your communications I have little to say: but that I have been stormstayed some weeks at Edinburgh being there to look over Dr Blacks Papers.[220] They will form I trust a very useful publication. When I heard of the Prime Consuls letter I was smitten with fear of our Answer & am certainly sorry that we should decline deliberation.[221] We minded our allies perhaps more than our Ennemies and avoided every remission of projected exertion under the notion of an opening Treaty: But for this I would have said that the cause in which we were engaged was the common cause of Europe. That we must concert with those who took an active part in it & made no doubt it would be matter of general joy to find / that the trustees of the French Nation whoever they were, were disposed to equity & Peace, & would willingly agree to measure of Common safety to France itself as well as its neighbours: but the existence of negotiation depended on the Prospect which France should give of desisting from the pretensions respecting its neighbours which gave occasion to the War.

My giving an opinion in the matter would appear ridiculous to Others: but you will forgive it.

The W.S.[222] has nobody to blame but me for placing him in a situation where the first access to business is so difficult. I was studying Philosophy and did not mind that when a W.[223] has got a business once into his hands it is a difficult to remove it as to remove an Estate which has been forty years in legal possession: so that both you & I must bear with those who have been seemingly restive in this matter, And still hope that accidents may come in our Favour. The Management of Dr Blacks Estate towards the discharge of Legacies &c &c is in the mean an importance piece of business & will engage us properly. I made offer of a / Visit to the States you mention and was appointed to dine with him in a party consisting entirely of his own family for he had then scarcely seen any body else in this Country where he came oppressed with detail business & merely as I believe by a little respite to recover his appetite for repeated doses of the same fare I had no opportunity of any serious talk. So much for a cover under which I meant to put three letters in one if the weight permit.

> I am most affectionately yours
> A Ferguson

Envelope reads (in Macpherson's hand): D^r. Adam Ferguson \ 20 Jany 1800 \ about answer of L^d / Grenville.

> Source: MSS EUR F291/97, 69r–70v.

34. Adam Ferguson to Sir John Macpherson

> Hallyards near Peebles
> 12 Octr 1801

My Dear Friend

I am, as usual, in your Debt for Letters; but you must not think me inattentive or indifferent to yourself or the Subject in hand. Too much as well as too little matter may fetter the tongue; The war and the Peace at once were surely too much for any Speculative Politician and I have almost forgot to wish you joy of what has come of Labours in which no one took a more copious load or was more sincerely concerned.[224] People may say what they please of former times, but the present I believe are better. One ministry quits the Helm, because from certain Circumstances, another ministry might do better.[225] This other lays hold with all its responsibility, and all the prospect of thankless return which the Peacemakers in this Country have repeatedly experienced; If this should be their lot I believe there is to some people a Secret pleasure in doing what fools disapprove, / you may now tell your Friend Otto,[226] and he may tell his friend Buonaparte;[227] that it is the neighbourhood of Britain, that makes such men as they are necessary to France, and the neighbourhood of France that makes a counterpart necessary to this Country. If either were destroyed Ruin or Degradation would ensue to the other. So may they long continue to foster the Race of Patriots and Heroes on both sides the Channel. So much for an Epithalamium to Peace. – I were not a right *Quid nunc* if I did not consider what is next to be done, How will Bonaparte manage his affairs? I believe with great ability; for he has not yet, to my knowledge, made a single false step since his first appearance. The more interesting question is what are we to do? Are we to think of nothing but Eloquence & Riches and Trade or are we seriously to ponder on our Posture of Finance and of safety? I believe I long since declared to you for Income Tax and Volunteer Corps.[228] / The latter carefully nursed with prospects of honour, publick attention and Manly Exercises. This may retain a generous Spirit in the Middle and more orderly part of the Community, & so far infect the whole as to make us a people capable of Arms & give us a force against Attacks at home proportioned to our population. I likewise return to my Idea of a Board of Education. – Smith in pursuit of his general Principle of Free Trade would explode Universities as well as limitations of Commerce, leaving every Age to fund Education as well as Trade suited to the exigency of its own affairs.[229] But I apprehend the *Public* must take some charge of both at least to check fraud & folly, and give a beginning at least to what once experienced will make way for itself. We may be asked what more would you have in the way of Education, than *Knowledge* and *Elocution: Sapere & Fari qua sentiat.*[230] Nothing more; if sapere means the Knowledge of mankind, their affairs & their Interest & *Fari* means qualification for / manly action, as well as Speech: men of one Generation do not always know how much there may be wanting in the next, until they have themselves entered on the scene in which they are required. Then the propriety of a *Noble Board*, composed of those who hold or have past through the higher offices of State, to open Channels of Instruction & Exercise for the rising age. God bless you & continue to make you mindfull of me even if I should get into Dotage and not be able to make you any return. I am my dear Friend

Your most affectionate humble servant
Adam Ferguson

I had almost forgot one of my great puzzles in this new Scene of things. What is to become of my Nestling Seaman?[231] He has served the greatest part of his Time as midshipman,[232] and the service tho' not neglected must be Stationary for some time. He is not altogether Spoilt for a landsman & is young enough for a Cadet: but even Asia itself must overflow with such Commodities for some time. –

Source: MSS EUR F291/97, ff. 84r–85v.

35. Adam Ferguson to Sir John Macpherson

St Andrews 28 July
1809

My Dear Friend

I might leave you to guess how long silence is to be accounted for, seeing that it will not be ascribed to indifference about your concerns. I could wish that what your Friends proposed had come to pass[233] but rejoice nevertheless that your mind as usual enjoys <u>what is</u> It has been more than half the business of my Life to proove that Good & Evil spring up within more than springs from without Without effect in steering my / own course of Life[.] I will not say be it known however that I wish the effect were greater. If so I should be less peevish than I now am under this delay of our furniture coming to occupy a house which is now open to receive us here. We are divided onto two collumns. One to urge our remove from the south the other to receive if here in the mean time there is an Embargo which detains the Vessel in which it is embarked. Such are the miseries of human Life which even the kindness and indefatigable / Application of our Friend H: Cleghorn[234] can scarcely asswage But the Tub of Diogenes which I once mentioned to you was not always the mansion of serenity and good humour.²³⁵ I have come to St Andrews to look for these in a Tub:²³⁶ but find the Vessel greatly changed from what I remember it. It has become a Town of much good company in the common sense without loseing what I hoped for the society of many well educated people of Fortunes like my own. May your lot ever be health such is the earnest Desire of your &c &c

A: Ferguson

Source: MSS EUR F291/97, ff. 88r–89v.

36. Adam Ferguson to Sir John Macpherson

St Andrews 13 April 1811

My Dear Friend

I have experienced much kindness on occasion of my Son's Shipwreck, tending to alleviate my suffering.²³⁷ & even to reach²³⁸ himself with some aid himself; but you may believe I did not mistake your silence: In this case words are of no avail. I always knew that shipwreck is one of the incidents to which the navy is which the navy is exposed, and that under this – his misfortune – the conduct of an officer may be not only blameless but meritorious. on this point conjecture is not satisfactory. and uncertainty is very painful. / I cannot have relief till the matter is decided by the Court martial, usually appointed on on [sic] such occasions: In other instances I should presume the Party to be blameless, till the contrary was made out: but here I dare not flatter myself in any degree, although the Character concerned ought to give me some assurance. But I have thus already said too much on this painful subject[.] Be so good as favour me with whatever is agreeable. The Prince I believe has won every heart in The Kingdom.²³⁹ His Conduct has been truly majestick & engaging. Yours &c &c – Adam Ferguson

Source: BL MSS EUR F291/97, ff. 90r–91v.

Notes

1. Peter John Cullen (d. 1797), one of the seven sons of William Cullen (see note 3). Along with two other of William Cullen's sons, Peter John was an East India Company servant.

2. Thomas Wyndham Goddard (c. 1740–83), East India Company soldier appointed commander-in-chief at Bombay in 1780 during the First Anglo-Maratha War (1775–82).
3. William Cullen (1710–90), a chemist and physician of high reputation who helped to establish Edinburgh Medical School as the leading European institution of its kind. He was close with the Moderate literati and was the personal physician of David Hume (1711–76).
4. Untraced.
5. Untraced.
6. See note 12 below.
7. Untraced.
8. Henry Dundas (1742–1811), first Viscount Melville, was appointed Solicitor General for Scotland in 1766 and Keeper of the Scotch Signet in July 1782, among several other positions in which he controlled patronage for Scotland, for which he was nicknamed the 'uncrowned king of Scotland'. He was also closely involved with the government's relations with the East India Company and was appointed to the Secret Committee in 1781 and then to the Board of Control in 1784, which he effectively controlled.
9. Possibly Macpherson to Carlyle, 29 October 1783, BL/MSS EUR F291/87, ff. 4r–11v.
10. Alexander Carlyle (1722–1805) was an integral member of the Moderate literati and a close friend of Ferguson. He studied at the University of Edinburgh and then at the University of Leiden before being ordained minister of Inveresk in 1748. He was a leader of the Moderate Party in the Church of Scotland and is now remembered for his *Autobiography* (published posthumously in 1860), an important source for the study of eighteenth-century Scotland.
11. Captain Alexander Macleod (c. 1715–90) made a small fortune in the East India Company navy. He purchased the barony of Harris around 1778 before winning a seat in the Commons for the rotten borough of Honiton in 1780.
12. Charles Francis Greville (1749–1809), MP for Warwick, had studied at Edinburgh University from 1764 to 1767 with his younger brother Robert Fulke Greville (1751–1824). The pair lived with and were tutored by Ferguson, who in turn placed them under his other young lodger John Macpherson.
13. Sir William Hamilton (1730–1803) was a famous antiquarian and vulcanologist and the British ambassador to the Kingdom of Naples from 1764 to 1800. It was on this journey back to Britain that Hamilton's nephew Charles Greville persuaded Hamilton to marry

his own mistress, Amy Lyon, better known as Lady Hamilton (bap. 1765–1815). Hamilton was the author of *Observations on Mount Vesuvius, Mount Etna, and Other Volcanos* (1772), *Account of the Discoveries at Pompeii* (1777), and *An Account of the Earthquakes which Happened in Italy, from February to May 1783* (1783).

14. Possibly Robert Douglas, twelfth Earl of Morton (d. 1729/30).
15. This was written shortly after Ferguson's major health scare in the early 1780s.
16. John Macpherson Ferguson (1784–1855) served in the Royal Navy, eventually attaining the rank of admiral. Ferguson had been hinting at naming a child after Macpherson since at least 1773, when he suggested adding 'McPherson' to the names of his first son (Sir) Adam Ferguson (1770–1854); see Merolle, *Correspondence*, I, 98.
17. John Home (1722–1808), a close friend of Ferguson and member of the Moderate literati, was a playwright most famous for *Douglas* (1756).
18. Untraced.
19. See letter no. 1 above.
20. Unidentified.
21. James Macpherson (1736–96) became famous across Europe in the early 1760s after he published 'translations' of the poems of Ossian. He became a close confidant and partner of John Macpherson in the late 1760s when the pair worked as hack journalists and then as agents for the Nawab of Arcot. They worked together until John's return from India in 1787, though their relationship had cooled and remained somewhat strained until the death of James in 1796. It has occasionally been assumed they were kinsmen, but this is true only in the loosest sense. The Skye Macphersons had broken away from the centre of the clan in Badenoch several generations previously.
22. Possibly John Cameron (?–1809).
23. 'Gentoo' was a term usually meaning 'Hindoo' but occasionally also applied more broadly to non-Muslim Indians.
24. Ferguson had been a sober vegetarian since a serious health scare in the early 1780s. His propensity to wear heavy furs even in milder weather led to the quip that he looked like a philosopher from Lapland.
25. A roc is a mythical bird of prey from Arabian culture and folklore.
26. By this point John Macpherson had been acting governor general of Bengal for several months, having taken the office on 8 February 1785.
27. Robert 'Bob' Ferguson (?–1830).

28. I.e. they were Loyalists during the American Revolutionary War.
29. George Johnstone (1730–87), a Royal Navy officer and politician. He was Governor of West Florida from 1763 until 1767 and recommended Ferguson as his successor, though Ferguson demurred. He served on the Carlisle Commission with Ferguson and was later appointed a director of the East India Company; he was also an MP at different points.
30. 'Whatever folly Kings commit' (Horace, *Epistles*, book 1, epistle 2), see Horace, *Satires, Epistles, Art of Poetry*, trans. H. R. Fairclough, revised ed. (Cambridge, MA, 1929), 262–3.
31. Ferguson married Katharine Burnet (1746–95) in 1767. She was the niece of his relative and close friend Sir Joseph Black (1728–99). They had four sons and three daughters.
32. Captain Joseph Burnett (1752–1833).
33. Ferguson knew before Macpherson did that Charles, Earl Cornwallis (1738–1805), had been appointed governor general of Bengal in February 1786.
34. 'Romulus, father Liber, Pollux and Castor, who, after mighty deeds . . . lamented that the goodwill hoped for matched not their deserts' (Horace, *Epistles*, book 2, epistle 1), see Horace, *Satires, Epistles*, 396–7.
35. Joseph Ferguson (d. 1799), second son of Adam and Katy Ferguson, a soldier who died in Bengal.
36. Dugald Stewart (1753–1828), moral philosopher, took up Ferguson's chair in that subject after he stepped down in 1785. His lectures were immensely popular and established him as the most influential man of the late Scottish Enlightenment.
37. William Pitt the Younger (1759–1806), prime minister in 1783–1801 and again in 1804–6.
38. George III (b. 1738, r. 1760–1820).
39. Ferguson's *History of the Progress and the Termination of the Roman Republic* (3 vols, London, 1783).
40. William Strahan and Thomas Cadell were leading London-based booksellers, from Scotland and Bristol respectively. They published the work of Hume, Smith and many others.
41. Robert Clerk (1723–97), a military man with intellectual interests that he shared with the Moderate literati, though he often disagreed with them. Alexander Carlyle described him as 'a very Singular [Man] of a very Ingenious and Active Intellect' but 'he was the Most Disagreable person to Converse, whom I ever knew'. See Alexander Carlyle, *Anecdotes and Characters of the Times*, ed. James Kinsley (Oxford, 1973), 231.

42. Sir William Pulteney (1729–1805), born William Johnstone, changed his surname to that of his wife, Frances Pulteney, in 1767 upon inheriting the considerable wealth of her family. He was an advocate and sat in the House of Commons from 1768 until his death in 1805.
43. General James Durham (1754–1840).
44. James Durham Esq. (1732–1808).
45. Biography unknown.
46. Alexander Russell (1760–1826) became an administrator in the EIC.
47. Likely the solicitor John Russell (1710–96).
48. Sir William Jones (1746–94) was a famed 'Orientalist' scholar who founded the Asiatick Society in January 1784, shortly after his arrival to serve as a judge for the East India Company in the High Court at Calcutta. Coincidentally, Macpherson had written to Ferguson a month earlier and mentioned the discoveries being made by Jones and his colleagues (Merolle, *Correspondence*, II, 316). His tenure there overlapped with John Macpherson's as governor general, and the latter loaned Jones Ferguson's *Progress and Termination of the Roman Republic* in 1785, and likely the *Essay on the History of Civil Society* in 1786.
49. John Zepaniah Holwell (1711–98) was a Dublin-born surgeon employed by the East India Company in Calcutta. He is most famous for his account of the 'Black Hole of Calcutta', which was probably exaggerated if not an outright fiction, but also served briefly as governor of Bengal in 1760 and studied Indian history and religion. The text to which Ferguson refers is likely the *Chartah Bhade Shastah*, which Voltaire used to undermine the historical authority of the Old Testament.
50. This was written in the midst of 'Balloonomania', which began in France with the flight of the Montgolfier brothers in 1783, and quickly spread to Britain.
51. Macpherson was created a baronet on 10 June 1786.
52. Thomas Robertson (life dates unknown) commanded the *Busbridge* Indiaman from 1785 to 1793; accessed 20 August 2021, https://threedecks.org/index.php?display_type=show_ship&id=29125.
53. François-Marie Arouet (1694–1778), better known by his pen name Voltaire, was a famous wit and an Enlightenment celebrity.
54. Gabrielle Émilie Le Tonnelier de Breteuil, Marquise du Châtelet (1706–49), was a leading French Enlightenment scientist. She is most famous for translating Newton's *Principia mathematica* (1686), but she produced a landmark study of physics (*Institutes de Physique*) that achieved notoriety. She and Voltaire were lovers

and intellectual partners, and lived in her husband's chateau in north-eastern France.
55. John Dalrymple (1673–1747), second Earl of Stair, a Scottish officer and diplomat.
56. 'He is worthy of your acquaintance.'
57. Reading conjectural; unidentified.
58. Macpherson was succeeded as acting governor general by Charles, Earl of Cornwallis (1738–1805), on 12 September 1786.
59. James Macpherson.
60. For the first letter see letter 241 in Merolle, *Correspondence*, II, 313–17.
61. Macpherson had suggested the money go to paying off the feu duties on Ferguson's farm at Bankhead.
62. Ferguson alludes again to Macpherson's supersession.
63. Both untraced.
64. Cornwallis, leading British general in the American War of Independence.
65. Reading conjectural.
66. Ferguson alludes to his journey to America as part of the Carlisle Commission to seek peace with the American colonies in 1778.
67. Robert Burns (1759–96), a Scots-language poet from Ayrshire, now revered as Scotland's national poet. It was on 11 February 1787 at Ferguson's house at Sciennes House Place in Edinburgh that a famous meeting happened between Burns and a young Walter Scott (1771–1832). See Merolle, *Correspondence*, II, 330.
68. Robert Burns, 'The Cotter's Saturday Night', in his *Poems, Chiefly in the Scottish Dialect* (Kilmarnock, 1786), 124–37. This was Burns's first published collection of poetry.
69. William Robertson (1721–93), principal of Edinburgh University, historian and a former moderator of the General Assembly of the Church of Scotland. An integral member of the Moderate literati.
70. A reference to the Moderate literati's support for Macpherson's Indian career, for which he had abandoned plans to become a professor.
71. See previous letter (no. 6).
72. Untraced.
73. A light, two-wheeled carriage pulled by a single horse.
74. Scots: to beat or strike.
75. Both letters untraced.
76. 'The hour calls not for such aid or such defenders', Virgil, *Aeneid*, trans. H. R. Fairclough and G. P. Goold (2 vols, Cambridge, MA,

1918), I, bk. 2, 521–2. Ferguson jokes about his ability to help, citing a passage in which Priam puts on his armour though Troy is at this point certainly lost.
77. Lindisfarne.
78. Seat of the Dukes of Gordon in Moray.
79. John Murray (1755–1830), fourth Duke of Atholl, a Scottish peer.
80. Probably Andrew Stuart (1725–1801), an MP and eventual author of *A Genealogical History of the Stewarts* (London, 1798).
81. The Grevilles.
82. Henry Dundas.
83. See previous letter, note 76. Macpherson, irked at his supersession in India, felt he had been mistreated by the Company and threatened to return to India, agitating for a pension. He was eventually bought off in early 1789 with a lump sum of more than £15,000. See 'Macpherson, John', *History of Parliament*, accessed 6 January 2022, https://www.historyofparliamentonline.org/volume/1754-1790/member/macpherson-john-1745-1821#footnote9_0xr6p9u.
84. This brief comment, likely alluding to the fallout of the Anglo-French commercial treaty of 1786, signals the beginning of a long preoccupation with international relations between Britain and France in the correspondence between Ferguson and Macpherson.
85. Probably Charles Greville.
86. Charles Greville.
87. Katharine Ferguson's father was James Burnet, a merchant in Aberdeen.
88. Alexander Gordon (1743–1827), fourth Duke of Gordon, a Scottish peer and holder of various offices and titles.
89. A reference to Franco-British antagonism following the agreement of the Eden commercial treaty of 1786.
90. William Eden (1744–1814), first Baron Auckland, was a diplomat and the chief negotiator in the commercial treaty with France of 1786. He had also served with Ferguson on the Carlisle Commission to America in 1778.
91. John Johnstone (1734–95), brother of George Johnstone and an East India Company servant from 1750 until 1765, when he returned to Britain with a considerable fortune that he used to purchase the Alva estate in Stirlingshire. He was MP of Dysart burghs from 1774 until 1780.
92. Reading conjectural.

93. Archibald Campbell (1682–1761), third Duke of Argyll, was the most influential Scottish politician of his day, by virtue of holding the Privy Seal of Scotland from 1721 and the Great Seal of Scotland from 1733. Later in the eighteenth century his role was taken over by Dundas.
94. Ferguson was using the gift from Macpherson to discharge the feu duty on Bankhead (see letter no. 6).
95. Ferguson's latest work had been published in 1783 and his next would be published in 1792.
96. 'Here are the hands, who for their country bled; And by their merits, made their memories loved', Virgil, *Aeneid*.
97. The pound Scots continued to exist after the Union of 1707 but at a much inferior rate – about twelve to one – to the pound sterling.
98. Biographical information unknown.
99. Long before the Regency Crisis, which played out in the winter of 1788–9, the cause of the Prince of Wales had been championed by the Whig opposition ('his Party'). The prince, who had come of age in 1783, notoriously lived beyond his means, and the Foxite opposition pressed for a larger allowance. In early 1786, his debts stood at £250,000. In 1787, Pitt finally agreed to pay off his debts and fund the renovation of Carlton House, on condition that the prince would furnish details of his affairs. George III also agreed to give his son an extra £10,000 from the Civil List. The prince's animosity towards Pitt was eased, but not for very long. In classic 'reversionary tactics', the opposition and the heir to the throne were united against the king's government.
100. Macpherson had by this time made himself a favourite of the Prince of Wales, having published a pamphlet titled *The Present Question, in the Constitutional Point of View* [1788?]. A copy is in BL, MSS EUR F291/176.
101. This is a clear reference to the reversionary tactics referred to in note 99.
102. Dundas.
103. Likely Adam Ferguson, *The History of the Progress and Termination of the Roman Republic*.
104. Jean Nicholas Démeunier (1751–1814) had published the first part of Ferguson's *Roman History* in three volumes as *Histoire des progrès et de la chute de la république romaine* (3 vols, Paris, 1784). In 1791, the remainder was published as volumes four to seven, translated by Jacques Gibelin.
105. 'Emancipated son of the soil.'

106. In Scots law: to invest with or give symbolical possession of inheritable property.
107. See letter 12.
108. I.e. orally.
109. Possibly Sir Archibald Macdonald (1747–1826), MP, to whom Ferguson refers in a letter to the Earl of Carlisle nine years earlier; see Merolle, *Correspondence*, I, 203–4.
110. Between one in five and one in six of adult males held the parliamentary franchise in eighteenth-century England and Wales, but significantly fewer in Scotland. The voting qualification of the English and Welsh counties was uniform: freehold property valued for the land tax at 40 shillings per year. The franchise for England's 203 boroughs was more complicated, and voting qualification could depend on a plethora of criteria, usually linked to property. Scottish county elections were in some ways similar to English 'rotten' boroughs. For example, eight of the twelve voters in Buteshire were relatives or friends of the Earl of Bute. The Duke of Argyll and later Dundas exerted an enormous influence over elections by virtue of their governmental connection rather than property. At the Scottish burghs, members were selected by burgh councils, with between twenty and thirty-three members, rather than by popular vote. Edinburgh was the only single-member Scottish burgh with an electorate of thirty-three.
111. From 1788 to 1793 Dundas introduced annual India budgets to the House of Commons.
112. Dundas.
113. Untraced.
114. Ferguson did undertake this trip in 1793–4, and a new edition of the *Roman History* was published in 1799.
115. This is the first reference to Ferguson's *Principles of Moral and Political Science; Being Chiefly a Retrospect of Lectures delivered in the College of Edinburgh* (2 vols, Edinburgh, 1792), in which Ferguson – who lectured from only a heading or short note – elaborated his moral and political philosophy in print. He had previously published a shorter version of his lectures: *Institutes of Moral Philosophy* (Edinburgh, 1769).
116. Macpherson's uncle, Captain Alexander Macleod (Esq. of Harris), died in January 1790.
117. Robert Ferguson.
118. Probably 'Ishara', listed in 1784 as a piece of land two miles below Serampore and just outside of Calcutta, once owned by Warren

Hastings. See W. Seton-Karr, ed., *Selections from Calcutta Gazettes of the Years 1784, 1785, 1786, 1787, and 1788, Showing the Political and Social Condition of the English in India Eighty Years Ago* (Calcutta, 1864), 49.
119. Joseph Burnett (1752–1833), a solder in the army of the East India Company.
120. Lit.: 'flight from the world'.
121. Ferguson's preference for the *vita activa* is evident here, but he is counselling Macpherson to take his snub by the Company in stride.
122. James Douglas (1702–68), fourteenth of Earl of Morton, was a Scottish natural philosopher and president of the Philosophical Society of Edinburgh from its foundation in 1737 until his own death. In 1746 he was imprisoned in the Bastille.
123. Probably a reference to Home's *The History of the Rebellion in the Year 1745* (1802). It is possible that Home had conceived of the project already in the aftermath of the Jacobite rising which ended on the battlefield of Culloden in 1746. His work began in earnest after his final play 'Alfred' (1778), which was unsuccessful. See Henry Mackenzie, 'Account of the Life of Mr. John Home', in *The Works of John Home* (3 vols, Edinburgh, 1822), I, 67–8.
124. In 1789 Carlyle put himself forward for the general clerkship to the General Assembly of the Church of Scotland, but was ultimately unsuccessful.
125. Sir Robert Myrton (1704?–74), second Baronet.
126. Untraced.
127. At this time Macpherson was pursuing his case for financial restitution from the East India Company.
128. Macpherson was a strong supporter of the Prince of Wales during the Regency Crisis and published a pamphlet in support of the cause (see above).
129. The cause of the Prince of Wales during the Regency Crisis and before (see letter 13) had been championed by the Foxite Whig opposition, held together by Burke's theory of party loyalty.
130. Robert Sloper (1729–1802), who in July 1785 was appointed acting commander-in-chief of the army in British India, until he was superseded by Cornwallis.
131. From Cicero's letters to Atticus. Lit.: 'In the dregs of Romulus, not in the Republic of Plato.'
132. Lauriston Castle is a sixteenth-century tower house to the east of Edinburgh that overlooks the Firth of Forth.

133. The translation of the *Progress and Termination of the Roman Republic*.
134. Possibly Jacques Gibelin, who replaced Démeunier as the translator of Ferguson's Roman history (see note 104).
135. Untraced.
136. Perhaps an early indication he was meditating the trip to Italy, undertaken finally in 1793–4.
137. Eventually published as the *Principles of Moral and Political Science* in 1792.
138. See letter no. 17.
139. Rev. Martin Macpherson (1743–1825) took over his father's parish on Skye upon his death in 1765.
140. Likely Rev. Roderick MacLeod (c. 1727–1815), who had been Professor of philosophy at King's College Aberdeen since 1749, and became the university's principal in 1801.
141. Likely Hugh McLeod (1730–1809), Professor of ecclesiastical history at Glasgow.
142. Brindisi, an Adriatic port city in Apulia.
143. Reggio di Calabria, the capital of Calabria, faces Sicily and is separated from it by the Strait of Messina.
144. Marsala, on the western coast of Sicily, site of a Phoenician city called Lilybaeum in Latin.
145. Ferguson used something close to this line in his most recent surviving letter to Macpeherson (Merolle, *Correspondence*, II, 341).
146. Roughly 'I have saved the work for old age'. Ferguson paraphrases Tacitus' explanation for his *Histories* (I.1).
147. Ferguson alludes to the third chapter of part 1 of *Don Quixote*.
148. William Robertson had passed away two months earlier, on 11 June 1793.
149. This letter is mentioned by Ferguson in Merolle, *Correspondence*, II, 354–5. It is the first letter of Ferguson's trip to Italy in 1793–4, undertaken in order to see the setting of the events in his *Roman Republic*, the second edition of which he was working on and which would finally be published in 1799. For an account of this European trip, see Merolle, *Correspondence*, II, 578–82.
150. Shakespeare, *Henry IV*: 'Well, To the latter end of a fray and the beginning of a feast Fits a dull fighter and a keen guest.'
151. Dunkirk had been under siege by coalition troops, but they were defeated at the Battle of Hondschoote (about 40 kilometres from Ostend), which took place between 6 and 8 September.

152. Ferguson's information was faulty. The Siege of Dunkirk was lifted following the defeat at Hondschoote and allied troops withdrew east.
153. Lit.: 'on the cobbles'.
154. Aachen, a city in the Rhineland, had been a Roman spa town and later was the favoured city of Charlemagne (748–814) and the place where most Holy Roman Emperors were crowned.
155. Life dates unknown. Barclay was related to the Quaker family of bankers in England and apparently spied for the government during the Revolutionary Wars. See Niccolò Valmori, 'Private Interest and the Public Sphere: Finance and Politics in France, Britain and The Netherlands during the Age of Revolution, 1789–1812' (PhD thesis, European University Institute, 2016), esp. 53–60.
156. This letter is damaged. Half of f. 51 is torn off.
157. Thomas Jenkins (1722–98), art dealer, painter and banker. He served as a de facto ambassador at Rome, there being no official British representative there.
158. Shakespeare, *The Tempest*, act 1, scene 1.
159. Charles Erskine (1739–1811) was born in Rome and educated at the Scots college there. From 1793 to 1801 he was papal envoy to Great Britain.
160. In the summer of 1793 a royalist revolt had taken control of Toulon with the aid of an Anglo-Spanish blockade. Republican forces laid siege to the city and finally prevailed in December. Here Napoleon Bonaparte (1769–1821) first began to make a name for himself as commander of the artillery.
161. Ferguson was elected a foreign member of the Berlin Academy in 1793; his thanks were read out on 19 December 1793. See *Mémoires de l'Académie royale des sciences et belles-lettres* (Berlin, 1798 [1792–3]), 6, 37.
162. Possibly Count Ewald Friedrich Graf von Hertzberg (1725–95), a Prussian statesman and man of letters.
163. Johann Heinrich Samuel Formey (1711–97) was from a Huguenot family and a prominent member of the German Enlightenment. In 1748, he was appointed perpetual secretary of the Berlin Academy of Sciences, to which he helped to elect Ferguson an honorary member.
164. A common valedictory phrase used often by Cicero. Ferguson used it occasionally with Macpherson and later translated it as 'If you are well so am I' (Merolle, *Correspondence*, II, 484).
165. Likely the Marquis Federico Mandredini (1743–1829), who Macpherson had met during his own European sojourn, and with

whom he had carried on a correspondence in 1792 that would later be published as *Correspondance entre un voyageur et un ministre, en octobre, et novembre, 1792* (place of publication unknown, [1796?]).

166. Ferdinand III (1769–1824), Grand Duke of Tuscany. Macpherson had cultivated close links with his father, Leopold II (1747–92), Grand Duke of Tuscany and Holy Roman Emperor, from 1789 until his death in 1792. See also letter no. 289 in Merolle, *Correspondence*, II, 361–2.

167. It is not clear which 'Museum' and 'Gallery' Ferguson means, but it seems likely he is referring to the Gallerie degli Uffizi – open to the public since 1765 – and possibly the Galleria dell'Accademia di Firenze, open from 1784.

168. Pius VI (r. 1775–9), born Count Giovanni Angelo Braschi (1717–99), who condemned the French Revolution and the suppression of the Gallican Church. In his Italian campaign of 1796, Napoleon occupied the Papal States, and in 1798 Pius was taken prisoner and sent to France as a result of refusing to cede temporal power.

169. Adam Walker, *Ideas, Suggested on the Spot in a Late Excursion through Flanders, Germany, France, and Italy, by A. Walker, Lecturer on Experimental Philosophy* (London, 1790), 442.

170. Ferguson had arrived on the Continent as the Flanders campaign of 1793 was underway and by the time he departed in 1794 the fighting had resumed once again.

171. John o' Groats is a village in Caithness, Scotland, and one of the most northerly inhabited areas of Britain.

172. The Revolution was at this point in its most radical phase. The constitution of 1793 was never implemented and the Republic was being ruled by a Jacobin dictatorship which declared 'Terror' the 'order of the day'.

173. This was a recurrent idea of Ferguson's, viz. that once France's foreign wars were over the country would descend into civil war; this meant that Ferguson, nervous about invasion, was also hopeful that making peace with France would be the real key to Britain's salvation.

174. These were tense times in Scotland. Dundas was trying to keep a lid on any potentially revolutionary activity and in the summer of 1794 Robert Watt (?–1794) was arrested for suspected republican activity – it was alleged he planned to take over key strategic points in Edinburgh – and executed in October.

175. George III was born on 4 June 1738.

176. Sir James Stirling (1740–1805), first Baronet of Larbert and Mansfield, was a banker and Lord Provost of Edinburgh in 1790–2, 1794–6 and 1798–1800.
177. Impressment by 'press gangs' refers to the taking of men into military or naval forces by compulsion. Press gangs could also be used by authorities as hired mobs to suppress disturbances, which is what Ferguson seems to refer to here.
178. Ferguson had met Pope Pius VI on his visit to Rome. See letter no. 23.
179. Unidentified.
180. Charles Erskine.
181. Ferguson's brother-in-law.
182. Untraced.
183. 'I gladly rejoice.'
184. This letter was written in the wake of the formation of the Pitt–Portland coalition government which had been formed in the summer of 1794. It brought key members of the Whig opposition into the cabinet and left a Foxite rump in opposition. The Whigs, many of whom were close to Burke, were seeking to bring more energy into the war effort against France.
185. Ferguson alludes to his belief that France would descend into anarchy and civil war if there was not a foreign foe to unite against.
186. Sir William Forbes (1739–1806), sixth Baronet of Pitsligo, was a banker and philanthropist.
187. She died on 23 March 1795.
188. Colin Morison (1732 or 1734 to 1809 or 1810), Scottish painter, sculptor and art and antiquities dealer. He arrived in Rome around 1754 and remained there until his death.
189. Lucius Appulius Saturninus (died late 100 BC), a populist politician.
190. Strabo (c. 64 BC to c. 24 AD), Greek geographer and historian. His *Geographica* presented a history of peoples and places from the different regions of the world known to both Greeks and Romans during the reign of Augustus.
191. 'Ury' is listed in the 1818 edition of John Jamieson's Scots dictionary as 'Clammy, covered with perspiration'; see his *An Etymological Dictionary of the Scottish Language* (Edinburgh, 1818).
192. Ferguson early adopted the position that international war was a Jacobin strategy for consolidating its internal political position in France.
193. Hugh Blair carried on a correspondence with John Macpherson over the same time as Adam Ferguson. Together with John Home,

they discussed the international political situation. Ferguson alludes to the *Correspondance entre un voyageur et un ministre, en octobre, et novembre, 1792*, which Macpherson was probably translating into English at the time.

194. 'Sabots' were wooden clogs worn by French peasants.
195. Like many of his contemporaries, Ferguson feared a French invasion, the prospect of which was a constant topic in his correspondence throughout this period.
196. Unidentified.
197. Par value means static value, unlike market value, which fluctuates.
198. Ferguson seems to have mixed up the dates, and likely refers to a debate on 30 December 1796 on foreign policy and peace prospects. See *Scots Magazine* 59 (January, 1797): 53–8.
199. The Austrian Netherlands was annexed by the First Republic in 1795, but Austria did not relinquish its claim over the province until the Treaty of Campo Formio, signed on 17 October 1797.
200. In early 1795, the old Dutch Republic fell after intervention from the French revolutionary forces. Its successor, the Batavian Republic, was founded with the armed support of France, and it became a sister republic.
201. Ferguson was a lifelong supporter of militias and mentioned it often in 1797 as he feared invasion by France (see, e.g., Merolle, *Correspondence*, II, 411). He visited Geneva in 1774 and spoke admiringly of its political system (see Merolle, *Correspondence*, I, 110–18).
202. It is not clear to what Ferguson refers but he often used Macpherson's franking privileges as an MP to send letters to his sons.
203. Macpherson spoke in the House of Commons on behalf of George Pollen's motion for peace with France made on 10 April 1797. This was the only time he spoke in parliament; see *The Parliamentary History of England*, vol. XXXIII (London, 1818), 423–4.
204. Lucius Sergius Catilina (108–62 BC), a Roman patrician who is best known for the second Catilinarian conspiracy, an attempt to subvert the Roman Republic and the aristocratic senate. Catiline was one of the key figures and chief villains in Ferguson's Roman history.
205. '[He has] Much eloquence, but not much wisdom', see Sallust, *The War with Catiline*, trans. John C. Rolfe (Cambridge, MA, 1921), 10–11.
206. 'To be wise and say as one feels', Horace, *Satires, Epistles*, 276–7.
207. George Augustus Pollen (1775–1808) was elected MP for Leominster in 1796 and on 1 March joined the 'armed neutrality', a group

of about thirty backbenchers – including Macpherson – who sought to end the polarisation between supporters of Fox and Pitt by starting a moderate party. On this, see esp. Macpherson's pamphlet: *Two Letters to a Noble Earl, from a Member of Parliament* (London, 1797).
208. Reading conjectural.
209. 'Vis medicatrix naturae', or 'the healing power of nature', is the Latin equivalent of a Greek phrase attributed to Hippocrates (c. 460–c. 370 BC), meaning that healing often happens naturally.
210. Likely Sir William Pulteney, MP for Shrewsbury.
211. Deborah Charlotte Nugent (1756–1813), née Dee, the former widow of Ferguson's friend George Johnstone, and subsequently wife of Charles Edmund Nugent (1759–1844), who from 1795 until 20 February 1797 commanded the *Caesar*, the ship on which Ferguson's son John served.
212. See letter no. 4, note 41.
213. 'Carthage must be destroyed.' Cato the Elder (234–149 BC) reportedly ended all of his speeches prior to the Third Punic War (149–146 BC) with the phrase.
214. John Macpherson Ferguson.
215. Texel is an island in the North Sea, just off the northern coast of the Netherlands.
216. Dogger Bank is a large sand bank in the middle of the North Sea.
217. Lucius Papirius Cursor (c. 365–c. 310 BC) was a patrician politician and general.
218. Ferguson refers to an article in the *Monthly Magazine* in which 'Sternutatorius' proposes to write a history of snuff and gives an outline of what the book would look like (*The Monthly Magazine and British Register*, vol. III, 1797: 339).
219. Dated according to the note and postage stamp on f. 70v.
220. For Ferguson's obituary of Black see essay no. 3 in Part II.
221. This is contrary to what Ferguson wrote to Carlyle two weeks later: 'Our Government I believe had good Reason for declining present overtures of Negotiation' (Merolle, *Correspondence*, II, 460).
222. Writer to the Signet, i.e. a solicitor entitled to supervise use of the King's Signet, the private seal of the early kings of Scots.
223. I.e. a Writer, a Scottish solicitor.
224. The Treaty of Lunéville in February 1801 marked the beginning of the end of the Second Coalition against the French Republic. The Treaty of Amiens the following year ended Britain's hostilities

with France, but a preliminary peace agreement had been signed in London in September 1801.
225. Pitt had resigned as prime minister in February 1801 over the issue of Catholic emancipation in Ireland, which he had promised in order to secure the Act of Union in 1800, but which George III strongly opposed. Between 1801 and 1804, Pitt was replaced by Henry Addington. Pitt returned to power in May 1804 until his death on 23 January 1806.
226. Louis-Guillaume Otto (1754–1817), French diplomat who negotiated peace with the British cabinet.
227. Napoleon Bonaparte (1769–1821), First Consul of France from 24 December 1799 until he proclaimed himself emperor on 18 May 1804.
228. Pitt had instituted the first income tax in Britain two years earlier in December 1799. Ferguson was a longstanding campaigner for a national militia. In his copy of the letter, Macpherson has underlined 'Income Tax' and 'Volunteer Corps', probably denoting their significance in this context (BL MSS EUR F291/97, f. 82v.).
229. Ferguson's friend Adam Smith had promoted free trade and criticised modern universities, especially those outside Scotland, in *An Inquiry into the Nature and Causes of the Wealth of Nations* (2 vols, 1776). Ferguson waxed lyrical about the book on its appearance, and cited it in his teaching and published lectures. He was critical, however, of Smith's promotion of the standing army. Both Smith and Ferguson were members of the Poker Club, which promoted a Scottish militia. See the introduction for more details.
230. Lit.: 'To know and to speak as one thinks.' This is a quotation from Horace's epistle to Albius Tibullus. See, e.g., *The Works of Horace, Translated Literally into English Prose*, ed. C. Smart (Edinburgh, 1777), II, 240–1.
231. Likely John Macpherson Ferguson.
232. In his copy of the letter, Macpherson added here 'Since made a Lieut. By Ld. Nelson' (BL MSS EUR F291/97, f. 83r).
233. A reference to Macpherson's campaign for financial restitution from the Company. Summarised in *The Case of Sir John Macpherson, Baronet, Late Governor General of India; Containing a Summary Review of His Administration and Services* (1808), and referred to by Ferguson in a letter of 16 September 1808 (no. 394 in Merolle, *Correspondence*, II, 509–10).
234. Hugh Cleghorn (1752–1837) was Professor of civil and natural history in the United College of the University of St Andrews.

235. Also referenced in Merolle, *Correspondence*, II, 509–10.
236. Macpherson had studied as an undergraduate at St Andrews between 1738 and 1743.
237. John Macpherson Ferguson had been commander of the *Pandora* sloop since October 1810. On 13 February 1811 it wrecked in the Kattegat Sea between Denmark and Sweden, a disaster in which twenty-seven men died.
238. Reading conjectural.
239. The Prince of Wales had been acting as regent since 5 February 1811, following his father's final and irrecoverable bout of mental illness. Macpherson had long fallen out of favour with the prince.

Part II

Essays

'Copy Dʳ Ferguson's opinions / Public affairs / <u>no Date French Revolution</u>'

Note on the Text

This undated essay is located approximately halfway through the papers in MSS EUR F291/97 (which are often but not always ordered chronologically). It comprises two large sheets folded into eighths, thus making four columns per side, with writing on every other column. Complicating any attempt to date the essay is the fact that it is labelled in Macpherson's hand as a 'copy [of] Dʳ Ferguson's opinions'. However, the essay itself is in neither Ferguson's nor Macpherson's handwriting. Yet it seems certain that the essay is by Ferguson in light of the attribution on the cover; the short paragraph format (which is clearly in line with Ferguson's style in his unpublished manuscripts published by Merolle and located in Edinburgh University Library MS.DC.1.42); and the intellectual content. We suggest that the essay might have been included with the letter sent by Ferguson to Macpherson on 26 September 1797 (Merolle no. 331), in which, in a discussion on foreign policy and the war, Ferguson noted to Macpherson that he included 'a full Sheet', which may have been this essay. Importantly, the paper used for the letter and for the essay are the same size (about 2 cm longer and 1 cm narrower than a modern A4), which is larger than that of the rest of the correspondence. The watermark on the paper in the new essay (a seated Britannia with the letters 'P' and 'B' on the left and right side of her, respectively, but without a date) seems to match with that used in the letter (Merolle no. 331), which is dated 1795, but does not match with any of the Britannias in EUL MS.DC.1.42. For contextualisation and discussion of the essay, see section 9 of the introduction (pp. 44–52, above).

Dr Ferguson's Opinion [on the French Revolution]' (1797?)

The French Revolution has formed the most dangerous Crisis that ever took place in Europe.

By that example the needy are invited to supply their wants, not by industry and labour the source of prosperity to themselves and their country; but by levelling degradation of ranks, and violation of property. They are taught to look for liberty in the subversion of all former authority and in serving the Government of their Country.

The majority of the People are needy and have the force of numbers to subvert the actual order of things in every state.

The existing war in Europe is an attack made by such Revolutionists, & an attempt to spread their contagion, to devalue the blame of their own distresses / on other nations, and by the pressure of external ~~want~~ war to keep their People united at home, to Justify under the alarm of danger from abroad the violence which their Leaders are disposed to commit on the Persons and Properties of their Opponents and fellow Citizens.

In other wars, nations have small losses to guard against, and small advantages to gain, and they advance or decline by particular victories or defeats.

In this war every advance is a triffle [sic] that does not ward off the danger of French contagion, and no particular loss merits consideration farther than it tends to keep up or to spread the contagion to be dreaded. –

France is a house on fire in the midst of a great Town, every neighbour ought to join in extinguishing the flame at once for his own sake, and for that of the unfortunate owner whose ruin alas is to be lamented and if possible / prevented.–

The French may be alarmed on their frontier, and distressed by every species of hostility, but their numbers, their enthusiasm, and their resources render them in a high degree invincible, and the most alarming hostilities from abroad do but confirm their union at home, for this purpose their Leaders have provoked such hostilities, and continue to prosper under their effects. They are hastening to bring their People into the condition of a wild military Horde independent of the accommodations & luxuries which appear necessary to other nations.

Their Policy and the attacks of their Ennemies combine to the same effects, and resemble the operations of an assailant who should begin with burning the suburbs of a Town at one extremity while the Garrison preparing for their own defence are burning it in the other.

What is to be done then in this War?

Let the Confederates engaged in it beware how they substitute any object of gain in place of the defensive cause in which they are engaged.

Let them remain firm in their confederacy, and sacrifice every other consideration to that of extinguishing the Flames in which their Country are in danger of being involved.

Hostilities therefore to prevent if possible the spreading of the contagion of France, & Declarations to explain the purpose of the allies to restore or preserve publick order comprehend the measures which seem to be required in this case.

The Influence of France may be restrained by sec'ring a Barrier to be opposed to its communication.

The People of France and of all Europe, by Declarations & Manifestos, may be informed of a purpose in the war merely defensive, verified by operations that carry no view to acquisition or conquest or any / other kind besides the Barrier in Question.

All the members of the confederacy ought to join in the manifestos published for this purpose, and in order to act in concert ought to form a Convention consisting of Deputies entrusted to frame and issue their declarations from a Joint authority.

In the first act or publication of this convention, let all the nations of Europe & the People of France more especially be invited to send their Deputies to consider of the best measures to restore or preserve the good order of nations, & to favor those who are now in distress in emerging from it.

If this candid and beneficent overture should be rejected by the present Rulers of France, it will at least satisfy the subjects of the powers at war that their object is reasonable, and merely defensive, and their success to be appreciated / not by the advantage they gain but by the approaches they make to general Peace and good order, for in the present Crisis any other advantage compared to these is a triffle.

Numbers of the People in France will learn to distrust the Leaders who reject such favourable offers, and a Party may arise in that Country more likely to extinguish the fire which now rages there than any efforts that could be made from abroad.

Mere indiscriminate and unexplained hostilities leave every Frenchman to imagine that his life and every thing he values in his country is at stake, and requires his utmost efforts to oppose them. his liberties he may suppose are to be sacrificed to the reestablishment of unlimited monarchy &ct. &ct. &ct.

Henry 4th
 alarmed with the overgrown power of the House of Austria proposed such a convention or Congress as is now mentioned.

But the Crisis which then subsisted is far short of that which now subsists in Europe.

Then every Sovereign had the hearty support of his own Subjects, now the danger is lurking in the bosom of every state, and if not well guarded is ready to burst out from thence.

Such a convention therefore may appear at all times a romantic idea, but at no time less so than the present, it might be the means of extricating the nations of Europe out of the present seemingly endless war, and even of restoring France itself to some measure of order consistent with the safety of other nations, and opening an / Aera of new liberty & happiness to that distracted Country.

Such a Convention if we may at all indulge as romantic an idea if continued, might save to Europe many articles of ruinous expence, & many a destructive war, by bringing differences under negotiation and friendly arbitration & enabling nations to concert together Proportional reduction of Troops & other expences, by removing obstructions to commerce &ct. &ct. &ct.

Source: BL MSS EUR F291/97, ff. 42r–45v.

Remarks on a Pamphlet Lately Published by Dr. Price, Intitled, Observations on the Nature of Civil Liberty, the Principles of Government, and the Justice and Policy of the War with America, &c. In a Letter from a Gentleman in the Country to a Member of Parliament (1776)

Note on the Text

The *Remarks* is Ferguson's pamphlet on the American crisis, written at an early stage of the armed conflict between Britain and the Thirteen Colonies.[1] It was a response to the dissenting minister Richard Price's immensely popular *Observations on the Nature of Civil Liberty, the Principles of Government, and the Justice and Policy of the War with America* (1776), which went through numerous London editions in its first year of publication, and was reprinted in Edinburgh, Dublin, Boston, New York, Charleston and Philadelphia. Price's pamphlet provoked many responses from the likes of John Shebbeare, John Wesley and James Stewart. Like the works of many of Price's other critics, Ferguson's *Remarks* was printed at the government's expense. It was well-received in London, and two years later Ferguson would be invited to accompany the Carlisle Commission sent to negotiate, unsuccessfully as it turned out, with General George Washington and the American Congress.

Though Ferguson's response to Price was respectful, he strongly supported the British state and constitution against Price's criticisms, and condemned any acts of hostility by the Americans, which he simply regarded as illegal and unjustified. He wrote:

> If . . . they took possession of their settlements by grants of the Crown, if they have been uniformly considered as British subjects, amenable to the law and under the protection of the state, what title have they now to withdraw their allegiance because their settlements were made in America, any more than if they had been on Hounslow-Heath or on Finchley-Common?

Many of his arguments are indeed legal in character, seeking to clarify fundamental questions about the right of sovereignty, contracts, property, and the ultimate purpose of government in providing security for individuals and preserving civil peace.

Citing Montesquieu, Ferguson disagreed with Price's definition of liberty as independence. This could not be the same as liberty, since 'if any citizen were free to do what he pleased, this would be an extinction of Liberty, for every one else would have the same freedom'. The danger of democracy and the tragic fate of the Roman Republic are key themes in Ferguson's pamphlet. It is evident from the references and examples in the pamphlet that he was working hard on his Roman history whilst writing it. He had written to Edward Gibbon in the spring of 1776: 'I have as you suppose been employed at any intervals of Leisure or rest I have had for some years, in taking notes or collecting Materials for a History of the Disstractions that broke down the Roman Republic & ended in the Establishments in Augustus & his immediate Successors', adding that 'I comfort myself that as my trade is the Study of human Nature I coud not fix on a more interesting Corner of it than the end of the Roman Republic.'[2] That the power of the people was not the same as their happiness was exemplified by ancient Rome, in which the liberty of the people decreased as their power increased, and finally 'perished at last by the very hands that were employed in support of the popular cause'. Ferguson would elaborate on this theme in his *History of the Progress and the Termination of the Roman Republic* (3 vols, 1783).

Notes

1. See Ronald Hamowy, 'Scottish Thought and the American Revolution: Adam Ferguson's Response to Richard Price', *Liberty and American Experience in the Eighteenth Century*, ed. David Womersley (Indianapolis, 2006), 348–87.
2. Merolle, *Correspondence*, I, 141.

[1]

REMARKS
ON A
PAMPHLET LATELY PUBLISHED
BY DR. PRICE.
In a Letter to a Member of Parliament.

SIR,

I SEND you some Remarks upon Dr. Price's Pamphlet, concerning which you do me the honour to desire my opinion. A gentleman who gives his name to the Public is intitled to have the fairest construction put upon his words, and I shall be extremely sorry if, in differing from Dr. Price, any expression escape from me that is too abrupt for the respect that is due to him. As I am a mere commentator, I am likely to be as dull as the rest of my fraternity, but shall, nevertheless, abide by the order, and confine myself to the matter, that is suggested by my Author.

[2] You will please to observe, that the Doctor rests his argument on a definition of Civil Liberty, which is therefore a principal subject of these Remarks. He considers Liberty under four general divisions, *Physical Liberty, Moral Liberty, Religious Liberty* and *Civil Liberty*.[a] The first is the *principle of spontaneity*. The second is the *power of following our own sense of right and wrong*. The third, the *power of exercising the religion we like best*. And the fourth, or Civil Liberty, is the *power of a civil society or state to govern itself by its own discretion*.

The Doctor, in the following inference from all these definitions collated together, puts Liberty in contradistinction to Restraint, and makes Restraint, in every case, the essence of Slavery. In all these cases, he says, *there is a force which stands opposed to the agent's own will and which, as far as it operates, produces servitude*. And he concludes the whole deduction with observing, that *as far as in any instance the operation of any cause comes in to restrain the power of self-government, so far slavery is introduced*. Nor do I think, he adds, *that a preciser idea than this of Liberty and Slavery can be formed*.[1]

[3] I am under the necessity, however, of owning, that this idea is somewhat perplexing to me. It does not appear, that upon this idea of Liberty any civil community can be formed without introducing

slavery. For even where the collective body are sovereigns, they are seldom unanimous, and the minority must ever submit to a power that stands opposed to their own will.

In this, however, the loss of Liberty may be supposed unavoidable; for it is common to say, that men, by entering into society, give up a part of their Natural Liberty.[2]

But there is yet another difficulty. If Liberty be opposed to Restraint, I am afraid it is inconsistent with the great end of civil government itself, which is to give people security from the effect of crimes and disorders, and to preserve the peace of mankind.[3]

The Liberty of any single man, in this sense of a freedom from restraint, would be the servitude of all. In Turkey, perhaps in Brandenburgh,[4] there are persons who pretend to this Liberty; but I believe that no one can devise a more plentiful source of slavery than this. The Liberty of every separate district or corporation in a state would be national independence; and as [4] far as the humour for it should spread, would threaten every community with the loss of every incorporated member that has a pretence for separation, or a fancy to set up for itself.

I confess I am somewhat surprised that Dr. Price, who quotes Montesquieu with so much regard on other occasions,[5] should have overlooked what he has said on this. Among the other mistaken notions of Liberty, this celebrated writer observes, *That some have confounded the Power of the people with the Liberty of the people.*[b] *That in democracies the people seem to do what they please; but that Liberty does not consist in doing what we please. It consists in being free to do what we ought to incline, and in not being obliged to do what we ought not to incline.*[c] We ought to remember, he continues, *that Independence is one thing, and Liberty another. That if any citizen were free to do what he pleased, this would be an extinction of Liberty, for every one else would have the same freedom.*[d]

If the Doctor persist in his definition of Civil Liberty, it will be difficult to support the high encomium which he bestows upon it. For it would be a real curse to numbers of mankind [5] to be left to do what they please. Certain instances we have had of this Liberty in the case of despotic princes, who were taught to think that they had a right to do what they pleased; but they were, in consequence of this Liberty, the completest wretches that have appeared in the history of mankind.

Whether we say or no with Montesquieu, that the power of the people is not the liberty of the people, it may be said with confidence, that the power of the people is not the happiness of the people. Corrupt and vicious men, assembled in great bodies, cannot have a greater curse bestowed upon them, than the power of governing themselves.

It is possible that the Doctor may have meant to qualify his definition and the encomium of Civil Liberty, by supposing, that it was preceded by Moral Liberty; and if he did, this would be rather an aukward way of informing us, that Liberty consists in the freedom to do what is just and innocent. In the mean time, and till Moral Liberty is fully established in the world, we shall do well to prepare some restraint for the inclinations of men, and be contented with a Liberty which secures to us the possession of our rights, while it restrains us from invading the rights of others.

[6] Here, however, I am obliged to look forward some pages,[e] and must confess, that the Doctor himself has qualified his description of Liberty in some such manner as this: *A free state, he says, at the same time that it is free itself, makes all its members free, by excluding licentiousness, and guarding their persons and property and good name against insult.* That is to say, when we bring together the two parts of the Doctor's description, that a free state produces servitude, to produce Liberty. Or, as he concludes the paragraph himself, that *Government restrains Liberty, when used to destroy Liberty.*

This collision of words, I confess, renders the precision of the Doctor's former idea somewhat suspicious; but we must be contented with the good meaning, and only regret, that the qualification of the general definition had not come sooner, and that it is not more uniformly kept in view through the piece. If a writer should insist, that the inhabitants of St. Giles's have a right to seize the houses in Grosvenor Square, and afterwards, upon a difficulty stated, should qualify his doctrine by saying, that he affirmed the right only on a supposition that they had [7] bought the subjects in question, and had paid for them, his doctrine might be true on the whole; but his manner of stating it, by leaving out so important a condition till it was required to solve an objection, especially if he dropt it, afterwards through the whole of his argument might appear somewhat exceptionable. It is probable that some of the parties concerned would be in such haste to avail themselves of the right, that they would not stay to think of the condition. And I apprehend with some regret, that the Doctor may have readers who will reason on his definition of Liberty, and think themselves entitled to do what they please, without attending to the qualification that is afterwards brought to explain it.

My impatience to have a satisfactory account of this important subject, by collating together the descriptions and limitations of my Author, has carried me a few pages too fast; I think myself now, however, authorised to conclude with the consent of the Doctor, that Civil Liberty is not precisely a power to do what we please, but the security of our rights; and that a person may be free, although contrary to his own will he is obliged to pay his debts, and even to contribute to the revenue of the state. And if the Doctor insists that Liberty still implies [8] a freedom from restraint, he will please to observe, that nothing can give a more complete freedom from unjust restraint, than the perfect security that we cannot be wronged. This is the freedom which Montesquieu holds forth to our esteem; and I presume, it is that Liberty on which Dr. Price bestows his encomium, notwithstanding his apparent partiality to the freedom of doing what we please. I now return to the place at which I met my Author.[f]

The Doctor, in every step of his argument, is somewhat hurried by his own definition. *In every free state, he says, every man is his own legislator: all taxes are free gifts for public services.*[6] It may be fair to ask in what part of the world such a state does, or ever did exist? Or what sort of laws thieves and pickpockets are likely to make against theft? Or how much of his property the miser is likely to bring to the coffers of the Public?

In most free states the populace have as much need to be guarded against the effect of their own folly and errors, as against the usurpation of any other person whatever. And the essence of political Liberty is such an establish-[9]ment as gives power to the wise, and safety to all. The exercise of power in popular assemblies has a mixture of effects, good and bad. It teaches a people, as it did the Athenians, to become wits, critics, and orators. It gives to every man one chance against being oppressed, in allowing him to appear for himself. But it places him when accused before rash, precipitate, prejudiced, and inequitable judges; he is no more his own legislator, than he is the master of the people. And he is in fact subject to a power, which is of all others the most unstable, capricious, and arbitrary: bound by no law, and subject to no appeal. For this reason, Mr. Montesquieu has very wisely said, that Democracy and Aristocracy are not by their nature free governments.[g]

They are inferior in this respect to certain species of monarchy, where law is more fixed and the abuses of power are better restrained.⁷

The Doctor farther observes,ʰ or concludes, from his definition, *that Civil Liberty in the most perfect degree can be enjoyed only in small states, where every member is capable of giving his suffrage in person, and of being chosen* into public [10] offices. It is true that democracy is tolerable only in small states; and the Doctor certainly means to speak of democracy, when he makes this inference on the subject of Liberty. But even in the smallest states, the preservation of public consistency and justice, the security of private rights, must ever recommend some mixture of aristocratical power, that may prove a check on the caprice of the people; and such a mixture took place in all the happiest institutions of antiquity.

The Doctor owns,ⁱ that although Liberty be most perfect in small states, it is not altogether banished from great ones: For, *where all the members of a state are not capable of giving their suffrages on public measures individually and personally, they may do this by the appointment of substitutes or representatives.*

In this concession, the Doctor begins to elude the force of his own definition; and when we consider how little in some cases the constituent may know of what his representative does,⁸ it appears, that by this device, men may be their own legislators, without so much as knowing that laws are enacted or proposed. And even [11] America, at the distance of three thousand miles of sea, may enjoy its freedom by sending substitutes or representatives to the Parliament of Great Britain.

This indeed is one of the happiest institutions of mankind, and might be of use in small as well as in great states, by giving every order of the people that share in the legislature of their country, which is necessary to guard their own rights, without enabling them to usurp on the rights of others. But I must still contend, that the Liberty of every class and order is not proportioned to the power they enjoy, but to the security they have for the preservation of their rights.

In stating this fortunate principle however, the Doctor very reasonably recommends a fair and adequate representation, and makes such a description of pretended inadequate representation, as I am afraid can hardly fail of being applied to the government of Great Britain.ʲ The representatives of seven millions are chosen by less than three hundred thousand, and the whole is attended with circumstances that make the Doctor exclaim, *it is an abuse of language to say, that* [12] *such a state possesses Liberty. And that rather than be governed in such a manner, it would perhaps be better to be governed by the will of One Man without any representation.*⁹

The fact in our history, I believe, is, that there never entered into the head of any person able to bring it about, except Oliver Cromwell,¹⁰ the idea of having the people of Great Britain represented. Persons of a certain description were in the way of attending the king in his wars and in his Parliaments. It appears that they considered this distinction rather as a burden than as a privilege. The kings were in use to grant exemptions to the officers of their court, and to others. The counties and boroughs that sent substitutes were obliged to give them wages; and sometimes, by the connivance of sheriffs, eluded the duty altogether. In process of time, however, a place in the King's Court of Parliament became of more consequence. Deputies became willing to serve without wages; boroughs revived their charters. Freeholders embraced their distinction as a privilege, and their representatives improved it into a formidable power, which became of the greatest importance to themselves and to their country. So little however are mankind commonly aware when they are laying in politics [13] the foundation of the best superstructures.¹¹ The spirit of the constitution, the design of the constitution, are the mere constructions of speculative men; at least, they only mean the effect of the constitution, which, notwithstanding the disdain of our Author, has been in many respects superior to the effect of any other constitution in the known world; and notwithstanding the high ideas of Liberty with which it is contrasted does actually bestow upon its subjects higher degrees of Liberty than any other people are known to enjoy.

It is known, that under all the defects of the British Legislation, the subject enjoys more security than was ever before enjoyed by any people; and this not accidentally, but by a very natural tendency of the constitution, by lodging legislation in the hands of persons interested in the justice of the laws which they make, and by giving to all the different orders of the state a power to reject or amend every law that is likely to be grievous on themselves. It is less material who elects, than it is who may be elected. For so long as no one can be elected without the qualifications of a British commoner, the interests of the Commons in the lower house is secure.

[14] The experience of Europe, Asia, and Africa, should convince Dr. Price, that it is not better to be governed by one man than by such a representation: but this hasty expression of the Doctor, shows the danger of going so fast in search of ideal perfection, which is apt to make us despise what is attainable and obtained, for the sake of something impracticable, and sometimes absurd.

It is of great moment to extend the participation of power and government, as far as the circumstances and character of a people will permit; but extremely dangerous to confound this advantage with Civil or Political Liberty; for it may often happen, that to extend the participation of power, is to destroy Liberty. When all the powers of the Roman senate were transferred to the popular assemblies, the Liberty of Rome *came to an end*.[12]

In general, to be free, is to be guided by one's own will; but licentiousness is its opposite.[k]

Dr. Price seems to forget his own definition of Liberty, and admits the restraint of crimes as necessary to it: nay, admits that Liberty is [15] not less infringed when the licentious multitude do what they please, than it is when a single person does so; although he seems to think, and perhaps justly, that the former infringement is the most repairable and the least pernicious of the two, p. 14.

Dr. Price has very justly observed, that the imputation of omnipotence to any government, except that of the strongest, the most numerous, or the greatest force, is absurd; and that even force cannot always secure obedience. It must be satisfied with the alternative of obedience, of tortures, or of death. Government, whatever be its origin, must employ various engines, of which force is but one; authority, respect, public confidence, persuasion, are the principal engines to be employed with the body of a well-meaning and innocent people: force is the engine to be employed against criminals and slaves. And the government of mere force, in every instance, either finds people slaves, or makes them so.

It is absurd to say, as some writers have said in the course of this paper-war, that there must be in every state one supreme uncontrollable power;[13] for this never yet existed in any state whatever. The despotic Prince, in search of [16] such a power, finds, that he changes the control of assemblies, councils, civil departments or of men of education and virtue only, to come under the control of Serjeants and Corporals. In our government, King, Lords, and Commons are not one power, but three collateral powers; any one of which may stop the motions of all the rest. This observation, however, takes nothing from the authority of their joint acts wherever they concur, nor had any one till now, from the extreme settlements of British subjects in the old world, to their utmost migrations in the new, doubted the validity of any such act. Dr. Price seems to regret that the efforts formerly made by our fathers in behalf of Liberty are no longer repeated; he should likewise regret, that our liberties are no longer attacked in the same manner as in the times of our fathers. The contest between the prerogative of the King and the privilege of Parliament is discontinued:[14] the King has influence enough in Parliament to obtain the necessary supports of his government, though, I hope, never to obtain the smallest resignation of the people's right. In the contest of our times, the parties are the pretenders to office and the holders of office. A noble contest, though an ignoble cause. I must call it a noble contest, as it is undoubtedly one principle of life in our constitution. It [17] leads one party to watch the motions of administration; and the other to be on their guard because they are watched. As the matter now stands, indeed, it is more the interest of opposition to stop the ordinary movement of government, than to prevent its abuses. If they can stop the ordinary course of government, the minister must withdraw to make way for themselves: but in preventing abuses, they only oblige him to change ill measures for good, and by this means to take a firmer hold of his power. I know that many ill consequences might be imputed to the state of our parties; but I am not for removing any one safe-guard to freedom, until we have found a better.[15]

Dr. Price infers from his argument, that no one community can have *any power over the property or legislation of another, that is not incorporated with it by a just and adequate representation.* P. 19.

In this passage, by the word Power, he certainly means the right to have such a power; for it is an undoubted fact, that many states have had the power. Even the admired and happy republics of Swisserland and Holland have their subject towns and provinces; and this nascent republic of New England too, if it [18] acquire the independence which, under the denomination of Liberty is projected for it, may come to have its subject towns and provinces, and, among the foremost, some of those who are now so ready to become partners of its revolt against the state.

I do not contend for the right to any such power in any actual case, but I contend not only for the reality of the power, but for the right likewise in some supposable cases. No writer on the law of nature,[16] that I know of, has denied that states or bodies politic may perform every act that any private party can perform; and if this be admitted, it follows, that they may, either by contract or forfeiture, become tributary or subject to another state or body politic, as much as a single man may become the servant or debtor of another single man by stipulation or forfeiture.

This maxim of the law of nature, I confess, does not bind the Americans to contribute to the supply of the British Empire, unless it can be shewn that they have received all the benefit of subjects; and therefore have stipulated to perform all the duties of subjects, by the same tacit convention that binds every inhabitant of Great Britain.

[19] I agree with the Doctor, that the subjection of one state to another is inexpedient, and often calamitous for both; but this will not preclude one member of the same state, who has always made common cause with another, from having a very just claim to expect a joint contribution to the common support.

After what has passed between Great Britain and her Colonies, whoever pretends that Great Britain should drop every claim of a return, and the Colonies refuse to make any return, under every possible security to their property, must have very high notions of the generosity incumbent on the one party, and as low notions of what is incumbent on the other. Nay, but they have traded with us, and this is enough:[17] and have not we traded with them? Have they given us their goods for nothing? Or have they been careful to receive value? Or have they taken less value than other nations would have taken? These questions should be answered before we are told that their trade has repaid us for all the blood and treasure we have expended in the common cause, and before it can be admitted that in the heights of prosperity, at which they may arrive, they are not bound under any form, or with any precautions, for the remainder of their property, to contribute any [20] part of it whatever to the common supplies of the Empire.

The Doctor owns that one state may become bound to indemnify another for an injury done them, or be bound to give security against future injury; but who can set limits to the possible rights thus established in the claim of one state against another. It is impossible to tell how long a state may be tributary, or how much it may pay before it has acquitted a debt of indemnification; or what precaution may be necessary to obtain, for the future, a sufficient security against injuries. The Romans, when they recovered Campania from its revolted inhabitants, and from Hanibal, thought proper, for their own future security, to abolish the Municipal Senate, and assemblies of that province: Such meetings they considered as a standing conspiracy against themselves. In this I shall not pretend to justify their conduct, but suppositions may be made that would be sufficient to justify it, and such as I shall neither be willing to make nor apply to the American Colonies: But let no one contend, that in the plenitude of madness, they may not forfeit more to the state, than any one would be willing to exact from them. I will not say what an imperious state, like that of the Romans, so often [21] quoted in a similar case, would have exacted and done; but if we are to hope that one party will not inflict the penalty, we may hope likewise that the other will not incur it.

Writers on the Law of Nature sustain the validity of a fair contract in all cases where the performance is possible or lawful.[18] That it is both possible and lawful for one corporation or body politic to submit themselves to the laws, and contribute to the supplies of another, no one will doubt; that all corporations, and bodies politic belonging to the same state are actually under such a contract, no body ever questioned.

No one can bind himself to receive the religious opinions of another, because his opinions are not in his power, but he may bind himself, if he pleases, to pay a shilling in the pound of his estate.

But can one generation bind another? No doubt, in every lawful contract, as much as any person can bind his heirs, or as much as the late King of France could bind the successors to his crown to leave Canada in the possession of the English.[19] The Doctor's reasoning on this subject[20] takes away the obligation of treaties, or at [22] best makes them temporary agreements, to last for the lives of those who made them.

It is confessed, that favours voluntarily conferred, cannot be stated as a ground of debt; but they who rest so much on the affection and attachment of the Colonies to the Mother Country, ought to allow something for the favours done by the Mother Country to her Colonies.

The Doctor attempts a distinction between the separation of parts in the same kingdom, and the separation of parts in the same empire,[21] which I confess I cannot comprehend; but if he lays so great a stress on the difference of names, he may be told, that Great Britain and its dependencies is not an Empire, but a kingdom. I see no warrantable part for mankind to act under either denomination, but to acquiesce in the government which Providence has given to their kingdom or their empire, until they are sure that they do not change it for the worse; and in this, reformers upon general principle, however sanguine, are far from being secure.

It is the fashion, however, I observe, with some writers, to give high expectations of the great perfection to which human nature is tending, especially in America for I think Old England, by their account, is degenerating. But a republic extending 1200 miles in one direction, and without any known bounds in the other, is still an experiment to be made in the history of mankind. Our ancestors made the experiment in vain, within narrower limits; they too had high expectations of what mankind were about to exhibit; they thought the millennium and the kingdom of Christ were at hand, but they found, in their stead, the iron reign of an usurper, supported by military force.[22] It is charity, perhaps, to pray that if the Colonies must break with us for ever, they may be more faithfully served by those they employ, than they themselves have served their country. The officer, perhaps, has not yet appeared, who, on that emergency, is to dismiss the Congress as Cromwell did the Parliament. But what title have they to hope for an exemption from the too common fate of mankind; the fate that has ever attended Democracies attempted on too large a scale; that of plunging at once into military government? The armies they form against their country will need no other title to become their masters. It is even fair to conclude, from the history of the world, that there is no time of more danger than those times of sanguine, of florid, and enthusiastic expectation, [24] in which mankind are bent on great and hazardous change.

Americans, however, may still be thought out of this question; they seek no innovation; they are the parties that contend for the ancient establishment.[23] Their plea, however, I hope is better founded than this.[1] The Parliament of Great Britain has made laws for the Colonies from their first establishments. The charters of the Colonies subjected them to taxes, and they have been taxed by acts of the British Parliament: Matters therefore were in their ordinary train, when the Americans stopt short, and would proceed no farther. I will not, however, insist, that the change of circumstances may not have required a change of policy; and that, as the Americans are growing rich, and have something that tempts rapacity, they ought to have better security for their property, than the continuance of former practice will perhaps bestow. But, in this view of the contest, what is to be done if the Colonies have a right to contend for new securities? Let them apply to the state with proper professions of duty, and representations of the dangers they apprehended; but no one [25] can pretend that the state ought to yield up the ordinary way of constituting a revenue, till a new and better way is substituted in its place.

The Doctor refers to the example of the Romans, and bids us consider how much they suffered for having been the tyrants of other nations,[24] and I shall never recommend to any state to follow their example.

Dr. Price[m] has deduced, from our leading principle, viz. *that every restraint on the will of man is an introduction of slavery*, a number of consequences that seem to him incapable of being disputed. There is, indeed, nothing that requires to be disputed, but his principle itself, for with that, the consequences must fall. Its application, as he observes, to the present question with America, is obvious; and the principle indeed seems to be made for the application, and is fitted to justify the desire of national independence, under the name of Civil Liberty. The change of words has a mighty effect, even in the frame of an argument. There is not an English gentleman, I believe, that would not shrink from the thought of reducing millions of his fellow-subjects to a state of servitude, and as few that will not be seized with indignation in [26] being told that the Colonies aim at independence, and will contribute no longer to the joint support of their common country.

We shall be told, however, that the Colonies do not aim at independence. — Yes, if they aim at the Liberty designed for them by Dr. Price. If they aim only at security to their rights and properties, let the question be fairly stated, and put in the train of pacific discussion.

The Doctor is pleased to say, that the question of right, with all liberal inquirers, ought to be; not what jurisdiction over them, precedents, statutes, and charters give, but what reason and equity, and the rights of humanity give: This, he says, *in truths is a question which no kingdom has ever had occasion to agitate*.[25] It is certainly the first time it ever was proposed that men having any political establishments, statutes, precedents, or charters, should at once demolish, cancel, or set aside all the maxims, records, or conventions on which every party must rely for the preservation of his property, and from which alone he can learn the relation in which he stands to the state, or to his fellow-subjects. Why has no kingdom ever had occasion to agitate such a question? Have no parties arose in politics before? Have no districts or corporations of the same community claimed privileges and [27] exemptions that have been disputed with them? It is well known that such questions have been agitated, and that parties uniformly referred to precedents, statutes, and charters for a determination. To bring questions of this sort to any supposed tribunal of reason, of equity, and humanity, is to set human affairs afloat upon the sea of opinion and private interest, and to deprive men of those charts, landmarks, and rules of sailing, by which they were in use to be guided, and to direct their cause.

It is certainly true, that no nation ever planted Colonies with so liberal or so noble a hand as England has done. But she has done so on the plan of those very charters, statutes, and precedents which are now to be set aside. And her having done so much for her Colonies, is surely an unfavourable topic from which to infer the right of her Colonies to do nothing for her. It is indeed to be lamented, that, in the place of argument, this controversy is hastening to employ the sword. Blessed were he that could bring it to a different issue. But I hope, that neither the Americans, nor the advocates that plead for them, will think, that every concession should come from Great Britain. They have hitherto said to the King of Great Britain, on his own territory, as the Romans said to [28] Pyrrhus and to Hannibal, 'You must evacuate this land before we will treat;' and if this were granted them, it is likely they would be ready to declare what further concessions they expect from the Crown and Legislature of their country.

The Doctor[n] proposes to determine the justice of the war by the object of it; and this he collects from a statute moved and carried in Parliament, under the auspices of a noble Lord, and of honourable gentlemen, who are the declared friends of America, and in whose intentions the Americans repose such confidence, that they have never once, as I have been told, complained of this declaratory law.[26] From this state of the case; that is, from the silence of America on this law, and from the friendly intentions towards America of those who obtained it; I am inclined to think, that this law cannot be the ground of the quarrel. I rather suspect, that we are going to war about taxation and property,[27] than about speculative, declarations of right; and that one party is very indifferent about laws that are to bring them nothing, and others about laws that are to take nothing from them. And on this supposition I [29] should think, the fair way of determining the justice of the claim, would be by stating two questions. The first, Whether the charters, statutes, and precedents; that is to say, whether the present constitution of Great Britain respecting her Colonies; has committed a power of Taxation over America, to the legislature of Great Britain. If this question shall be decided in the affirmative, as I am persuaded it must be so decided, it will follow, that the Legislature of Great Britain has yet incurred no blame in urging a claim in which they were justified by the constitution of the state.

I however most willingly admit a second question. Has the situation of affairs undergone any change that require a change of policy and of measures, that deserve the attention of the Legislature, and on which the Colonies ought to be heard with candour and patience, so as to avoid, if possible, inconveniencies to which, in a new situation, old precedents, and even statutes and charters might carry us?

The principal changes in our circumstances are, that our Colonies, under the influence of charters and statutes, have increased in resources and in people: that Great Britain is heavily burdened, and that now, from being at an or-[30]dinary expence in nursing and protecting her Colonies, she would gladly draw some share of the public supplies from thence. This situation, I confess, is new, and may require some suitable policy. If the Parliament of Great Britain, as formerly, be to grant the money of the Americans; the latter may think their property not secure. At the same time, if any party independent of the Parliament of Great Britain be to grant money to the Crown; this constitution loses one of its principal securities, the dependence of the Crown for supplies on the Commons of Great Britain.

Here is a difficulty, on which it is not surprising that parties should differ, and inadvertently get into a very hearty quarrel, in which both may suffer extremely before any one is able to find a solution.

In stating the question, I have passed over many things which other persons may think of great consequence, in order to come at what I apprehend every one will think so.

I do not write in order to persuade my correspondent, that the Legislature of Great Britain should retain their unlimited power of granting the money of America. But I write under a [31] deep conviction, that the Americans ought to contribute to the supplies of the empire. And that they ought now, before an indemnity is granted for the past, to specify the taxes on which they will establish a revenue for the state, and which, without augmenting the burden on them, may increase with their resources their population and the immunities given to their trade; but subject to no other alteration, without the consent of Parliament and their own. Or if they choose rather to pay some fixed proportion of what the Commons of Great Britain from time to time levy on themselves, let them have it in the mode which they themselves, or better judgments than mine, can determine.

They have been told, that the Parliament of Great Britain will not tax them, if they are pleased to tax themselves. No specific tax, no specific sum has been mentioned to them; and yet this proposition, coming from the Commons of Great Britain, has, by themselves and by their advocates on this side the water, been termed an insult. The plain English, I am afraid, is, that the Americans do not think any supply from thence due to the state of Great Britain. Or, that their advocates do not think they ought to grant any such supply till they themselves are in power. The Americans may [32] flatter themselves, that if the party that now opposes Government,[28] were in power, they would obtain every favour and every concession. But they may be assured, that no Minister in the councils of the King will surrender the undoubted right of this country, to require from America some share in the supplies which are necessary to support the Imperial Crown and the Empire of Great Britain. If precautions be wanting to secure the rights of that people in the mode of attaining this necessary end, the parties may still have an opportunity of entering into a candid and fair discussion of this subject. Commissioners are soon to be appointed by the King, who are to accompany his fleets and armies across the Atlantic, doubtless with the humane and merciful intention to spare, by pacific means, if that is yet possible, the effusion of blood.

In this light the Colonies ought certainly to consider this lenient measure. And if they do, I think they ought to be ready on their part, to meet the advances of the King with dutiful representations of the securities they deem necessary in the future administration of government respecting them.—If no such step is taken, we may fairly conclude, that they are intoxicated with the idea of separation and independence, and that they are re-[33]solved not to grant supplies in any mode or in any proportion whatever. And if this be their resolution, I am afraid the sword must strike as well as be raised; and till they exculpate themselves from the design of withdrawing their allegiance, and every reasonable mode of supply from the Crown of Great-Britain, the wounds they receive will appear to come from the hand of Justice, and will remain unpitied by many persons, who are far from wishing to invade their liberties.

It is likely that the councils of the King will incur more censure for the reluctance with which they have armed the kingdom against this revolt, than they will for any supposed precipitation in urging matters to extremities. But it is a noble error to have been slow in believing that British subjects, unmolested in their religion or in their liberties, still in possession of that government by which they had arrived at so much prosperity, untouched in their property by any unprecedented invasion; and if assailed, only assailed by penal statutes, to make compensation for an outrage done to the property and the trade of their fellow-subjects: It was, I say, a noble error to be slow in believing that British subjects, under this description, would have drawn upon themselves and this nation all the horrors of a civil war. If we were taught to think them pusilanimous, they were certainly [34] taught to think our councils irresolute, distracted, and unstable; but both, I hope, will return from their errors, and exchange the sword for a more rational mode of arbitration.

Dr. Price, being to consider the justice of the war, recites all the pleas that may be offered by the state in support of coercive measures. Those pleas he supposes to be, *The necessity of war to preserve the unity of the empire: our superiority: our pretensions as the parent state: the return due for our benefits: our sovereignty in the territory of America.*[29] The Doctor will own, that union is at least a desirable object, and will pardon our endeavours to preserve it, by the same means that states, the most moderate, have employed for this purpose; the policy of a common interest, a common sense of duty, and the authority of a common government. If any one contend, that we ought to rely on either of the former principles to the exclusion of the latter, and that we ought to resign either the authority or the force which government on occasion must exert, I should suspect that he does not wish to have us united, nor even to leave us possessed of the common resources for the preservation of peace and good order, that all nations have employed within their dependencies.

[35] I mean not to argue from the second topic. Nations do not found obligations of allegiance and duty on difference of wealth, numbers of people, or the supposed precedency of scholars and learned men. I hope the remaining title, however, will not be so slightly treated. The name of Parent State is not an empty sound. It carries the authority by which civil rights are established and modified. If America derive nothing from this authority, why did its settlers take any charters from the crown of Great-Britain?[30] Or if they were emancipated by these charters, why is not their emancipation expressed in some such terms as the following? *Whereas certain persons mean to depart this our kingdom and form states apart, we hereby emancipate such persons, discharge their allegiance to us, and discontinue our protection.* If, on the contrary, they took possession of their settlements by grants of the Crown, if they have been uniformly considered as British subjects, amenable to the law and under the protection of the state, what title have they now to withdraw their allegiance because their settlements were made in America, any more than if they had been on Hounslow-Heath or on Finchley-Common?[31] The charters, the precedents, the statutes on which this right of the state is founded, can no more be disputed than the charters, precedents, [36] and statutes on which the constitution of the state, respecting any other part of its power, is established. The utmost any party can plead is, that circumstances are changed, and require a new system of policy, or at least some additional precautions, to give to the British subjects of America the same security, or a security as nearly as possible the same, with that which is enjoyed by their fellow-subjects at home.

Exaction of gratitude is but an ungracious plea; the fact is, that the state protected and encouraged that part of her subjects on the same mixed motives of political interest and affection, that she protects and encourages every other member of the community, and there is no other member that has not an equal title to reject the claim of gratitude. It may again be repeated, that considering what has passed between Great Britain and her Colonies, the Americans will be found to act an odious part in this contest; they are not satisfied with the enjoyment of their municipal governments, and such a mode of contributing to the supplies of the empire, as may be consistent with the safety of their persons and their properties.

The sovereignty of a territory, and the property of its land, every where admits of a [37] distinction. The state is undoubtedly sovereign of all the territory on which any of her subjects, under her protection, and by her charters and grants, have made any settlements; and the territory of North America was, and is subject to all the claims of sovereignty under the limitation of statutes and charters. I write from memory, but appeal to the original deeds, whether some of them did not give an exemption from Taxation during a limited time,[32] with an evident implication, that at the expiration of that term they should be subject to taxation like other British subjects. And whether others did not limit taxation to specific duties, mentioned with a like implication, that the right of taxation was entire while the exercise of that right was restricted.

But Dr. Price is willing to plead,° that the Colonies did settle under the faith of charters, and we must admit, that they have a right to all the immunities and exemptions granted them by statute, or by charter under the authority of statute; but let not their advocates plead the authority of charters in one page and reject them in the next. It is certain, that the Colonies were planted on the authority of law, and [38] never aspired to establish their privilege on a higher base. It is likewise probable, that all of them, at their first settlement, would have embraced, as an ample security of their property, an exemption from every burden besides that of parliamentary taxation. How far this security may now be deemed sufficient, I am willing to leave as a subject of better and more able discussion.

The remainder of Dr. Price's observations on the justice of the war tend to prove, that the past or present state of the constitution respecting the Colonies, is not precisely what it ought to be in the present state of the empire, nor such as it ought to be in the event of farther changes, of which he has stated the possible contingency; and in this I do not pretend to decide, but hope that persons better qualified will bring it to proper trial, not of force, but of political expediency and national wisdom.

Dr. Price, in the 2d Section of the 2d Part of his Pamphlet, in which he inquires, *whether the war with America is justified by the principles of the constitution*, affects to consider the Americans as a separate people; and inquires, *whether the war be made to establish our constitution among them.*[33] If this question has any meaning at all, [39] I apprehend it should stand, Whether, by the present constitution of the state, the Legislature of Great Britain is in possession of a right to impose taxes and to enact laws binding in America? If they be in possession of such a right, have they been known to abuse it? They have been in possession of the right, and scarcely at all exerted it. But the Americans are now alarmed, and think that this right may be abused; let them come forward, therefore, and urge the precautions necessary to be taken against this abuse. If they will accept of no security below that of independency, and total separation of commonwealth; this, I apprehend, they must acquire at the point of the sword. But other and better remedies for the evil may yet be expected from the councils of a state that has been as remarkable for moderation, as for resolution in the conduct of great affairs.

Advocates in this cause perpetually quote the spirit and principles of the British constitution against the letter and the fact. Do they mean its primaeval state, the intention of its founder, or something else, that they fancy concerning it? Its primaeval state is very little known; and if it were, could not be admitted as the rule of proceeding in opposition to subsequent establishments and compacts.[34] In that stage which is [40] called the feudal constitution, the King, had his domain of royal estate, and had no other claim on his subjects but their personal services in his wars. When he wanted some extraordinary supply, he summoned his vassals together, and made his proposition to them for that purpose; they deliberated and refused, or granted sometimes in commutation for military services, and sometimes as a voluntary gift. The Constitution was gradually raised upon these foundations. The Parliament became what it is, and the state in possession of a maxim, that the King can raise no supplies without consent of Parliament. This is the origin, and this is the fact in our constitution; and right or wrong, till within these few years, or few months, within the British territory of Europe, Asia, Africa, and America, Parliament was supposed omnipotent and irresistible:[35] what change may now be made to accommodate forms to new situations, I hope may still be determined by a better decision than that of the sword. But, till that is determined, I hope, that every good subject will pay a proper respect to the fact, and the letter of the constitution, whatever fancy he may have about the spirit of it. We may wish for improvements in the laws of the state, but till these are made, we must abide by the law as it stands.

[41] In the next Section,[p] Dr. Price brings in question the policy of the war with America. There is, in fact, no apology can be made for any war, besides the necessity of it to maintain some right, and some right that is worth contending for at this expence. Whether Great Britain has any such right now at stake,

and by what steps this right came to be brought in hazard, are two separate questions.

I must maintain, that until our union is legally dissolved, the American Colonies are a part of the British empire. That acts of sovereignty, from which Great Britain might, or did derive, material advantage, were exerted by the legislature of Great Britain. That the act of navigation,[36] the acts limiting trade, the appointment of governors and other civil officers, the establishment of a revenue, however inconsiderable, were all of them acts of sovereignty, in which the state and people of Great Britain are deeply interested. That the interest of Great Britain, constituted by these acts of sovereignty, is now in imminent hazard; and in all human probability, to be secured by that force alone with which the state shall appear to be armed in support of its own rights. So much has been said [42] for the Americans in this country, and they have met with so little control in their own, that their pretensions are likely to rise. If they prevail by force in reducing the power of legislation, will they not take the same opportunity to reduce the navigation act, and other every right of sovereignty? What is to hinder their proceeding to assume that independency, which is so roundly prescribed to them under the denomination of Liberty? Are they not getting fast into a situation, in which the sovereignty of the Crown is likely to become as odious, at least to their leaders, as the power of the Legislature itself? One man is brought from behind the counter, to be member of a sovereign Congress; another to be one of five that wield the executive power of a great empire: others are promoted proportionally, though to inferior stations; and may entertain hopes of rising to the highest: one man is raised from a dealer in horses to be a general, another from a barber to be a colonel; all of them, I make no doubt, well qualified for the stations they fill: but whether they be or no, likely to be fond of their dignities, and unwilling to part with them; ready to employ all their authority, all their credit, all the force they can command to prevent the return of peace, which must bring the downfal of their power, and send them again to [43] their trades and their obscurity; what but a proper force, and a proper aspect of determination, on the part of Great Britain, can bring such persons as these to reason, or deliver out of their hands the bulk of the sober and the industrious people of America? who, seeing their properties and their peace at stake, will be glad to return to the bosom of the state, and be happy to receive such satisfaction on the future security of their property and civil rights, as I hope no generous or candid mind can ever entertain any idea of refusing them.

Men are indeed, as Dr. Price observes, too apt to be governed by the lust of power, by revenge, and by other detestable passions.[37] But are these passions unknown in America? Have the leaders in this revolt no ambition, no revenge to gratify, or would it be prudent in any administration to trust to the moderation and candor of parties, who have soared already so high above the condition of subjects, and who have such an interest in perpetuating a breach to which they owe so much personal consequence?

It may be confessed, that as matters now stand, the Americans are not likely to acknowledge the most evident rights of Great Britain, farther than those rights are supported by force.

[44] But it will be asked, How came we into this situation? Is not the war, though necessary now, the sequel of many unnecessary steps, that being discontinued in time, would have prevented it entirely? It may be so, and so have been the greater number of wars that have afflicted mankind. Disputes arise, provocations become reciprocal, and evils accumulate. The beginnings are admitted, because no body perceives the end; and every fool is a wise man after the event has shown him what was coming.

I am willing to own, that Dr. Price is inclined to censure measures, rather than to strike at men. That for this purpose he recals to our memory, the policy of many years, fraught with instruction to those who are now to act on the scene of public affairs. He predicts, though I hope rashly, the loss of America;[38] and to make us sensible how much we are to lose, he paints in the most favourable colours, the happy state at which that country at the beginning of these hostilities had arrived, and the growing importance of its trade to Great Britain. I hope, however, it will be remembered, that the Colonies arrived at this happy state under the influence of British policy, and under the undisputed right of the British Legislature to bind them in all cases whatsoever: and as we have so long prospered together, under [45] this policy; that the Doctor's prediction may still prove false; that a moderate share of public spirit and good intention, on that side of the water as well as on this, may still save to all parties their reciprocal advantages, without incurring the inconvenience that either apprehends. But for this purpose, as we are perpetually alarmed with the hundreds of thousands that the Americans can arm, I am afraid that Britain must not come to the conference unarmed, or in a st[ate] to be insulted.

I write in every page on the supposition that negotiation may take place;[39] and who, but infernal spirits, would ever go to war with any other intention than to obtain an equitable peace. The party on whose side the aversion to treaty lies, will be answerable for the consequence.

As for the trade of America, I am ready to allow it as high as the advocates of America are pleased to make it. Be it granted that we sold them our goods at our own price; but unless this price was a higher than we received from other markets, unless it was better paid, I do not see why this trade is preferable to any other vent for our commodities. Even if the price were higher, which I am told it was not, the slow [46] returns of this market rendered it less profitable than many others we have had and still may have.

But have the Americans a right to withdraw their trade from our merchants and manufacturers, as well as their supplies from the state? If they have not, why should it be supposed that they mean to carry the lines of separation beyond the bounds which they themselves, and their advocates, affect to prescribe. Trade is the child of interest, and will follow where its parent leads. But the right of sovereignty must be maintained by authority, and sometimes by force. The subjects of Great Britain do not claim a right of sovereignty, neither in Europe nor in America; but they expect from each other, and from the Americans, the reasonable co-operation of fellow-subjects; and the state itself must maintain its sovereignty in both. If any part of the monarchy withdraw its allegiance, the remainder must repel such an insult with their blood.

We are, in this argument, threatened with the attacks of enemies from abroad, while we are engaged in a war with our Colonies.[40] But the advocates of America, it is hoped, do not wish that the state of Great-Britain should bow [47] the head to foreign nations, as well as to her own subjects. If our quarrel be momentous and just, we must support it or perish, be the enemy who he will. But we have had our wars, and none of our enemies have yet had cause to rejoice in the effect of their arms against us. I am, however, inclined to believe, that this alarm, as it is injurious to the honour of nations with whom we are at peace on the faith of treaties, so it is injurious to their sagacity, and discernment of their own political interest. What are they likely to gain by erecting the colonies of North-America into a power independent of Britain? Will their own Colonies become more dutiful after this example of a supposed successful revolt? Or will they have less to fear in behalf of their West-India settlements, from this rising confederacy, than they have from Britain? The new enemy will be nearer to those settlements, and have many more advantages in seizing them, than the old.

Few persons are qualified to enter the lists with Dr. Price, on the subject of accounts and calculations;[41] but this alone will not enable us, in particular cases, to decide the great questions of national right. Paper-currency and public debt are the consequences of a fortunate constitution, and of an unlimited credit both public [48] and private. They have given us the advantage in many a contest to forces superior to our own; and the evil, though great, by our Author's account, is susceptible of a cure.[42] It is probably in order to urge this cure, that the desperate state of the patient is so much explored. Such admonitions go home to Ministers of State, who can verify or disprove the facts, and will not be shaken by false allegations. The people, however, are in more danger, and in the most flourishing time of the Public, may suffer as much from a false alarm of bankruptcy, as they could from a real one. A false and wanton alarm of fire, in a crowded theatre, has cost many lives; but they who alarm us so loudly on the subject of public credit, may have the consolation to know, that their own accounts are not fully credited, otherwise we should have the people of England crowding into every avenue that leads to the Bank, and treading each other to death, with an eager haste to get forward while any cash was to be had for their paper.[43]

Most people, however, believe, that it is not necessary for a great kingdom to have all its riches in cash; and even the example of the Americans, whose advantages Dr. Price is not on the present occasion inclined to decry, will serve to prove, that a people, with no better [49] resource than a paper circulation, may rush into the midst of alarming convulsions. The Americans have reason to believe, that their country will be a seat of war, and yet carry on their operations with paper. *Will not the landing of a few troops on their coasts, insurrections threatening a revolution of government, or events that produce a general panic, operate in America as they would do in Europe?*[q] And put an end there, as it would any where else, to the subsistence of armies, and to every species of traffic that depends on the faith of paper, or the credit of a government that supposes a revolution in order to give it any being.

But if in the present contest with America our revenue is likely to decline, and if the whole of it be scarcely adequate to the difficulties in which we are involved; this does not appear a proper argument to convince us, that we ought not to expect any aid from America; nor is it a very liberal apology for the Americans refusing to bear any part of the burden, of which a considerable part was incurred in their own cause. In their cause singly, if they persist and prevail in gaining that Liberty of independence which is now pointed out to them; but in our [50] common cause if they continue united with us, and bear a just proportion of our burdens.

In stating the *honour of the nation as affected by the war with America*,[44] Dr. Price supposes, that the claims of the state are wrong, and that the resistance of the Colonies is just. On this supposition, the argument is unanswerably for him; and the concessions of justice, however late, would, at least to our fellow-subjects, be honourable. But this, I humbly conceive, is begging the question. Hitherto the State has proceeded in the tract of precedents, and followed the rules of law and of charters. If a change be expected, the grounds of it should be laid in amicable representation, not in open war and hostility. Nations are like private men, they may commit errors, but must not suffer themselves to be kicked even into reason. When the parties are once armed, a great nation must attend to its reputation, as well when it sheaths as when it employs the sword. If the Americans refuse upon any terms, whether in conjunction with, or in subordination to the Parliament of Great-Britain, to furnish any part of the public supplies, it is by no means necessary, in order to justify the use of the sword against them, that they invade this island. If a person refuse the payment of his just debts, he may be [51] compelled to do right in his own habitation, no less than if he had actually entered with violence the house of his creditor.

We are said to assume as much power over the Americans as either the Genoese or the French could assume over the Corsicans. The State of Great-Britain had assumed nothing but the power of protecting her Colonies, when her constitutional powers in America began to be denied, and her authority spurned. What has happened since is surely matter of regret, at least, if not of just censure, to the warmest friends of America. A daring breach of peace and violence to property was committed, and went unpunished. Direct war has been levied in return for penal statutes. And instead of reparation to their fellow-citizens for the damage done by the citizens of Boston, we are told, that they are an independent republic, and no longer accountable to the laws.

We are bid to think of the allies of the Romans in Italy, how they claimed to be enrolled as citizens of Rome; how they fought, and how the state perished in the struggle. The claim of those allies was, by every reasonable person, thought to be fraught with disorder and public ruin. It was strenuously opposed by the most [52] candid and virtuous citizens of Rome. The multitude of the people, in the place of assembly, but too often made a scene of confusion. It was not thought necessary to bring an accession of the whole populace of Italy to swell the tumult. The event of the war was fatal to Rome; not because the claim of the allies was refused, as Dr. Price seems to insinuate, but because it was granted; and the sequel proved a striking example of what the Doctor does not seem to apprehend, that the power of the people is not the good of the people. Their liberty sunk as their power increased, and perished at last by the very hands that were employed in support of the popular cause.[45]

We are bid to consider[r] how far we are likely to succeed in the present war. The reader will please to observe, that success in war is a term of uncertain meaning. It may stand for the extermination of an enemy on the one hand, or for the most equitable terms of peace that can be obtained on the other. If the Doctor means the first, I hope that we shall not succeed. If he means the second, I hope we shall succeed; and if the Americans be actuated by any thing short of frenzy, they will not resign [53] their property and their peace, burn their own towns, and fly to the desert, as the Doctor insinuates, to avoid embracing us once more as their brethren, and concurring with us upon some equitable and safe ground, in supporting the common cause of the state. This I shall call victory; and a victory to all the ingenuous and well-informed natives of America, as well as to those of the same description in Britain

Some individuals among them, who meet in Congress, or stand at the head of armies, as the Lords of America, may think, the reunion of the Empire a defeat; but to every one else, I hope, it will appear a new æra of prosperity, and glory to the state.

Dr. Price supposes,[s] contrary to the lesson of independence, which, under the denomination of Liberty he has read to the Americans, that they may still be willing to remain in the bosom of the state, and on the same bottom with their fellow-subjects in Britain: But in what sense, and to what effect, remain on the same bottom with us? Will they acknowledge the law of the state, and contribute some reasonable proportion toward its support? Will they be contented with a reasonable security, admitted in [54] the form of granting this supply, that it shall not be augmented without their own consent? If ever any such proposal had come from America, I am persuaded it might have served as the foundation of friendship, and terminated in some happy arrangement. But if, by maintaining their union with us, they only mean to continue the practice of calling upon our fleets and armies to defend them when attacked, without contributing any thing to support the power that protects them, I do not see what interest the state has in this union. Nay, but they are willing to leave us the command of their trade. I confess I do not see the wisdom of this policy on the part of America; we are arrived at an age of experience, in which all parties might see the expedience of exchanging restrictions on trade for compensations in revenue. If the state were disposed to oppress, she might do so as effectually by restrictions on trade, as by impositions of taxes. And I believe, that if the Parliament of Great Britain, in its disputes with the Crown, had chosen rather to leave the trade of the people at its mercy, than to grant its supplies, the Public would have long since suffered severely by the choice.

I am sorry that Dr. Price should endeavour to flatter the Americans on a supposed aversion of [55] the people of Great Britain to this war, or impute to this circumstance the supposed flow progress made in recruiting the army. The nursery of the army in this country consists in the supernumeraries of our manufacturers, and labouring hands.[46] Had the American leaders, by shutting their ports on our traders, distressed us as they proposed, recruits for the army would have been but too easily found; but as matters now stand, our armaments must increase with their usual pace. If, to avoid loading the public, by means of new levies, with an enormous half-pay list at the end of the war, it is to be opened with a supply of foreign troops, I hope it will close with them too; and that in whatever manner the first army that goes to America is composed, it will satisfy the people of that country that peace with Great Britain is better than war.

I am farther sorry, that Dr. Price should flatter the Americans on the subject of their own strength, and of our weakness. If the Doctor were pleased to recollect a few more of the passages of history, with which he is so well acquainted, he would observe, that no general, being to invade a country, thought himself obliged to have an army in numbers equal to the natives; and that most of the unhappy con-[56]quests recorded in the history of mankind were made with small armies, who, having the superiority of discipline, made a progress the more rapid that their numbers were few: in short, that small armies have done more than I hope the arms of Great Britain will have to do in America; they have reduced, and kept in subjection, extensive countries, replenished with numbers of people, not of the weak and effeminate alone, but of the most warlike and fiercest nations that are known in history.

The Romans, a little before the second Punic war,[t] mustered in Italy seven hundred thousand foot, and seventy thousand horse; yet this country was invaded by Hannibal with twenty thousand foot, and six thousand horse:[u] The greatest part of it was reduced, and remained in the hands of this enemy for sixteen years. With how small an army did Caesar reduce four hundred independent Certons, and fierce nations in Gaul? With how few did he afterwards invade Italy itself, and with how few did he reduce the whole Roman Empire? Were the Saxons that landed in Britain superior to the Britons; the Danes to the Saxons, or the Normans to the English? On this point, therefore, I should be sorry to flatter the Americans. The distractions [57] that arise in a country that is invaded, turn the superiority of numbers into disorder and weakness. The Americans have not yet met the British soldiers on the plain, and when they do, their numbers, I imagine, will not avail them much.

I have as high a sense of what men ought, and will do, in defence of their liberties, as any man: But I flatter myself, in the present case, that, unless the Americans mistake independence and separation of commonwealth for Liberty, that they will not think themselves called upon to try the force of this principle. I should willingly, with Dr. Price, in the close of his pamphlet, or while he is hastening to the conclusion,[v] rejoice in the prospect of a power growing in America that shall astonish the world. If it were not proposed to raise this power by dismembering the state of Great Britain, and by stripping her of a branch she has nourished with so much care, and which by having partaken with her in every national advantage, is now in condition to bear an equitable part in her burdens; and which certainly, on every principle of justice, human and divine [58] is not now entitled to say, we need you no longer, and will take no farther part in your affairs.

I confess that I think, when the cause of our country is at stake, impartiality is but a doubtful virtue. It may be noble to wish that our country should do no wrong, and it may be lawful to stay her hand when rashly lifted up against the weak and the helpless; but when swords are drawn, to beat down that of a friend while the enemy is striking, I am afraid, is perfidy.

The Americans, it is true, are not come here to invade us; but they with-hold the rights of Great Britain, and oblige us to invade them, which is a no less justifiable ground of hostility. When citizens of Great Britain anticipate with joy the independent or separate greatness of America, it is natural to suppose, that they think the dismemberment of this empire will bring us back only to what we were about a century ago; diminish our luxury, give a check to many vices, and by landing us down a few steps on the scale, only renew our endeavours to remount again. This, however, is not of a piece with the history of mankind; nations in their progress, though weak and inferior to [59] their neighbours, spurn their condition, and continue to advance from the bottom to the top of the scale. But nations that have been high can seldom bear a fall; they sink in the scale with a retrograde motion as rapid as they advanced. Is Great Britain then to be sacrificed to America; the whole to a part, and a state which has attained high measures of national felicity, for one that is yet only in expectation, and which, by attempting such extravagant plans of Continental Republic, is probably laying the seeds of anarchy, of civil wars, and at last of a military government, so much that, in this great contest, Dr. Price might have ventured to say, that the friends as well as the enemies of America *may not know what they are doing*?

I am happy to find in the conclusion of this Pamphlet,[w] that Dr. Price, notwithstanding the language of independence which he has taught the Americans, is pleased to repeat with some expressions of approbation, a motion for peace, suggested by a noble Lord,[47] in which the union, dependency, and participation of America in the burdens of the Empire are included as part of the plan. The proposal does honour to the noble Lord; and if it had actually come from [60] America, I should have thought it an equitable ground upon which to open a council of deliberation with the most friendly intentions. I should have prayed that, while the deliberations were open, parties would agree to a cessation of arms, and a suspension of penal statutes. But I see not the use of fabricating plans, of which the first step always is a concession on the part of the state, without any overture of submission on the part of its subjects. These subjects have treated plans of the minority with the same contempt that they have treated acts of Parliament or resolutions of the majority, and seem to be determined to bring this contest to an issue more agreeable to the enemies of Great Britain than to its citizens and friends.

P.S. I know not how the tenets of any party may be affected by what I write, but my paper is now in your hands; if you publish it, I shall become the Author of a Pamphlet; and in that case beg of you to remember, that we Pamphlet-writers of every condition mistake ourselves for statesmen, and so decide and advise without reserve. But that, not being singular, you will treat me no worse than you have done others of the same description. Our esteem with many is fallen; but our consequence with a warm-hearted and reasoning people, who like [61] to be consulted in their own affairs, merits the interposition of the best informed and best intentioned persons in the kingdom. My small pretentions being only to a share of the last gratification, I hope to meet with some indulgence to the first. And am,

Your's, &c.

THE END

Notes

a. [Richard Price, *Observations on the Nature of Civil Liberty, the Principles of Government, and the Justice and Policy of the War with America* (London, 1776),] sect. I., p. 2.

b. [Montesquieu,] *De l'Esprit des Loix* [3 vols, Geneva, 1748], livre ii [*sic*; i.e. 11]. c. 2. [I, 313. 'on a confondu le pouvoir du peuple avec la liberté du peuple'.]

c. Ibid., c. 3. ['Il est vrai que dans les Démocraties le peuple paroît faire ce qu'il veut; mais la Liberté politique ne consiste point à faire ce que l'on veut. Dans un État, c'est-à-dire, dans une Société où il y a des Loix, la liberté ne peut consister qu'à pouvoir faire ce que l'on doit vouloir, & à n'être point contraint de faire ce que l'on ne doit pas vouloir.']

d. Ibid., 313–14. ['Il faut se mettre dans l'esprit ce que c'est que l'indépendance, & ce que c'est que la Liberté. La Liberté est le droit de faire tout ce que les Loix permettent; & si un Citoyen pouvoit faire ce qu'elles défendent, il n'auroit plus de Liberté, parce que les autres auroient tout de même ce pouvoir.']

e. [Price, *Observations on the Nature of Civil Liberty*,] pages 12 and 13.

f. [Price, *Observations on the Nature of Civil Liberty*,] page 4.
g. [Montesquieu,] *Esprit des Loix*, liv. ix. c. 5. [*sic*: bk. 11, ch. 4, I, p. 314. 'La Démocratie & l'Aristocratie ne sont point des États libres par leur nature.']
h. [Price, *Observations on the Nature of Civil Liberty*,] page 7.
i. [Price, *Observations on the Nature of Civil Liberty*,] page 7.
j. [Price, *Observations on the Nature of Civil Liberty*,] page 10.
k. [Price, *Observations on the Nature of Civil Liberty*,] pages 11, 12.
l. See [James Macpherson,] *The Rights of Great Britain Asserted Against the Claims of America* [(London, 1776)].
m. [Price, *Observations on the Nature of Civil Liberty*,] part II., page 31.
n. [Price, *Observations on the Nature of Civil Liberty*,] part II., sect. i., page 34.
o. [Price, *Observations on the Nature of Civil Liberty*,] page 40.
p. [Price, *Observations on the Nature of Civil Liberty*,] page 50.
q. [Price, *Observations on the Nature of Civil Liberty*,] page 77.
r. [Price, *Observations on the Nature of Civil Liberty*,] section V [94–103].
s. [Price, *Observations on the Nature of Civil Liberty*,] page 101.
t. Polyb. lib. ii. c. 24. [*The General History of Polybius. In Five Books. Translated from the Greek by Mr. Hampton* (London, 1756), 133.]
u. Ibid. lib. iii. c. 60.
v. [Price, *Observations on the Nature of Civil Liberty*,] page 103.
w. [Price, *Observations on the Nature of Civil Liberty*,] page 103.

1. Price, *Observations on the Nature of Civil Liberty*, 4–5.
2. See, e.g., John Locke, *The Second Treatise of Government*, in *Two Treatises of Government*, ed. Peter Laslett (Cambridge, 1988), ch. 9, §130, 353. In 1764, Ferguson borrowed from the Edinburgh University Library the second volume of Locke's *Works*, which included the *Two Treatises*. See J. B. Fagg, 'Ferguson's Use of the Edinburgh University Library: 1764–1806', in *Adam Ferguson: History, Progress and Human Nature*, ed. Eugene Heath and Vincenzo Merolle (London and New York, 2008), 61.
3. This argument is now mainly associated with Hobbes, but it had become mainstream via the natural law tradition and writers such as Samuel Pufendorf. Hume wrote that '[man] is engaged to establish political society, in order to administer justice; without which there can be no peace among them, nor safety, nor mutual intercourse. We are, therefore, to look upon all the vast apparatus of our government,

as having ultimately no other object or purpose but the distribution of justice, or, in other words, the support of the twelve judges.' See Hume, 'Of the Origin of Government', in *Essays, Moral, Political and Literary* (Indianapolis, 1987), 37.
4. Ferguson refers to the Ottoman Empire and Prussia, which are meant to exemplify two autocratic states.
5. Price, *Observations on the Nature of Civil Liberty*, 18, 29.
6. Price, *Observations on the Nature of Civil Liberty*, 6.
7. See Hume, 'Of Civil Liberty', in *Essays*, 94: 'But though all kinds of government be improved in modern times, yet monarchical governments seem to have made the greatest advances towards perfection. It may now be affirmed of civilized monarchies, what was formerly said in praise of republics alone, *that they are a government of Laws, not of Men*. They are found susceptible to order, method, and constancy, to a surprizing degree.'
8. For contrasting views of the role of members of parliament at this time, see *Mr. Edmund Burke's Speeches at His Arrival at Bristol, and at the Conclusion of the Poll* (London, 1775) and [Catharine Macaulay,] *An Address to the People of England, Scotland and Ireland on the Present Important Crisis of Affairs* (London, 1775), in *Political Writings*, ed. Max Skjönsberg (Cambridge, 2023), 145–61.
9. Price, *Observations on the Nature of Civil Liberty*, 10–11.
10. Oliver Cromwell (1599–1658) was a general in the Wars of the Three Kingdoms and Lord Protector between 1653 and 1658.
11. See the introduction for the importance of unintended consequences in Ferguson's social and political thought.
12. Ferguson had at this point begun working on his history of Rome, eventually published in 1783. This is reflected in his loans from the Edinburgh University Library, which between 1769 and 1776 included works on Roman history and other Latinist works by Aelianus Tacticus, Ammianus Marcellinus, Appian, Julius Caesar, Catullus, Cicero, Cassius Dio, Theodorus Regnerus de Bassenn, Jean-Charles de Folard, Dionysius of Halicarnassus, Eusebius, Josephus Flavius, Florus, Benno Caspar Haurisius, Horace, Livy, Ovid, Onofrio Panvinio, Stephanus Winand Pighius, Plutarch, Polybius, Charles Rollin, Seneca, Italicus Silius, Suetonius, Tacitus, Antoine Terrasson, Pierre-Joseph Thoulier d'Olivet, Tibullus, Varro, and Obadiah Walker. See Fagg, 'Ferguson's Use of the Edinburgh University Library: 1764–1806', 57–64.
13. See, e.g., James Otis, *The Rights of the British Colonies Asserted and Proved* (London, 1764), 12.

14. This argument formed part of the conclusion in David Hume's *The History of England* (6 vols, 1754–62); see esp. *The History of England from the Invasion of Julius Caesar to the Revolution in 1688* (6 vols, Indianapolis, 1983), VI, 530.
15. For Ferguson on party, see Max Skjönsberg, 'Adam Ferguson on Partisanship, Party Conflict, and Popular Participation', *Modern Intellectual History* 16 (2019): 1–28.
16. Ferguson borrowed Samuel Pufendorf's *Law of Nature and Nations* (1672, translated into English in 1703) from the Edinburgh University Library in 1776; see Fagg, 'Ferguson's Use of the Edinburgh University Library', 62.
17. Price, *Observations on the Nature of Civil Liberty*, 39.
18. See note 16 and Ferguson, *Institutes of Moral Philosophy* (Edinburgh, 1769), part I, ch. 8: 'Law of Acquisition by Contract'.
19. Under the terms of the Treaty of Paris of 1763, which concluded the Seven Years' War (1756–63), France ceded New France (Canada) to Britain.
20. Price, *Observations on the Nature of Civil Liberty*, 25–6.
21. Price, *Observations on the Nature of Civil Liberty*, 26–7.
22. Ferguson refers to the English Revolution, extreme Puritan sects such as the Fifth Monarchists (or Fifth Monarchy Men), and the military dictatorship of Cromwell.
23. This was a key argument in Edmund Burke's *Speech on American Taxation* (London, 1774).
24. Price, *Observations on the Nature of Civil Liberty*, 29–30.
25. Price, *Observations on the Nature of Civil Liberty*, 32.
26. Ferguson refers to the first Rockingham ministry's Declaratory Act 1766, which accompanied the repeal of the Stamp Act 1765. At the time of Ferguson's pamphlet, the Rockingham Whigs – led by Charles Watson-Wentworth, second Marquess of Rockingham (1730–82) – and its spokesperson Burke posed as the friends of America in parliament, in opposition to the ministry of Lord (Frederick) North (1732–92).
27. Ferguson refers to the Townshend Duties, which placed indirect taxes in America on glass, lead, paints, paper and tea, imported from Britain. In 1770, Lord North repealed most of these duties, but fatally kept the tax on tea.
28. I.e. the Rockingham Whigs.
29. Price, *Observations on the Nature of Civil Liberty*, 35–40.
30. By 1775, Virginia, New Hampshire, Massachusetts Bay, Rhode Island, Connecticut, New York, New Jersey, North Carolina, South

Carolina and Georgia were crown colonies. Pennsylvania, Delaware and Maryland were proprietary colonies.
31. Two areas of land in the south of England.
32. For instance, the Charter of Massachusetts Bay 1629 granted an exemption from all royal taxes, subsidies and customs for seven years and from all taxes for twenty-one years, apart from a 5 per cent duty on imports from England.
33. Price, *Observations on the Nature of Civil Liberty*, 48–50.
34. Ferguson shared his scepticism of ancient constitutionalist arguments in favour of reform with Hume, who criticised '[t]hose who, from a pretended respect to antiquity, appeal at every turn to an original plan of the constitution, only cover their turbulent spirit and their private ambition under the appearance of venerable forms'. See Hume, *History*, II, 525. It was also key for Burke's criticism of parliamentary reform. On this, see esp. J. G. A. Pocock, 'Burke and the Ancient Constitution: A Problem in the History of Ideas', *Historical Journal* 3 (1960): 125–43.
35. See William Blackstone, *Commentaries on the Laws of England: Book the First*, 2nd ed. (Oxford, 1766), 160–1. Ferguson borrowed Blackstone's *Commentaries* from the Edinburgh University Library in 1769 and 1770; see Fagg, 'Ferguson's Use of the Edinburgh University Library', 58.
36. The Acts of Navigation 1651 and 1660 restricted trade within the British Empire.
37. Price, *Observations on the Nature of Civil Liberty*, 51, 55.
38. Price, *Observations on the Nature of Civil Liberty*, 59.
39. Ferguson would himself later participate in the peace negotiations, as part of the unsuccessful Carlisle Commission in 1778.
40. America held talks with France about an alliance from late 1776, which eventually came into effect in February 1778. Eventually, Spain and the Dutch Republic also entered the war on the American side.
41. Besides moral philosophy and theology, Price was known for his works on political economy, including *Observations on the Expectations of Lives, the Increase of Mankind, the Influence of Great Towns on Population, and Particularly the State of London, with Respect to Healthfulness and Number of Inhabitants* (London, 1769) and *Observations on Reversionary Payments; On Schemes for Providing Annuities for Widows, and for Persons in Old Age; On the Method of Calculating the Values of Assurances on Lives; and On the National Debt* (London, 1772).

42. In his more positive appreciation of public debt, Ferguson differed not only from Price, but also from Hume and to a lesser extent Smith; see the introduction.
43. Despite his alarm, Hume invested his own funds in government stock; see E. C. Mossner, *The Life of David Hume*, 2nd ed. (Oxford, 1980 [1954]), 409–10.
44. Price, *Observations on the Nature of Civil Liberty*, 87–94.
45. Ferguson would elaborate on this theme in his *History of the Progress and the Termination of the Roman Republic*. See Max Skjönsberg, 'Adam Ferguson on the Perils of Popular Factions and Demagogues in a Roman Mirror', *History of European Ideas* 45 (2019): 842–65.
46. For a similar argument, see Hume, 'Of Commerce' (1752), in *Essays*, esp. 260–2.
47. William Petty, second Earl of Shelburne (1737–1805).

Minutes of the Life and Character of Joseph Black, M.D. (1801)

Note on the Text

Ferguson's biographical essay of the famous chemist Joseph Black, who passed away in 1799, was composed in 1801 and published by the Royal Society of Edinburgh in 1805.[1] Black was a distant blood relative on his mother's side, as well as his wife's uncle. Ferguson and Black had been longstanding colleagues at the University of Edinburgh, where the latter held the professorship in medicine and chemistry from 1766. Ferguson was highly indebted to Black, who was also a physician; in 1780, when Ferguson suffered a major attack of paralysis, Black cared for him as he made an unexpected full recovery. Ferguson's biographical sketch provides details of his skills as a physician.

Among other notable things, it is revealed that Black's father, born in France, was acquainted with Ferguson's intellectual hero Montesquieu, who, like Black's father, traded in wine in Bordeaux. The essay also discloses details of Ferguson's life, as he wrote of himself in the third person. Ferguson had himself started his academic career as the Professor of natural philosophy at Edinburgh in 1759, before he transferred to the chair of pneumatics and moral philosophy in 1764. Though he wrote to Gilbert Elliot in September 1759 that 'I like my Situation very well, & begin to admire S[ir] Isaac Newton as I did Homer & Montesquieu',[2] it is clear that his primary interests eventually reverted to moral and political philosophy. He clarified in a footnote in this essay on Black that 'his own studies have been so different, that he would not, if he could, charge his mind with any of its [chemistry's] practical details'.

The biographical sketch is of interest not only because of its details about Black and the history of science, but also for its picture of the Scottish Enlightenment's social environment more broadly.

We learn, for instance, that Black was a member of the Poker Club – the militia club that lasted from 1762 to 1784 – whose name, as Ferguson tells us in a footnote, came about through 'whimsical accident'. Ferguson has influentially been credited by the diarist Alexander Carlyle for coining the name, which his formulation in this essay at least calls into question.[3]

Notes

1. *Transactions of the Royal Society of Edinburgh* (Edinburgh, 1805), V, part III, 101–17.
2. Merolle, *Correspondence*, I, 38.
3. *Autobiography of the Rev. Dr Alexander Carlyle; Containing Memorials of the Men and Events of His Time* (Edinburgh, 1861), 419–20; John Robertson, *The Scottish Enlightenment and the Militia Issue* (Edinburgh, 1985), 118.

[101] II. Minutes of the Life and Character *of Joseph Black*, M. D. *Addressed to the Royal Society of Edinburgh.*

[Read Aug. 3. 1801.]

THE merits of studious men are to be estimated by the aids they have given to the advancement of science, or the literary monuments they have left with posterity; but if the public be gratified by their labours in these respects, readers are generally willing also to be told, who and whence they were.

JOSEPH BLACK, the person to whom these minutes relate, successively Professor in the Universities of Glasgow and of Edinburgh, Member of this Society, and of other royal and public institutions in Europe; having made important discoveries, and having laid the foundations of many others, towards erecting a fabric of science, which has since been raised to a considerable height; and having been himself distinguished for modesty and felicity of manners, as well as correctness of understanding, and ingenuity of research, — will, it is hoped, be thought worthy of notice on these accounts. He was born on the banks of the Garrone, in France, in the year 1728. His parents were Irish and Scots. His father, JOHN BLACK, a native of Belfast in Ireland, was settled in the wine-trade at Bourdeaux. His mother was a daughter of ROBERT GORDON, of the family of Halhead in Aberdeenshire, who was likewise settled in the same trade, and at the same place, and in consequence of his success, was enabled to purchase, with additions, the estate of his elder [102] brother, greatly encumbered by the debts of those who had possessed it for some generations preceding. The mother of JOSEPH BLACK, and the mother of JAMES RUSSEL,[1] late Professor of Natural Philosophy in the University of Edinburgh, were sisters and the mother of ADAM FERGUSON, Professor of Moral Philosophy, was their aunt; a circumstance which was the origin, though not the cement, of a friendship subsisting between them through life.

WHILE Mr BLACK, the father, lived at Bourdeaux, the great MONTESQUIEU, being President of the Parliament or Court of Justice in that province, honoured Mr BLACK with a friendship and intimacy, of which his descendants, to this hour, are justly proud. They preserve letters, or scraps of correspondence, that passed between the President MONTESQUIEU and their ancestor, as they would titles of honour descending in their race. On a paper wrapped round a bundle of such letters, the following note is found in the handwriting of JOSEPH BLACK. 'My father was honoured with President MONTESQUIEU'S friendship, on account of his good character and virtues. He had no ambition to be very rich; but was chearful and contented, benevolent and liberal-minded. He was industrious and prudent in business, of the strictest probity and honour, very temperate and regular in his manner of life. He and my mother, who was equally domestic, educated thirteen of their children, eight sons and five daughters, who all grew up to men and women, and were settled in different places. My mother taught her children to read English, there being no school for that purpose at Bourdeaux.'

SO much may suffice for an account of JOSEPH BLACK'S parentage. No words, added to those used by his son, to delineate the father's character, can improve it; and nothing more is wanting, to account for the regard with which he was honoured by the President MONTESQUIEU. This illustrious personage, [103] together with a great simplicity of heart in himself, had a glowing sense of modest merit in others, and a partiality also for the manners and institutions of the British nations, which he thought singularly happy, and in respect of which, he willingly listened to any important details. On being made acquainted with BLACK's intention of leaving Bourdeaux, he wrote to him a letter, in which, with other expressions of kindness, are the following: 'I cannot be reconciled to the thoughts of your leaving Bourdeaux. I lose the most agreeable pleasure I had, that of seeing you often, and forgetting myself with you.'[a]

A FEW years before Mr BLACK retired from business, his son JOSEPH, in the year 1740, being about twelve years of age, was sent home in order to have the education of a British subject; and having, for some years, gone to school at Belfast, or its neighbourhood, was sent to continue his education at Glasgow College, where he passed through the ordinary course of preparation for any of the learned professions to which he might devote himself; and upon his father's requiring him to make a choice, he took to medicine, as agreeable to the habit of physical studies which he had already acquired.

IN entering on this pursuit, he became connected with the celebrated WILLIAM CULLEN, M.D.[2] then Professor of Medicine at Glasgow, and was distinguished through life by this ingenious man with an uncommon degree of friendship and confidence, which he did not fail to acknowledge and to return. In continuing the same studies afterwards at Edinburgh, he, as well as Adam Ferguson, lived with their relation JAMES RUSSEL, whose singular correctness, and precision of thought, in various branches of science, could not fail to be of use to all who approached him.

[104] BEFORE JOSEPH BLACK offered himself a candidate for a degree in medicine, he had already made his discovery of Fixed Air; that is to say, of an elastic fluid, which being fixed in calcareous and alkaline substances, is dispelled from them in their calcination by fire, or effervescence with acids, leaving a residuum, which, in the absence of this air with which it had been combined, becomes caustic; a quality which it retains until the air of which it was deprived is again restored.[3] Pure chalk, or pure calcareous matter of any form, in this experiment, loses about two-fifths of its weight, or, more accurately, forty-one parts in the hundred. Here, accordingly, is a ready way of assaying limestone or marl, to ascertain its purity or its value, to the husbandman in particular, who would employ it to improve his soil.

THE air obtained in this experiment has its peculiar qualities. Besides that of being fixable in stone, it is heavier than common air, its specific gravity being nearly double. Flame is extinguished, and animals are suffocated in it equally as in water. By this discovery, notwithstanding the ingenious and copious observations of Dr HALES[4] and others, on the subject of what were called Factitious Airs, it was reserved for BLACK to give a spur and a new direction to the researches of science.

FROM this beginning, great progress has been made in distinguishing varieties of elastic fluid, and in ascertaining the composition of the atmosphere itself. Chemistry was become a favourite study in France, as it had long been in Germany, and the report of a new species of air was every where received with avidity. The experiments of BLACK were repeated, and the inferences confirmed by ingenious men both at home and abroad; though by some in Germany the result was at first contested, and a controversy arose, in which it does not appear that BLACK took any part, nor does any doubt now remain of the fact, as stated by him, or of the inferences he drew from it.[b]

[105] AN elastic fluid, indeed, of the same qualities, has been since obtained from various sources; from vinous fermentation, from the earth itself, laid open in grottos or fissures, from mineral springs, from the breathing of animals, and from the combustion

of charcoal. This air is found to have the properties of an acid; and the French chemists, being led by their experiments to consider it as produced by the union of the principle of charcoal with vital air, have laid aside the appellation of Fixed Air, and have substituted that of Carbonic Acid Gas in its stead.

IF the researchers to which the observation of fixed air gave occasion, had terminated here, the accession to science, though important, had been comparatively small. The composition of the atmosphere, the distinction of vital and mephitic air, the effects of respiration, and the conjectural theories of combustion and animal heat, might have remained unknown.

HERE, however, no mean progress has been made, and names too numerous to be recited in such minutes as these, will, on account of their part in these studies, go down, with well-merited lustre, to future ages. Nations may hereafter contend for the honour of such discoveries as were made by LAVOISIER,[5] PRIESTLEY[6] and others,[c] not merely of single or insulated facts, but of a magnificent order existing in nature, for the continuance of vegetation and animal life. Even France and England, though [106] rich in the treasures of science, and each having much to boast of its own, may, in the future, as in times part, be jealous of what is gained by its neighbour; it is pleasant, however, to observe, that the individuals chiefly concerned were untainted with such illiberal passions. LAVOISIER, in sending to BLACK a copy of his experiments on respiration, tells him: 'It is but just you should be one of the first to receive information of the progress made in a career which you yourself had opened, and in which (he says) all of us here consider ourselves as your disciples.'[d] To this BLACK replied, with a just admiration of what the French chemists were doing, and, as might be expected from his modesty, without reference to any merit of his own.

NEARLY about the same time that BLACK made the discovery of fixed air, his mind was already at work on the phenomena of latent heat. Among his papers are found some note-books, in which he had inserted observations and queries, medical, chemical, and miscellaneous; accompanied with particular references or allusions to times and circumstances, which serve to fix dates within certain limits at least. In one book, the notes appear to have been written while he was a student at Edinburgh, or candidate for his degree, in the year 1756; at which time he made or published his discovery of fixed air. In this book are contained conjectures and queries relating to the cold produced in the liquefaction of salt and snow, and in general in the solution of salts in water. Seeming to have the doctrine of latent heat in his view, 'Is it not,' he says, in one place, 'owing to this that all bodies, in becoming fluid, have occasion for more heat than in their solid state?' In another place he says, [107] 'Does not the heat produced in the slacking of quicklime, arise from the sudden fixing a part of this fluid (water) into a solid state? Is not this the case in the setting of gypsum?' In the same way he accounts for the intense cold produced by ice and nitrous acid, applies the principle again to all saline solutions, and ascribed the slow granulation of salt to the re-appearance of heat, 'Is not ice,' he says, 'crystallized water? and does it not always feel cold, because it melts on our handling it? This is similar to the solution of salt in water.' These notes, from circumstances intermixed, appear to have been written as early as 1756. In a following note-book, which, from circumstances also, does not appear to be of a later date than the year 1757, there are several queries, of the same nature with those above mentioned, particularly with respect to the curious observation of FAHRENHEIT,[7] that water, if not disturbed, will cool below 32 degrees without freezing, but the moment it is disturbed, it raises the thermometer to 32 degrees, and freezes. 'Is not this,' he says, 'the heat that is unnecessary to ice?' In the same note-book conjectures are carried still farther, and applied to the production of vapour. A way is mentioned to estimate the quantity of heat which is employed and disappears in the formation of vapour, and cannot afterwards be discovered by the thermometer. 'Place a phial,' he says, 'with water, close-corked in a stove; open it suddenly, and see how much of it is converted into vapour, while the water comes down to the boiling point.' Observations to the same effect are continued through six small note books; in different places of which, it is observed, that animal heat originates in the lungs, and that heat always accompanies the production of fixed air.

FROM these notes, it appears, that the experiments in which BLACK evinced his doctrine of latent heat to the satisfaction of his pupils, were not made at random, or without previous apprehension of the fact, as it appeared in the ordinary course of na-[108]ture or chemical phenomena. 'Heat,' he observed, 'is in nature the principle of fluidity and evaporation, though, in producing these effects, it is latent in respect to the thermometer, or any sensation of ours; and as matter, otherwise quiescent, becomes voluble and volatile in liquid and in vapour, heat may be considered in nature as the great principle of chemical movement and of life. If it pass through vacuity as well as through body, as it certainly does in its communication from the sun to the planets, we must consider it not as an accident in bodies, but as a separate and specific existence, not less so than light or electric matter;[e] and though agreeing with these in some of its effects, in its nature possibly different from either.' But such was BLACK's caution not to outrun the course of actual evidence, that he declined any discussion of the question, relating to the absolute nature of this magnificent power in the system of nature.

MY reading in chemistry does not enable me to say, how far the doctrine of latent heat is, in these precise terms at least, admitted as a principle in the received theories of combustion and animal heat but, to my limited apprehension, it appears to be the only solid foundation of any theory that proceeds upon the supposed decomposition of signifying or vital air, manifesting a light and heat previously latent in such air. We can have no direct proof of latent heat in the atmosphere, or permanently elastic fluids, and it is from analogy only that we assume it to exist in such fluids. The maxim of Newton, indeed, may be applied here, that what is uniformly observed in any department of nature, as far as our experience reaches, may be safely deemed general within such department; and the heat which we find [109] disappear in liquefaction and evaporation, we may safely assume as existing also, though in a latent state, in every fluid of a similar form. Even BLACK admitted, that in the atmosphere, under all the manifest changes of its temperature, there may be, and probably is, a very great measure of latent heat.

SUCH were the scientific discoveries of BLACK, when residing as a student at Glasgow or at Edinburgh, at least before his nomination to a professorship at either place. When his friend Dr CULLEN was removed from Glasgow to Edinburgh, BLACK was appointed to succeed as Professor of Medicine at the former place;[8] and following his example as lecturer on Chemistry also, was, from this time forward, more employed in detailing particulars already known, for the information of his pupils, than in pursuing any series of investigations for himself.

IN entering upon this task, it became matter of course to define the science, and even in this our Professor gave a specimen of his character, and the modesty of his pretensions, in a matter formerly enveloped in mystery, and the affectation of magical power.

THE science of nature, indeed, is interfiling in all its branches, whether they rise into the heavens, or sink into the bowels of the earth. We are placed in a busy scene, and have our safety and accommodations at stake, in the midst of operations and changes that greatly affect them. The principles that operate in our system are the objects of our science, and when known, become the instruments of our art, towards procuring what it has pleased Providence to make the conditions of our preservation and well-being. In respect to these principles, science becomes an accession of skill to every manufacturer, and to every labourer of the soil, as it is to the contemplative an opening into the interior springs, which are employed in the production of so much beauty and order in the system of nature around us; and this is the rank of importance, which, without the pretentions of [110] alchemy, or the mysteries of supernatural power, the chemist might assume to his studies. But, in these, BLACK still saw no more than research and inquiry, far short of complete science or comprehensive system, and he characterized the study on which he was to enter, by the use of its principal instruments, Mixture and Heat. If discoveries have since raised it to a higher rank among the branches of natural science, he himself has contributed his share in the progress it has made. He had published his discovery of fixed air, in a pamphlet, about the time that he obtained his degree in medicine;[9] but that of latent heat was never otherwise published than as a part of his academical course. His pupils, indeed, being numerous, and from different parts of the new, as well as the old world, made his doctrine sufficiently known.[f,10]

AFTER a few years employed by CULLEN in the first profession to which he was appointed at Edinburgh, he was removed to a different branch of the medical school; and BLACK, as before, being called to succeed him, was, on the 17th of April 1766, admitted Professor of Chemistry at Edinburgh. His talent for communication being no way inferior to that which he possessed for observation and inference, his manner of acquitting himself in his new situation gave additional lustre to the schools of science, and rendered him one of the principal ornaments of the University, in which he continued, for about thirty years, to teach the different branches of chemistry, with a reputation always increasing. His style was characterized by the most elegant simplicity. His address in performing experiments was remarkable, [111] and in the impression he made, subjects perplexed or intricate became perspicuous and clear of superfluous or questionable matter. To the last, and under symptoms of declining health, his mind gave proofs of strength undiminished. In speaking, his voice, though low, had an articulation which made him be distinctly heard through every corner of a spacious hall, crowded with some hundreds of his pupils: and the simplicity of his expression, if not eloquence, had, to those who listened for information, something more engaging and powerful than any ornament of speech could produce.

AVERSE to hypothesis or vain conjecture, his science was a just comprehension of facts, and might be adopted by any artist who consulted him, with as much safety as he relied on any practice he himself had experienced. His time and attention being devoted to the communications which his pupils had a right to expect from him, very much limited his practice as a physician. But where he was called or could attend, his manner was singularly acceptable. Without flattery, or uncommon pretentions to skill, he won the confidence of his patients, and, with unaffected concern for their benefit, was often successful in mitigating their sufferings, if not in removing their complaints. He was, in short, a physician of great repute, in a place where the character of a physician implies no common degree of liberality, propriety, and dignity of manners, as well as learning and skill. Never being anxious to bring himself forward into public view, little may remain with posterity to distinguish him as an author, unless his executors should think proper to publish the notes from which he used to prelect, and which, notwithstanding the subsequent progress of science, may still be of use to the student, as a most solid foundation on which to proceed in his studies.[11]

AMONG the few things published by himself in his own time, we may reckon his Thesis or inaugural essay, *De Acido a Cibis* [112] *orto, et de Magnesia Alba:* — *Experiments on Magnesia, Quicklime, and other Alkaline Substances*, printed between the years 1754 and 1756:[12] — *Observations on the Effect boiling has upon Water, in making it freeze more readily*, inserted in the fifty-fifth volume of the Transactions of the Royal Society of London, for the year 1774: — *Analysis of the Waters of some Hot Springs in Iceland*, made at the request of his friend Mr STANLEY, who brought the specimen for his inspection; inserted in the third volume of the Transactions of the Royal Society of Edinburgh: — *Two Letters*, one published in the year 1784, by Professor CRELL, in the tenth volume of his Collections; the other addressed to Monsieur LAVOISIER, and published in the *Annales de Chimie*.

Minutes of the Life and Character of Joseph Black 183

WITH these notes of our Author's professional distinction, readers will not expect any tale of adventures or remarkable events, which the lives of studious persons seldom afford; and we must conclude with a few lines of character, such as those who are placed in like circumstances may understand as spoken of themselves, and for their advantage.

HIS aspect was comely, his manner unaffected and plain, and as he never had any thing about him for ostentation, he was at all times precisely what the occasion required, and nothing more. Much as he was engaged in the details of his public station, and chemical exhibitions, his chamber never was lumbered with books, specimens of natural history, or the apparatus of experiments; nor did any one ever see him hurried at one time to recover any matter which had been improperly missed at a former. Every thing being done in its proper time and place, he ever seemed to have leisure in store, and he was ready to receive his friend or acquaintance, and take his part with complacence, in any conversation that occurred. No one ever, with more ease to himself, refrained from professional discussions of any sort, or, in mixed company, more willingly left the subject of conversation [113] to be chosen by others. Many years member of a society[g] composed of men of the highest rank, of Judges, lawyers and military men, as well as citizens and professed men of letters;[13] he kept his place with propriety, and in this group never betrayed any awkward peculiarity of his education or calling. His more intimate associates and friends, besides those of his own profession CULLEN and MONRO,[14] were JAMES WATT,[15] now of Birmingham, an engineer of the first order, whether ancient or modern, and who has happily united, in the grounds of his art, chemical as well as mechanical science; Mr GEDDES[16] of the Glass-works at Leith, an eminent manufacturer, who well knew the value of his friend's suggestions. Such intimates as these could scarcely allow BLACK to relax from the toils of his professional studies. But he had others, for whom his profession had no charm, and whose attachment to him, as to one another, arose from the experience of ingenuity and candour, rather than the identity of studies, or agreement of opinions. Such were DAVID HUME, Esq; Dr ADAM SMITH, JOHN HOME, ALEXANDER CARLYLE and JOHN CLARK[17] of Elden, of whom the last, without having ever been at sea, instructed the navy itself in naval tactics. At the head of either list, however, in respect to BLACK'S habits of intimacy, ought, perhaps, to have been placed JAMES HUTTON,[18] who made up in physical speculation all that was wanting in any of the others. It may be difficult to say, whether the characters of BLACK and HUTTON, so often mentioned together, were most to be remarked for resemblance or contrast. Both profound in [114] physical science, and rigid adherents to fact, in exclusion of hypothesis or vain conjecture. Both of consummate humanity and candour. BLACK was serious, but not morose; HUTTON playful, but not petulant. The one never cracked a joke, the other never uttered a sarcasm. BLACK was always on solid ground, and of him it might be said, *Nil molitur inepte*.[19] HUTTON, whether for pleasantry or serious reflection, could be in the air, speculate beyond the laws of nature, and treat the common notion of body, with its magnitude and figure, as a mistake. In these speculations BLACK never took any part, farther than to be diverted with any play of fancy, or refinement of thought, which, he well knew, in the case of his friend HUTTON, did not preclude the use of correct and sober reason when the subject required it, or was within its cognisance. The researches of HUTTON were unremitted, and his reference to the order and arrangement of this, which he called a Living World, was judicious and happy.[h] Unreal as corporeal subjects were in his apprehension, he established a lucrative manufacture, on principles of chemistry, and was for many years of his life keenly employed in the practice of agriculture. To this he was led by becoming a proprietor of land on the death of his father, when he hastened to Norfolk, where, he had formerly lived with a farmer, to observe the husbandry of that country. There he purchased a plough, hired a ploughman, and brought both on the post-chaise with him to Berwickshire. The neighbours were diverted with this assortment of company and baggage, and no less with the attempt which followed, to plough with a pair of horses with-[115]out a driver. This joke, however, has become serious, and is now the general practice from one end of Scotland to the other.[i]

IN returning to BLACK from this enumeration of his intimate friends, serving, perhaps, to disclose his character no less than any other circumstance relating to him, we but hasten to the conclusion of a life no less distinguished by correctness and propriety of conduct, than by ingenious reasoning, and scientific research. Fully entitled to the appellation of *Frugi*,[j] — that seemingly cant expression, of which the old Romans were so [116] fond, that they used it to denote the foundation, or the summary of all the virtues, he carried into his private affairs the same order and good conduct which he employed in his professional duties; and he reaped, through life, the benefit of his attention to this particular, in the ease of his circumstances, and in the power it gave him, on occasion, to assist a friend, or contribute to the attainment of any public convenience. From those, indeed, who can mistake remissness or improvident waste for generosity, BLACK may have incurred the imputation of penury. But the proofs of this charge, if ever it were brought, in his case were not to be distinguished from the effects of sound reason and good sense. No one ever struck the proper medium more exactly than he did. His expences were regulated, but no wise sordid, or unbecoming his station. His house was spacious; and his table, at which he never improperly declined any company, was elegant and plentiful, rather above than below his condition. His contributions for public purposes were liberal, and his purse was always open to assist a friend. Much of his practice as a physician arose from his previous connection with the patient as a friend; and he was as assiduous where he would not accept, or where he could not expect a fee, as in the most lucrative part of his profession.

HIS own constitution never was robust; and every cold he caught, or any approach to repletion, affected his breast so much as to occasion a spitting of blood. This he guarded against, by restricting himself to a moderate or abstemious diet.[20] As his infirmities increased with age, he met them with a proportional attention and care, regulating his food and exercise by the measure of his strength; and thus preventing the access of disease from abroad, he enjoyed a health which was feeble, but uninterrupted, and a mind undisturbed in the calm and chearful fuel of his faculties. A life so prolonged had the advantage of present ease, and the prospect, when the just period mould arrive, of a calm dissolu-[117]tion. This accordingly followed, on the 26th of November 1799, and in the seventy-first year of his age, without any convulsion, mock, agitation or stupor, to announce or retard the approaches of death. Being at table, with his usual fare, some bread, a few prunes, and a measured quantity of milk diluted with water; and having the cup in his hand when the last stroke of his pulse was to be given, he appeared to have set it down on his knees, which were joined together, and in this action expired, without spilling a drop, — as if an experiment had been purposely made, to evince the facility with which he departed. So ended a life which had passed in the most correct application of reason and good sense to all the objects of pursuit which Providence had prescribed in his lot. His effects, when looked into, shewed how much he had profited by the order and just arrangement he had ever maintained in his affairs; amounting almost to double of what any one thought his income or his frugality could have enabled him to acquire. The whole was disposed of by will, without specifying any sum, in a neat and satisfactory manner. Being divided into ten thousand shares, it was parcelled to a numerous list of relations, in shares, in numbers, or fractions of shares, according to the degree in which they were proper objects of his care or solicitude.

THIS account of JOSEPH BLACK, however inadequate to the merit of its subject, is inscribed to the President and Members of the Royal Society of Edinburgh,

By their faithful Associate,
And humble servant,
ADAM FERGUSON,
Hallyards, in Tweeddale,
23d *April* 1801.

Notes

a. 'Je ne me sais point à l'idée de vous voir quitter Bourdeaux. Je perds le plaisir le plus agréable que j'eusse, qui étoit de vous voir souvent, et de m'oublier avec vous.'
b. Vid. *Opuscules Physiques et Chimiques* par M. [Antoine Laurent] LAVOISIER [Paris, 1774].
c. To LAVOISIER we owe the discovery, that atmospheric air is not homogeneous, but composed of nearly three parts of azot, which is not of any effect in respiration, otherwise than as it dilutes the remaining fourth part, or the vital air, which, without being so diluted, would be too intense either for the purpose of animal respiration or of common fire.

   To PRIESTLEY we owe the discovery, that the well-known corruption or waste of vital air, in the burning of fuel, or the respiration of animals, is repaired in the vegetation of plants.

   If in science there might be any choice of truths, I would willingly hope that the decomposition of water may be found a mistake.

d. 'Il est bien juste, Monsieur, que vous soyez un des premiers informés des progrès qui se font dans une cariere que vous avez ouverte, et dans laquelle nous nous regardons tous comme vos disciples.'
e. It is no doubt a mighty increment in science, to have found such powerful substances operating, as the writer of these minutes apprehends, without gravitation, inertia, or impenetrability, the great bases and columns of the mechanical philosophy.
f. The writer of this article has little more than heard of chemistry as a branch of general science, and fondly embraced any doctrine as it seemed to connect with the system of nature; but farther, his own studies have been so different, that he would not, if he could, charge his mind with any of its practical details; and he pleads the reader's indulgence, if, under this defect in treating of BLACK, he happens to subjoin a description of the man to so imperfect an account of his science.
g. This society formed itself, about the year 1770, upon a principle of zeal for the MILITIA, and a conviction that there could be no lasting security for the freedom and independence of these islands, but in the valour and patriotism of an armed people. It became known, by some whimsical accident, by the name of the *Poker Club*.
h. He, too, had carried his Audits so far as to obtain a degree in medicine; but an attempt to consult or see him would have been met with a laugh, or some ludicrous fancy, to turn off the subject.
i. HAVING said so much of HUTTON in this occasional notice, so far short of his merits, it may not be improper to prepare those who may consult him as an author, to meet with a disappointment for which his friends could never rightly account. Though uncommonly luminous and pleasant in conversation, he was obscure, unintelligible, and dry in writing, to an equal degree. His favourite specimens of natural history, he used to say, were GOD's Books, and he treated the books of men comparatively with neglect. This may, in some measure, account for his want of style or his indifference to language. In company, he spoke to be understood by such as were present, and when obscure, was called upon to explain himself. But alone, he was not aware that others could be at a loss for a meaning so clear to himself. From this circumstance, (notwithstanding many volumes written in the last years of his life, more numerous, perhaps, than all he ever read that were written by others, except the voyages and travels, from which he was perpetually collecting facts to complete his view of the terrestrial system), his very ingenious conceptions, to be received as they ought, must come from some other pen than his own.

j. [I.e. frugal] ON this subject we may consult the following passage of CICERO, *Tusc[ulanae] Quaest[iones]* lib. iii. c 300. 'Sed quia, nee qui, propter metum, praesidium reliquit, quod est Ignaviae; nec qui, propter avaritiam, clam depositum non reddidit, quod est Injustitiae; nec qui, propter temeritatem, malè rem gessit, quod est Stultitiae, *Frugi* appellari folet. Eas tres virtutes, Fortitudinem, Justitiam, Prudentiam, frugalitas est complexa; etsi hoc quidem commune est virtutum: omnes enim inter se connexae et jugatae sunt. Reliqua igitur et quarta virtus, ut sit ipsa Frugalitas. Ejus enim videtur esse proprium, motus animi appetentis regere et sedare; semper adversantem libidini, moderatam in omni re servare constantiam, cui contrarium vitium Nequitia dicitur.' [But because neither the man who through fear has deserted his post, which is a proof of cowardice, nor the man who through avarice has failed to restore a trust privately committed to him, which is a proof of unrighteousness, nor the man who through rashness has mismanaged a business transaction, which is a proof of folly, are usually called 'frugal', 'frugality' has come to include the three virtues of fortitude, justice and prudence: though this is a feature common to the virtues; for they are all mutually linked and bound together. Therefore I count 'frugality' by itself as left to be the fourth virtue. For it seems to be its special function to guide and compose the eager impulses of the soul and, by a constant opposition to lust, to preserve on every occasion a tempered firmness: and the vice which is its opposite is 'worthlessness.' See Cicero, *Tusculan Disputations*, trans. J. E. King (Cambridge, MA, 1927), 244–7]

1. James Russell (d. 1773) gave up his career as a surgeon to take up the chair of natural philosophy at Edinburgh in 1764 after Ferguson transferred to the chair of moral philosophy.
2. William Cullen (1710–90), Professor of medicine at Glasgow in 1751–5, at Edinburgh from 1755 until 1766, Professor of the theory of physic from 1766 to until 1773, and finally Professor of the practice of physic from 1773 until 1789.
3. One of Black's best-known achievements was the rediscovery of 'fixed air' (carbon dioxide).
4. Stephen Hales (1677–1761), English clergyman who made major contributions to a range of scientific fields.
5. Antoine Laurent Lavoisier (1743–94), French nobleman and chemist.
6. Joseph Priestley (1733–1804), English Unitarian minister and man of letters.
7. Daniel Gabriel Fahrenheit (1686–1736), physicist and scientific instrument maker.

8. In 1756.
9. *Dissertatio medica inauguralis, de humore acido a cibis orto, et magnesia alba: Quam, annuente summo numine, ex auctoritate Reverendi admodum Viri, D. Joannis Gowdie, Academiæ Edinburgenæ Praefecti; nec non amplissimi senatus academici consensu, et nobilissimae facultatis medicae decreto; Pro Gradu Doctoratus, summisque in medicina Honoribus ac Privilegiis rite et legitime consequendis; eruditorum examini subjicit Josephus Black Gallus, Ad diem 11 Junii, horâ locoque solitis* (Edinburgh, 1754).
10. Over 200 students regularly subscribed to Black's lectures annually.
11. Two years later, John Robison, Professor of natural philosophy at Edinburgh, published *Lectures on the Elements of Chemistry . . . by the Late Joseph Black, MD . . . Now Published From His Manuscripts* (2 vols, Edinburgh, 1803).
12. See note 9.
13. Including Ferguson himself, as well as Hume and Smith. For the Poker Club, see *Autobiography of the Rev. Dr Alexander Carlyle*, 419–23.
14. Alexander Monro *secundus* (1733–1817), Professor of medicine and anatomy at Edinburgh, as his father, Alexander Monro *primus* (1697–1767), had been.
15. James Watt (1736–1819), engineer and scientist, from Greenock. Invented an improved version of the steam engine in 1776.
16. Archibald Geddes, glassmaker and former student of Black's.
17. John Clerk, of Eldin (1728–1812), naval writer.
18. James Hutton (1726–97), farmer and naturalist, is known as the founder of modern geology.
19. '[He] makes no foolish effort.' See Horace, *Satires. Epistles. The Art of Poetry*, 462–3.
20. Ferguson himself became vegetarian after his near-death experience in 1780.

Biographical Sketch: Or, Memoir of Lieutenant-Colonel Patrick Ferguson (1817)

Note on the Text

Adam Ferguson composed this essay for the *Encyclopedia Britannica* late in his life at an unknown date, but it was deemed too long by the editor and was not published in his lifetime. Instead, it was printed posthumously in Edinburgh in 1817. It is a biographical sketch of the army officer Patrick Ferguson (1744–1780), who is sometimes referred to as Ferguson's cousin, though he is unlikely to have been a close relative. Both Patrick Ferguson's mother's family and his father, Lord Pitfour (1700–77), were well-connected with leading figures of the Scottish Enlightenment, including Hume, and close to the Johnstone family, as was Ferguson himself. Patrick Ferguson was named after his uncle Patrick Murray, Lord Elibank, one of Hume's closest friends, who had a Jacobite past. According to Ferguson's account, the young Patrick Ferguson had supposedly advocated for a Scottish militia in the 1760s, when the two possibly became acquainted, though his contributions have not been identified.

Patrick Ferguson is perhaps best known for having experimented with rifles in the years before the American Revolution, and an experimental rifle corps was formed for service under his command in North America, armed with his breech-loading rifle. When stationed in America, he recruited a unit of 150 loyalist volunteers, sometimes referred to as 'Ferguson's Scottish corps'. On 22 May 1780, he was an inspector of a militia in North and South Carolina and Georgia, with instructions to enlist as many men as possible for Britain, and managed to recruit 4,000 loyalists. He was said to have been 'one of the rare few among British officers who generally knew how to treat the loyalist militiamen with proper respect, encouragement and sympathy.'[1] This may have enticed the interest of Adam Ferguson, who was a longstanding advocate of militias. In the biographical sketch, Ferguson cites two works of David Ramsay (1749–1815), one of the first native historians of the American Revolution, including his later *History of South-Carolina* (1809). Ferguson's essay describes Patrick Ferguson's death at the Battle of Kings Mountain, which was also written about by Ramsay alongside its crucial impact on the war in his *History of the American Revolution* (1789):

> The fall of Ferguson was in itself a great loss to the royal cause. He possessed superior abilities as a partisan, and his spirit of enterprise was uncommon. To a distinguished capacity for planning great designs, he also added the practical abilities necessary to carry them into execution. The unexpected advantage which the Americans gained over him and his party, in a great degree frustrated a well concerted scheme for strengthening the British army by the co-operation of the tory inhabitants [i.e. the loyalists], whom he had undertaken to discipline and prepare for active service . . . . Henceforward they waited to see how the scales were likely to incline, and reserved themselves till the British army, by its own unassisted efforts, should get a decided superiority.[2]

Notes

1. William Thomas Sherman, *Calendar and Record of the Revolutionary War in the South: 1780–81*, 10th ed. (Seattle, 2018), 31.
2. David Ramsay, *History of the American Revolution* (2 vols, Philadelphia, 1789), II, 177–8.

[5] FERGUSON, LIEUTENANT-COLONEL PATRICK, was killed in the action at King's Mountain, South Carolina, 7th October 1780. The esteem and affection of his brother officers dictated the following Epitaph, which was inserted in the New York Gazette of 14th of February 1781:

IF AN ARDENT THIRST FOR MILITARY FAME,
A SOCIAL AND BENEVOLENT HEART,
AN UNCOMMON GENIUS,
A MIND GLOWING WITH PATRIOTIC FIRE,
REPLETE WITH USEFUL KNOWLEDGE,
AND CAPABLE
OF PRESERVING UNDER DIFFICULTIES
WHERE GLORY WAS IN VIEW,
CLAIM OUR ADMIRATION;
THE FATE OF
MAJOR PATRICK FERGUSON,[a]
WHO POSSESSED THESE AND OTHER VIRTUES
IN AN EMINENT DEGREE,
AND WHO FELL
WARRING AGAINST DISCORD,
IRRESISTIBLY
CLAIMS OUR TEARS.

[6] SUPERIOR military genius is but rare among the gifts of nature; and of those who are endowed with it, many are stopt short in the early stages of a profession of which they are forward to incur the dangers. Such as survive those dangers, and attain to eminent stations in the service of their country, are secure of their fame. For those who fall prematurely it is but fair, as often as they can be distinguished, to affix to their memory the marks of honour they covet, and for which the votaries of profit will not surely contend with them.

If the young man who is the subject of the present article had escaped the dangers to which he was so often exposed, it is probable that the annals of his country would have spoken more fully for him

He was second son of JAMES FERGUSON, Esq. of Pitfour,[1] one of the Senators of the College of Justice, and Lords Commissioners of Justiciary in Scotland, by ANNE MURRAY,[2] daughter of ALEXANDER LORD ELIBANK;[3] and, with this descent, fortunately united in his own character, the calm judgment and exalted abilities of his father, with the vivacity and genius of his mother's family.

[7] Those who associate ferocity with the military character, will hardly believe in what degree a person so fond of the military life, was humane and compassionate to his enemies, as well as affectionate and generous in his friendships. But these dispositions, however in appearance little suited to war, are the appurtenances of great courage; and bring along with them a passion for scenes of hardship and danger, in which magnanimity, in all its exertions, has the free'st scope.

Whatever circumstances there may have been to be regretted, in the origin and progress of a war between Great Britain and her revolted colonies, there never was any service in which the officers of the British army appeared to more advantage. Diligent, obedient, indefatigable, and humane as well as brave, they generally prevailed in the fortune of arms, and moved through the streets, villages and farms of those who were in arms against them, as in the country of a friend; a *general* character we are happy to prefix to the particulars which occur to be mentioned, relating to the person who is the subject of this article.

He was born in the year 1744; and, having early chosen the life of a soldier, was sent to finish his [8] education at a military academy in London, where he acquired the elements of fortification, gunnery, and other arts subservient to his intended profession. Of these he afterwards pursued the study in real situations—in action as well as on paper; and was sagacious, original, and inventive in the application of expedients to actual service.

His first commission was purchased for him at the age of fourteen, in the Royal North British Dragoons; and he gave, while yet a boy, many striking proofs of sensibility to the military character, and of his spirit in supporting it. Of these, which were indeed habitual to him, it may not be improper to mention two instances; one in particular, in Germany, when, not having completed his 16th year, being on horseback a few miles in front of the army, with another young officer of the same regiment, (SIR JOHN MITCHELL,[4]) they fell in with a party of the enemies' hussars, and, finding it necessary to retire, were pursued. FERGUSON, in passing a ditch, dropped one of his pistols; but thinking it improper for an officer to return to camp with the loss of any of his arms, he re-leaped the ditch in the face of the enemy, and recovered his pistol.

They halted, imputing probably his confidence to some support which he saw at hand, al-[9]lowed him to repass the ditch, join his companion, and regain their camp undisturbed.

The other happened at Paris some years after, with an officer in the French service, who spoke reproachfully in his presence of the British nation. This insult he not only resented on the spot, but surprised his antagonist next morning with a visit before he was out of bed. 'This is well, young man,' said the other: 'I have paid such visits, seldom received them; but it is fair to tell you that I am reputed one of the best swordsmen in France.'— 'That is not the question now,' said FERGUSON: 'You are in my debt, let us find a fit place to settle our accounts.' They accordingly went to the Boulevards together; FERGUSON considering how he might deprive this swordsman of the advantage of his superior skill, and the other regarding with security and contempt so young an antagonist. As soon as they had drawn, FERGUSON rushed within his adversary's point, seized the hilt of his sword, and in the scuffle was so fortunate as to get possession of it. 'You are a brave fellow,' said the other; 'and I shall certainly do you justice whenever our affair is mentioned.'

[10] He had scarcely finished his first campaign, when he was disabled by sickness; and having been for some months confined under the care of the physicians and surgeons of the army,[b] was sent home when in a condition to be removed. His words, in a letter to his friend General WATSON,[5] some time after, are as follows: 'I am now entirely recovered, and might serve the next campaign with ease, had not the fears of my parents prompted them to apply for an order for my joining the light-troop; by which means I am deprived, for these many years to come, of the only chance of getting a little insight into my profession.'

Being much at home from the year 1762 to the year 1768, he entered warmly into the question which was then agitated relating to the extension of the militia laws to Scotland. He saw no difficulty in combining the character of a soldier with that of a citizen, so far as was necessary for the defence of a country in which citizens enjoy such invaluable privileges; and some of the ablest and most intelligent publications which appeared in the public prints of the time, were of his writing.[6]

[11] In 1768 a company was purchased for him in the 70th regiment of foot, then in the West Indies, and he soon after joined that part of it which was in Tobago, where he was of great service

in quelling very formidable insurrections of the negroes; but after much distress in this situation from bad health, he went to North America, and returned to Great Britain in 1774, where he remained about two years.

During this interval a dispute with the North American colonies was verging to a civil war; and the boasted skill of the Americans in the use of the rifle, was held out as an object of terror to the British troops, whom it was said the American marksman could unofficer by lodging his ball from a distance, within the compass of the smallest mark.

These rumours set FERGUSON'S invention to work on a new species of rifle, which he could load at the breech without the use of a rammer, and in such quick repetition as to fire seven times in a minute. The riflemen, in the meantime, might be stretched at full length on the ground, so as to have the cover of a parapet behind even a consolidated mole-hill, or the least inequality of the earth's surface.

[12] The first exhibition of this invention was made before Lord TOWNSHEND,[7] then master-general of the ordnance.[c] It was afterwards practised by some private men of the Guards at Windsor, that the King might have an opportunity of seeing its effects. When his Majesty[8] was pleased to give orders for that purpose, a few men who had learned the use of the rifle were brought to perform in his presence, but, being overawed, in their first attempts shot wide of the mark: 'They would not,' said [13] the captain, 'be so embarrassed in presence of your Majesty's enemies.'

FERGUSON then took a rifle himself; and of nine shots which he fired at the distance of a hundred yards, put five balls into the bull's-eye of the target, and four within as many inches of it. Three of these shots were fired as he lay on his back, the other six standing erect. Being asked how often he could load and fire in a minute, he said seven times; but added pleasantly, that he would not undertake in that time to knock down above five of his Majesty's enemies. The recollection of which he was capable in the most arduous situations, gave him at all times the ease of an experienced courtier.

He wished to be employed in the armaments which were then preparing for the continent of North America, and was accordingly indulged with instructions to the Commander-in-chief, to have a corps of volunteers draughted from the regiments on the American service, to have them armed in his own way, and put under his command.

This commission was agreeable to him, chiefly because it gave him a species of separate command, and left him to conduct a corps which was formed [14] upon a principle different from that of the rest of the army. He gave a signal specimen of its services at the battle of Brandywine, when, being advanced in the front of the column commanded by General KNYPHAUSEN,[9] and supported by the rangers under Colonel WEMYS,[10] he scoured the ground so effectually that there was not a shot to annoy the column in its march. His merit on that occasion was acknowledged throughout the army, and fully stated in the reports of the day to the Commander-in-chief, by whose order the following letter was written to him by the Adjutant-general.
'*Head-quarters, 12 September 1777*,

Sir,
The Commander-in-chief has received from Lieutenant-general KNYPHAUSEN the most honourable report of your gallant and spirited behaviour in the engagement of the 11th, on which his Excellency has commanded me to express his acknowledgements to you, and to acquaint you, Sir, that he shall with great satisfaction adopt any plan that can be effected to put you in a situation of remaining with the army under his command.

For the present, he has thought proper to incorporate the rifle corps into the light companies of the respective regiments. I am very happy [15] to be even the channel of so honourable a testimony of your spirited conduct, and of that of your late corps. And I am, Sir, with perfect esteem and regard, Your most obedient humble Servant, (Signed) J. PATERSON, Adjt. Gen.[d,11]
Capt. Ferguson, commanding the Rifle Corps.'

His corps, though advanced immediately before, suffered considerably less than the rangers, from the advantage of being able, wherever they came under the enemy's fire, to use their arms as they lay on the ground. The rangers had seventeen [16] men killed, and FERGUSON'S corps only two men wounded, of whom he himself was one.

While he lay with a part of his riflemen on the skirts of a wood, in the front of General KNYPHAUSEN'S division of the army, the following circumstances happened, which he relates in a letter to a friend: 'We had not lain long,' he says, 'when a rebel officer, remarkable by a hussar dress, passed towards our army, within a hundred yards of my right flank, not perceiving us. He was followed by another dressed in dark green, or blue, mounted on a bay horse, with a remarkably large cocked hat. I ordered three good shots to steal near to them, and fire at them; but the idea disgusted me. I recalled the order. The hussar, in returning, made a circuit, but the other passed again within a hundred yards of us, upon which I advanced from the wood towards him. On my calling, he stopped; but, after looking at me, proceeded. I again drew his attention, and made signs to him to stop, levelling my piece at him, but he slowly continued his way. As I was within that distance at which, in the quickest firing, I could have lodged half a dozen of balls in or about him before he was out of my reach, I had only to determine; but it was not pleasant to fire [17] at the back of an inoffending individual, who was acquitting himself very coolly of his duty; so I let him alone. The day after I had been telling this story to some wounded officers who lay in the same room with me, when one of our surgeons, who had been dressing the wounded rebel officers, came in and told us they had been in forming him, that General WASHINGTON[12] was all the morning with the light troops, and only attended by a French officer in a hussar dress, he himself dressed and mounted in every point as above described. I am not sorry that I did not know at the time who it was.'

'Farther this deponent sayeth not, as his bones were broke a few minutes after.' He received a ball in his right arm, which so shattered the joint of the elbow as to render it doubtful whether amputation would not be necessary. He was for some months disabled from service, and, although he preserved his arm, never recovered the use of that joint; but, with a spirit peculiar to himself, so assiduously practised the use of the sword and of the pen with his left, that he scarcely seemed to have incurred any change but a difference in his hand-writing. What mortified him most was, that during his confinement the rifle corps, deprived of its leader, was broke up, as mentioned in the above [18] letter from the Adjutant-general, the rifles lodged in the store of spare arms, and the men returned to their respective regiments.

As FERGUSON was now no more than a mere volunteer with the army, the regiment to which he belonged being stationed at Halifax in Nova Scotia, it was at the discretion of the Commander-in-chief[13] whether he should be employed at all; but every one concurred in favouring his pretensions, and in doing justice to his merit; and, what is uncommon, he shewed an ardour for distinction and eminence without exciting proportional envy. His brother officers ever mentioned him with esteem and kindness. One of them who kept a journal of the war, observed of FERGUSON, that, though careless of his own life to a fault, he was ever attentive to the means of preserving those under his command.[14] Another who has had occasion to publish his eulogium to the world, among other expressions of esteem and regard, gives the following account of his character:

'That in private life his humanity and benevolence were conspicuous, his friendship steady and sincere. To a distinguished capacity for planning the greatest designs, he added the ardour necessary to carry them into execution; his [19] talent for enterprize attracted the notice of the whole army. Military tactics had been his early and favourite study; considered as a scholar, his genius was solid, his comprehension clear, and his erudition extensive.'[e]

FERGUSON was the friend of every man's merit, and had no enemy to his own. His being employed, though out of his turn, did not give offence to officers of the same rank with himself. In the autumn of 1778, he had the command of a detachment that embarked at New York, on board of a little squadron, consisting of the Zebra, the Vigilant, the Nautilus, some gallies and small armed vessels, under the command of Captain COLLINS[15] of the Zebra. The troops under Captain FERGUSON amounted to three hundred; and their instructions were to destroy a nest of rebel privateers which infested the trade of New York, from Little Egg harbour in the Jerseys. This small armament sailed from Sandyhook on the 30th of September, but, meeting with contrary winds, could not reach the port to which they were destined, though within half a day's sail, until the 5th October. During this interval the enemy, having had intelligence of their coming, put to sea with some of their larger vessels, [20] and removed others over the bar into shallow water. The latter, however, were burnt to the number of ten or twelve privateers, by Captain COLLINS, who got over the bar with his small craft, while the troops were employed in destroying their haunts and storehouses on shore.

While Captain COLLINS lay in the harbour waiting for fresh orders, in consequence of the report he had made to his commander at New York, intelligence was brought by an officer who deserted from the enemy, that POLASKI,[16] an adventurer from Poland, and reported to be the same who had carried off the person of his Polish Majesty with many circumstances of audacity and cruelty, and now in the service of the American Congress, lay up the country with three companies of foot, three troops of horse,

Biographical Sketch . . . of Patrick Ferguson

and a detachment of artillery; and that about a mile in his front, there was a gully, or creek, with a narrow bridge upon it, which he had neglected to occupy. This last circumstance encouraged Captain FERGUSON to hope that the enemy might be surprised, and, in any event, a retreat be secured by seizing the bridge. For this purpose he embarked with about two hundred and fifty of his detachment in boats, set off at eleven at night, and, after rowing about ten miles, landed at four in the morning within a mile of the pass which he was to [21] seize. He left fifty men for its defence, and advancing rapidly, surprized POLASKI before break of day, killed several officers, amongst whom were one lieutenant-colonel, one captain, one adjutant, and about fifty private men.[f]

[22] In the following spring, it was proposed to push the war from New York up the North River, and to dislodge the enemy from the posts of Stonypoint, and Ver Planks Neck, which they occupied upon that communication. When Sir HENRY CLINTON[17] [23] moved upon this service, Captain FERGUSON at the head of a detachment was advanced, as on former occasions, before the army, and became a busy actor in the operations that followed.

Stonypoint being surprised by a party of the kings troops, Ver Planks Neck was deserted, as no longer tenable under its exposure to the guns of the other. Colonel WEBSTER[18] and Captain FERGUSON being stationed at Ver Planks, Stonypoint was again surprised, and recovered by the enemy, its guns turned upon Ver Planks, and a heavy fire continued from thence, and from a galley which the enemy had brought to bear upon it. This attack, however, was firmly sustained by Colonel WEBSTER, until the galley being sunk by a shot from his battery, Stonypoint was again retaken upon a second march of Sir Henry Clinton to that quarter. It appearing that the facility with which this post had been so often taken and retaken, was [24] owing to a defect in the works, the charge of reforming or supplying that defect was intrusted to FERGUSON,—an appointment unusual, as he did not belong to the corps of engineers, who nevertheless do not seem to have taken umbrage at it.

That FERGUSON, (who had by this time attained the rank of major,) might erect what works he thought proper, it was proposed that he should remain in the defence of the place. Flattered with this opportunity to execute what he had often been meditating, he proceeded to realize some of his favourite ideas; and while he looked for an attack with all the anxiety of a person who waits the result of an interesting experiment, he had the mortification to receive an order to evacuate Stonypoint, and join the army at New York, now destined to carry the war into a different quarter of the continent. In a letter to a friend on that occasion, full of regret, he says, 'Never did a fond mother leave her favourite child with more reluctance than I did that place.' He had the consolation, however, of being promoted to the rank of Lieutenant-colonel in America, and the prospect of being employed with distinction in the operations which were then projected.

[25] When the fleet and transports, with the army on board, were about to sail from Sandyhook, they had orders, in case of separation, to rendezvous at Tybee in the province of Georgia; at this place a small division of the army was put on shore, under the command of Major-general PATTISON of the Royal Artillery,[19] with orders to penetrate into South Carolina, that the attention of the enemy might be directed to him, whilst the fleet again put to sea, and appearing suddenly before Charlestown, should land the army without opposition near that place.

Of the first division, FERGUSON, with a detachment of regulars, and Major COCHRANE,[20] brother to the Earl of DUNDONALD,[21] with some companies of the British Legion, made a part. These two officers were employed to reconoitre the country, clear it of enemies, and collect boats and waggons for the use of the main body that followed. In this service, they both co-operated with cordiality and spirit; and as in their fates,[g] at no great interval of time, they equally became objects of public and private regret, it is impossible for a person in doing [26] justice to the one, not to consider the other with like affection and esteem.

> Fortunati ambo, si, quid mea carmina possunt;
> Nulla dies unquam memori vos eximit aevo.[h]

Having on this march from Georgia to South Carolina taken different routes, they had each of them intelligence of one MACPHERSON,[22] who had assembled a body of rebels at his own plantation, nearly on that which the troops were to take on their march to Charlestown, and both at the same time formed a resolution to surprise this enemy. FERGUSON arrived first, and finding that MACPHERSON had abandoned the place, took possession of it. Major COCHRANE arriving soon after in the night, and supposing the enemy still to be there, instantly proceeded to force his way; FERGUSON, as usual at the head of his men, opposed this attack, and attempting to parry a bayonet with his sword, received a thrust in the only arm of which he had any use; but while he raised his voice, to encourage his men, he was known to his friend Major COCHRANE, who immediately put a stop to the conflict. FERGUSON called for the man who had wounded him, and giving him a piece of money, commended his alacrity, [27] saying, 'We should have known our friends sooner from their mode of attack.'

This wound for some time had an alarming appearance, and, under the effects of the climate, threatened him with the loss of his other arm. In this state of it, however, it was necessary for him to continue his march, and he rode between two orderly men who were appointed to attend him, while he himself, to have the command of his horse, was occasionally obliged to hold the reins of the bridle in his teeth.

In a little time after he joined the army near Charlestown his wound took a more favourable turn, and he was soon in condition to take the field with his former activity. He was employed with Colonel TARLETON[23] during the siege of Charlestown, in clearing the country of parties of the enemy, who attempted to straiten the quarters of the army; and, while on this service, falling in with one of their convoys, he took two hundred horses, forty waggons, all their baggage, spare arms, and accoutrements, with fifty prisoners, without the loss of a man.[i]

[28] After the reduction of Charlestown, among the dispositions which were made to restore and preserve the province, it was proposed that the well affected should be armed in their own defence; and FERGUSON, who at this time held the rank of lieutenant-colonel in America, was appointed major to the 71st regiment, on the British establishment, and entrusted with the charge of marshalling the militia over a great extent of the country; a service for which he was particularly qualified, by his generous disposition and conciliating manners.

In the proclamations he was intrusted to frame, the people of South Carolina were called upon by him to restore the civil government of their country, under the favourable conditions then offered by the King and Parliament of Great Britain.

A numerous militia was accordingly soon enrolled, being allowed to name officers for themselves; and, as those officers were to act as civil magistrates also, a caveat was entered against the choice of any person who was likely to abuse his trust, by withholding from any peaceable citizen that protection to which he was entitled.

[29] FERGUSON exercised his genius in devising a summary of the ordinary tactics, for the use of this militia; and had them divided in every district into two classes;—one, of the young men, the single and unmarried, who should be ready to join the King's troops, to repel any enemy that might infest the province;—another, of the aged and heads of families, who should be ready to unite in defending their own townships, habitations, and farms. In his progress among them he soon gained on their confidence, by the attention he paid to the interests of the well-affected, and by his humanity to the families of those who were in arms against him. 'We come not,' he observed, 'to make war on women and children,' giving them money to relieve their distresses; but said, 'he hoped they would excuse him, if meeting with their husbands or brothers in the field, he should use them a little more roughly'.

Soon after the conduct of the war in that quarter had devolved upon Lord CORNWALLIS,[24] a detachment of regulars, joined with a body of militia, under the command of Colonel FERGUSON, was destined to cover the interior country, and the left flank of Lord CORNWALLIS'S army on its march towards North Carolina and Virginia.

[30] Having advanced towards Ninety-six, about two hundred miles from Charlestown, acting with vigour and success against different bodies of the rebels, who remained to dispute the possession of the country with him, he had intelligence from Colonel BROWN,[25] who commanded the King's forces at Augusta in Georgia, that a body of rebels, under the command of a Colonel CLARKE,[26] who had been recently repulsed in an attempt upon the post of Augusta, was retreating by the back settlements of Carolina. To this intelligence Colonel BROWN added, that he himself meant to hang on the rear of this enemy, and that if FERGUSON would cut across his route, he might be intercepted, and his party dispersed. As this service was perfectly consistent with that in which he was employed, FERGUSON gave way to his usual ardour, and pushed with his detachment, composed of a few regulars and militia, into Tryon county.

In the meantime, numerous bodies of back settlers west of the Alleghany mountains, hitherto believed favourable to the British cause, were in arms, some of them with a view of seizing upon the presents intended for the Creek and Cherokee Indians, which they understood were but slightly guarded at Augusta. Others had assembled upon the alarm of enemies likely to visit them from South [31] Carolina. These meeting with Colonel CLARKE secured his retreat, and made it expedient for BROWN to discontinue his pursuit and return to his station at Augusta, while FERGUSON having no intelligence of that event, still continued the march undertaken at his request. The enemy which he now alone and unsupported was likely to encounter, is described as follows by an officer who served the campaign in South Carolina: 'A swarm of backwood's men, the wild and fierce inhabitants of Kentucky, and other settlements westward of the mountains, under the Colonels CAMPBELL[27] and BOON,[28] with those of HELSTON, POWELS VALLY, BARCLAY, BOTTETOURT, AUGUSTA, and FINCASTLE,[29] under the Colonels CLEVELAND,[30] SHELBY,[31] SIVIER,[32] WILLIAMS,[33] BRAND,[34] and LACY,'[35] had assembled suddenly and silently upon the report of a booty to be seized at Augusta.[36] They were mounted on horseback, and by the rapidity of their motions well qualified to act by surprise.[j]

When FERGUSON had intelligence of BROWN'S retreat, and the appearance of a new enemy, he halted, with a view of returning to the parts of the country he had left. At the same time, he dispatched a messenger to Lord CORNWALLIS, to inform [32] his Lordship of what had passed,—of the enemies he had to deal with,—and of the route he had taken to avoid them; earnestly expressing his wish, that he might be enabled to cover a country in which there were so many well affected inhabitants; adding, that for this purpose he should halt at King's Mountain, hoping that he might be there supported by a detachment from his Lordship, and saved the necessity of any further retreat.

This letter having been intercepted, gave notice to the enemy of the place where FERGUSON was to be found; and though a duplicate sent on the following day was received by Lord CORNWALLIS, it came too late to prevent the disaster which followed.

The enemy having selected a body of chosen men, mounted on fleet horses, performed their march sooner than otherways could have been accomplished. They were in number so superior to FERGUSON'S detachment, and so well acquainted with all the approaches to his position, that they made arrangements to surround him and to cut off his retreat.

[33] On this sudden emergence FERGUSON'S detachment was immediately in arms, and rushing with the bayonet on the

first body of the enemy that presented themselves, forced them to retire; but while they gained this advantage in front, they were attacked on the flanks by a fresh enemy. To these also the regulars presented their bayonets, and repulsed the enemy in three several attacks. 'As often as one of the American parties was driven back,' says Ramsay, the American historian, 'another returned to their station. Resistance on the part of Colonel FERGUSON was in vain; but his unconquerable spirit refused to surrender. After having repulsed a succession of adversaries pouring in their fire from new directions, this distinguished officer received a mortal wound.'[37]

He had two horses killed under him, while he remained untouched himself; but he afterwards received a number of wounds, of which it is said any one was mortal, and, dropping from his horse, expired, while his foot yet hung in the stirrup.

The spirit which thus refused to be subdued, being now no more, the officer on whom the command devolved, though brave and equal to the trust, was compelled to accept of quarter for himself and the few men that remained under his command.

[34] The first reports of FERGUSON'S death, though vague and uncertain, were received by his friends in the army as a matter to be hourly expected: 'If not now,' they said, 'it must be soon, in the continual danger to which he exposes himself.'

He had estimated the part which became him to act, as the leader of such parties as were hitherto put under his command: in such services, he conceived, that he was not only to project what should be done, but to lead in the execution of it. His courage was considerate and calm. He says, in a letter to a friend, 'I thank God more for this than for all his other blessings, that in every call of danger, or honour, I have felt myself collected, and equal to the occasion.' Anxious to reconcile his parents to the risks to which he was so frequently exposed, he makes the following observation: 'The length of our lives is not at our own command, however much the manner of them may be. If our Creator enable us to act the part of men of honour, and to conduct ourselves with spirit, probity, and humanity, the change to another world, whether now, or fifty years hence, will not be for the worse.'

Of the millions who were born on the same day or year with Colonel FERGUSON, the longest liver [35] will die at no great interval of time, and none in a manner more worthy of the part which Providence had assigned him to act.

The body lay stripped on the ground, while the men lately under his command, now prisoners of war, desired leave to bury his remains with what they termed the honours of a soldier's grave; but this request, addressed to the recent feelings of a ferocity which resented the opposition even of the most generous enemy, was refused. This token of respect and affection, however, was paid to the deceased, by the inhabitants of a neighbouring village, who, having experienced his humanity, gave the body a decent interment in their own burying-ground.

Having noted the respect and affection expressed for Colonel FERGUSON by his brother officers, in the epitaph prefixed to this memoir; the person who offers this imperfect sketch, hopes that he will be pardoned the ambition of erecting this monument also to his memory.

THE END.

Notes

a. Major Ferguson was promoted to the rank of Lieutenant-Colonel some time before his death;— a circumstance which seems to have been unknown to his brother officers at *New York*.
b. The late Dr [John] ARMSTRONG [1709–79], author of the celebrated poem of the *Art of Preserving Health, &c* [(London, 1744)] was then physician to the British forces in Germany, and formed upon that occasion the warmest friendship and affection for young Cornet FERGUSON, which continued to his death.
c. The following account of this exhibition will be found in the Chronicle of the *Annual Register* for 1776, of date the 1st of June.

'Some experiments were tried at Woolwich before Lord Viscount TOWNSHEND, Lord AMHERST, Generals HERVEY and DESAGUILLERS, and a number of other officers, with a rifle gun, upon a new construction, by Captain FERGUSON of the 70th regiment; when that gentleman, under the disadvantages of a heavy rain and a high wind, performed the following four things, none of which had ever before been accomplished with any other small arms. 1st, He fired during four or five minutes at a target, at 200 yards distance, at the rate of four shots each minute. 2dly, He fired six shots in one minute. 3dly, He fired four times per minute, advancing at the same time at the rate of four miles in the hour, 4thly. He poured a bottle of water into the pan and barrel of the piece when loaded, so as to wet every grain of the powder, and in less than half a minute fired with her as well as ever, without extracting the ball. He also hit the bull's eye at 100 yards, lying with his back on the ground; and, notwithstanding the unequalness of the wind and wetness of the weather, he only missed the target three times during the whole course of the experiments. The captain has since taken out a patent for the said improvements.'

d. It was well known in the army that the Commander-in-chief, Sir WILLIAM HOWE [(1729–1814)], had taken umbrage at the rifle corps having been formed without his being consulted. It was therefore perhaps not to be expected that he would exert himself to support it. The use of which it had proved, to the great satisfaction of the army, seems to have prevented him from taking active steps to its prejudice, until Captain FERGUSON was wounded at Brandywine; of which Sir WILLIAM took advantage, and reduced the corps without consulting him. It seems extraordinary, however, that Sir WILLIAM should have carried his chagrin so far as to take no notice, in his official letter to the Secretary of State, of the conduct of Captain FERGUSON, and of the behaviour of the rifle corps in the action of Brandywine, notwithstanding he had given him the public thanks stated above on the occasion. Upon that circumstance being discovered, when the London Gazette, containing Sir WILLIAM's official letter, arrived in America, Captain FERGUSON sent a copy of these thanks to the Secretary of State.

e. MACKENZIE'S Strictures [i.e. *Strictures on Lt. Col. Tarleton's History 'of the Campaigns of 1780 and 1781, in the Southern Provinces of North America'. Wherein Military Characters and Corps are Vindicated from Injurious Aspersions, and Several Important Transactions Placed in their Proper Point of View. In a Series of Letters to a Friend, by Roderick Mackenzie, Late Lieutenant in the 71st regiment. To which is Added, a Detail of the Siege of Ninety Six, and the Re-capture of the Island of New-Providence* (London, 1787), 65].

f. This little enterprise is thus detailed in the London Gazette of 1st December 1778.

EXTRACTS *of a* LETTER *from General Sir* HENRY CLINTON [see note 17], *Knight of the Bath, to Lord* GEORGE GERMAINE, *dated October 25, 1778.*

'In my letter of the 8th inst. I mentioned that my move into Jersey was partly to favour an expedition sent to Egg harbour. I have now the honour to inclose copies of two reports made to me by Captain FERGUSON of the 70th regiment, who commanded the troops employed upon that service, to which I beg leave to refer your Lordship for an account of its success, under direction of that very active and zealous officer. *See Gazette for 1st Report of 10th October.*

REPORT *of* Captain FERGUSON *of the 70th Regiment, to his Excellency* Sir HENRY CLINTON, *dated Little Egg harbour*, October 15, 1778.

Sir,

Since the letter which I had the honour of writing to you on the 10th instant, Captain COLLINS has received a letter from Admiral GAMBIER, signifying that the Admiral and you are both of opinion, that it is not safe for us to remain here, as the army is withdrawn from the Jerseys, and ordering our immediate return; but as the wind still detained us, and we had information by a captain and six men of POLASKI'S legion, who had deserted to us, that Mr POLASKI had cantoned his corps, consisting of three companies of foot, three troops of horse, a detachment of artillery, and one brass field-piece, within a mile of a bridge, which appeared to me easy to seize, and from thence to cover our retreat, I prevailed upon Captain COLLINS to enter into my design, and employ an idle day in an attempt that was to be made with safety, and with a probability of success. Accordingly, at eleven last night, 250 men were embarked, and, after rowing ten miles, landed at four this morning, within a mile of the defile, which [22] we happily secured, and, leaving 50 men for its defence, pushed forward upon the infantry of this legion, cantoned in three different houses, who are almost entirely cut to pieces. We numbered among their dead about 50, and several officers, among whom, we learn, are a lieutenant-colonel, a captain, and an adjutant. It being a night attack, little quarter could of course be given, so that there are only five prisoners. As a rebel Colonel Proctor was within two miles, with a corps of artillery, two brass twelve-pounders, one three-pounder, and the militia of the country, I thought it hazardous with 200 men, without artillery or support, to attempt any thing farther, particularly after Admiral GAMBIER'S letter.

The rebels attempted to harass us in our retreat, but with great modesty, so that we returned at our leisure, and reimbarked in security.

The captain who has come over to us is a Frenchman, named BROMVILLE. He and the deserters inform us, that Mr POLASKI has, in public orders, lately directed no quarter to be given; and it was therefore with particular satisfaction that the detachment marched against a man, capable of issuing an order, so unworthy of a gentleman, and a soldier.

It is but justice to inform you, Sir, that the officers and men, both British and Provincials, on this occasion, behaved in a manner to do themselves honour.

To the conduct and spirit of Captain COX, Lieutenant LYTTLETON, and Ensign COTTER, of the 50th regiment, and of Captain PETER CAMPBELL of the 5d Jersey Volunteers, this little enterprise owes much of its success, as well as to the arrangements of Captain COLLINS of the navy, and attention of Captain CHRISTIAN, who accompanied the embarkation.

I have the honour to be, &c.
(Signed) PAT. FERGUSON, Capt. 70th Reg.

P.S. The dispatch vessel not having got to sea last night, I am enabled to inform you, that our yesterday's loss consists of two men of the 5th, and one of [23] the Provincials missing, and two of the 5th slightly wounded; Ensign CAMPBELL of the 2d Jersey Volunteers has received a stab through the thigh.

We had an opportunity of destroying part of the baggage and equipage of POLASKI'S legion, by burning their quarters; but, as the houses belonged to some inoffensive Quakers, who, I am afraid, may have sufficiently suffered already in the confusion of a night's scramble, I know. Sir, you will think with us, that the injury to be thereby done to the enemy, would not have compensated for the sufferings of these innocent people.'

g. Major COCHRANE having been sent, by Sir HENRY CLINTON, to apprise Lord CORNWALLIS [see note 24] of his approach, by courage and perseverance reached York-town with the intelligence, when he soon after had his head carried off by a canon-ball, while standing by his Lordship's side.

h. Aen. Lib. IX. ver. 456. ['Happy pair! If my poetry has any power, no day shell ever blot you from the memory of time'. See Virgil, *Aeneid*, trans. H. R. Fairclough and G. P. Goold (2 vols, Cambridge, MA, 1918), I, 144–5.]

i. Letter dated Charlestown, 15th May 1780, Captain FLETCHER'S M.S. account of Colonel FERGUSON.

j. Vide [David] Ramsay's *Revolution of America*, chap. 19 [Ramsay's *The History of the American Revolution* was first published in Philadelphia and New York in 1789, and in London the following year.]

1. James Ferguson (1700–77), a Scottish advocate and second Laird of Pitfour, a large estate in Buchan. He became Dean of the Faculty of Advocates in 1760 and was elevated to the bench as Lord Pitfour in 1764. Friend of Hume.

2. Anne Murray (1708–98) married James Ferguson in 1733.
3. Alexander Murray, fourth Lord Elibank (1677–1736). With his wife Elizabeth (d. 1756), daughter of George Stirling of Keir, he had many children, including Anne Murray, Hume's close friend Patrick Murray, fifth Lord Elibank (1703–78) and the Jacobite agent Alexander Murray, Jacobite earl of Westminster (1712–78).
4. Sir John Mitchell was made cornet in 1755 and lieutenant in 1761, and resigned in 1769. See Edward Almack, *The History of the Second Dragoons: The Scots Greys* (London, 1908), 225.
5. Possibly Sir Brook Watson (1735–1807), MP and Lord Mayor of London, with a military career, and served as commissary-general in North America.
6. Untraced.
7. George Townshend, first Marquess Townshend (1724–1807), Viscount Townshend from 1764 to 1787. Master-general of the Ordnance in the North ministry between 1772 and 1782.
8. I.e. George III.
9. General Wilhelm von Knyphausen (1716–1800) commanded Hessian auxiliaries on behalf of Britain in the American Revolutionary War.
10. Almost certainly James Wemyss (1748–1833); see Randy A. Purvis, 'Major James Wemyss: Second Most Hated British Officer in the South', *Journal of the American Revolution*, 27 November (2018), accessed 29 July 2021, https://allthingsliberty.com/2018/11/major-james-wemyss-second-most-hated-british-officer-in-the-south/.
11. James Paterson was adjutant general of the army of William Howe (1729–1814) from 18 April 1776 to July 1777, accessed 29 July 2021, https://founders.archives.gov/documents/Washington/03-05-02-0295.
12. George Washington (1732–99), general and later first president of the United States.
13. I.e. General Howe.
14. Untraced, though Patrick Ferguson is mentioned in many journals of the war, including *An Historical Journal of the American War. Extracted from the Publications of the Massachusetts Historical Society* (Boston, 1795) and *The American Rebellion: Sir Henry Clinton's Narrative of His Campaigns, 1775–1782*, ed. W. B. Willcox (New Haven, CT, 1954).
15. Commander Henry Collins.
16. Kazimierz Michał Władysław Wiktor Pułaski (1745–79), Polish military commander who travelled to America on Benjamin Franklin's recommendation and became a general in the continental army.
17. Sir Henry Clinton (1730–95), army officer who replaced Howe as commander-in-chief for North America in 1778.

18. Probably James Webster (?1743–81), lieutenant colonel from 1774.
19. James Pattison (1723–1805).
20. Major Charles Cochrane (1749–81).
21. Archibald Cochrane, ninth Earl of Dundonald FRSE (1748–1831).
22. Possibly Donald Macpherson (1755–1829).
23. Sir Banastre Tarleton, first Baronet (1754–1833).
24. Charles Cornwallis, first Marquess Cornwallis (1738–1805), a leading British general in the American Revolutionary War.
25. Almost certainly Thomas 'Burnfoot' Brown (1750–1825), a British Loyalist during the American Revolution, with the rank lieutenant colonel.
26. Elijah Clarke (1742–99), American military officer and Georgia legislator.
27. William Campbell (1745–81).
28. Daniel Boone (1734–1820), militia officer and frontiersman.
29. Holston, Powell Valley, Berkeley, Botetourt, Augusta and Fincastle are towns and counties in Virginia.
30. Benjamin Cleveland (1738–1806), American pioneer and officer in the North Carolina militia.
31. Isaac Shelby (1750–1826), American soldier and later the first and fifth governor of Kentucky.
32. John Sevier (1745–1815), American soldier and one of the founding fathers of the state of Tennessee.
33. James Henderson Williams (1740–80) held a colonel's rank in the South Carolina militia.
34. James Brandon (1734–90), pioneer in Rowan County, North Carolina, and an officer in the North Carolina militia during the American Revolution.
35. Edward Lacey (1742–1813), a Revolutionary War soldier, born in Shippen Township, Cumberland County, Pennsylvania, and the son of Edward Lacey, a native of England. He ran away from home and accompanied William Adair to Chester District, South Carolina.
36. Mackenzie, *Strictures on Lt. Col. Tarleton's History*, 58–9.
37. David Ramsay, *The History of South-Carolina: From Its First Settlement in 1670, to the Year 1808* (2 vols, Charleston, 1809), I, 383.

Part III

Appendices

Appendix A: Further Correspondence in MSS EUR F/291/97

The vast majority of the papers in the folder are letters from Ferguson to Macpherson. There are, however, a few copies of letters from Macpherson to Ferguson, as well as letters sent to Macpherson by Ferguson's friend in St Andrews Hugh Cleghorn, his two sons John Macpherson Ferguson and Adam Ferguson, and his nephew Robert 'Bob' Ferguson. They pertain mostly to the circumstances of Ferguson's death.

1. Sir John Macpherson to Adam Ferguson[1]

To D^r. Ferguson.–
    Brompton 24th November 1800.
My Dear Friend.–

You wished to see my Memorial relative to the Debt due to me by the late Nabob of Arcot before I gave it in: It was presented in April last as you have seen by the Copy which I lately sent to you from Tunbridge Wells: The Appendix, of which you have likewise received a Copy has not been yet given in officially but the papers, from which it has been extracted were shown to M^r. Dundas and he was so good to inform me in a Note that he had perused them. This was all I could desire at the Time.

Those papers contained much of the interior secret of India administration: But not until more of that secret is laid open to you, can I be justified even in your Opinion for the Sacrifices, which I found it necessary to make to the public cause. To you I may without injury to others or seeming arrogance in my own favor unfold the truth. You will know it all with the incontrovertible proofs if you survive me. Let me give you a hasty glimpse of it while we are both in this Scene.

The D^r. and C^r. History of the late Nabob of Arcots Debt to me is a simple transaction of a Bill of Exchange drawn by me upon him through the House of Drummond in January 1779 and formally accepted by him: A partial payment was made upon it at the time to my Attorneys Sir Charles Oakeley / and M^r. Casamajor: The remainder of the Bill is still unpaid and is reconfirmed by the present Nabob with Interest by a [Simind?] or Deed under his hand and Seal in which he laments his incapacity to discharge the Debt of so faithful a friend. The amount on the 1st of April 1798 was one Lack 18,861 Pagodas.

But the real History of this Debt would be in fact the history of our oppressions of the Ally, who first introduced us to territorial power in India, and whom the Crown and the Nation were pledged with the Company to protect in his rights.

The position of India in 1781 was not unsimilar to that of this Country in 1800. The Company were immersed in War. The public resources were exhausted, they had passed into the hands of the Companys Servants and their Native Agents. And how was I able with all the Confidential Powers, which you see explained in M^r. Robinsons Letter, to assist in meeting and relieving that public distress? Exactly as the present distress of their Country must be met and relieved by our present rulers – by sacrificing all that is personal to a Spirit of union by drawing resources out of the hands that held it to support the Public cause – were you to ask the India Directors and some Members of the India Board where the real supplies were bound for the public Service in India from 1781 to 1786 they could not tell you. But the papers alluded to in N$^{o's}$ 3. 4. And 5 of the Appendix explain the Mystery.

The fact was that on my Arrival at Madras, in August 1781, and visiting the Nabob with Lord Macartney, instead of asking him for my own Money I induced him, in union with his Lordships to assign all his remaining revenues to the Company. On my / arrival in Bengal instead of wishing to remove the native Decons of the revenue and put in office such as would owe their places to my influence, or, instead of sending new residents to the tributary Courts, I urged M^r. Hastings to make those in Office recover all arrears of revenue and Tribute. Hence were obtained, without noise, those immense extra-resources which you see attested in the official Statement of the Accountant General of Bengal of the 9th of April 1783.

But all these resources would have been inadequate had not I written to M^r. Hastings on the first week of my arrival at Calcutta that Oeconomy and reform could alone recover India and that to those ends I was ready to forego half my own Salary. The reform was begun soon after M^r. Hastings return from Benares to Fort William and much to his honor. But he had written to the Company before my arrival that he would be obliged to suspend sending them any Goods or what is called the Investment of the year. I wrote to them that an Investment must be found and regularly continued: when we met and composed our different dispatches – an accident and the Confidence of a friend led me to a great discovery; and what does not public distress discover in the end? In N°. 4 you see papers alluded to which proved that the Companys Investment could be provided at a reduced price of 27 per cent that measure was enforced; and we opened a loan on the proceeds of the Sales of that Investment in Europe at a very distant period of payment; In a week One Million and £200,000 were paid into our Treasury by the Companys Servants on the faith of Bills granted on the proceeds of Goods so cheaply provided. This measure was continued with redoubted advantage 1st to the Country which kept back the Specie 2ndly to the Company who gained profit upon Credit and 3rdly to the lenders of the Money subscribed who only wished to realize it in any given time in England. But this great and salutary / measure unveiled one of the great sources from which private fortunes were acquired by the Companys Servants: I Was aware of this and wrote to the Company a separate Letter in March 1783 conjuring them to 'avoid all retrospection': unfortunately for their own Interests they neglected my advice.

    I come now to the Denouement of the history of India Fortunes, or the Secret of India. All fortunes that had been acquired in the Companys Service prior to the establishment of large Salaries by Law and the Orders of the company were necessarily acquired through the Native Agents were employed in the Administration of the Revenues or the Provision of the Companys Goods. The Money acquired by lawful prize money, loans of money or the common concerns of Trade is but comparatively trifling. India has no Mines and the Native, once he hoards hard wealth, never, in almost any emergency, will touch it: Hence it follows that the real wealth of India springs from its agriculture and manufactures; and it is immense on two principles. 1st because the Harvests are double and sometimes triple within the Year 2dly because from habit and religion the Industrious Native is satisfied with a trifling part of the Value of his labor and gives the rest to Government; Happy People! Happy Country! Secured by various circumstances from Oppression, though eternally exposed to Invasion and foreign Dominion.

It will naturally occur to you that in order to raise a revenue from the agriculture and manufacture of Millions of Men so circumstanced it can only be raised by a regular general System of minute Assessment and Collection: The <u>Science</u> of that System is in the hands of particular Casts; and the language and figures of that Science were long a Mystery carefully concealed from the Companys Servants. /

Thus you see that no fortunes could be acquired but by a Substraction from the public revenue or from the alledged Cost of Contracts for providing the Companys Goods. While the Native Agents who had the Conduct of those transactions were in fact the Media for the Companys Servants to acquire an Independence or affluence. As a political philosopher you will say that no disposition of things could be better in the beginning both for the Conquerors and the Conquered. <u>We</u> were in fact the <u>Servants</u> and <u>they</u> remained our <u>Masters</u>: and those Bonds of Confidence and Friendship, which united the Native Agents and the British Masters, while the private fortunes of the latter passed through the hands of the former were favorable to both and hence perhaps the peculiar liberal and generous Character of our Countrymen, who have made fortunes in the East. Hence may likewise be accounted for the want of proof in those accusations which have led to India disputes trials and Impeachments. The fact is the parties accused knew not how their fortunes were in general acquired and they attributed to the Gratitude of their Native Servants or Banians the Money which they had in fact sequestered from the Public Revenue.

With this Key in your possession you may at once comprehend the real history of all the Parties that from the days of Lord Clive to those of John Macpherson agitated the Councils of India, the Direction in Leaden Hall and our parties in Parliament about making and unmaking Nabobs Raja's and Zemindars and about the Nominations of Nuncomars and Gungaving-sings to superintend the revenues of Bengal &c. &c.

It fell to my Lot and owing to the distresses of the period of my Service in Bengal, to discover <u>the whole Original Native System or Arcana of the Revenue</u> Accounts, as well as to ascertain the real reduced expence at which the Companys goods could be / <u>fairly</u> provided. I put both these discoveries into Operation in the short period of my Government and had the happiness of seeing that the antient revenue System would at once secure the Natives from Oppression and realize a Superior Revenue to the State, while the middle men, as they are called in Ireland and who are the Scourges of every Country, would be checked in their peculation, and while the Companys Servants who had gradually acquired the languages of the Country and the Secret of the Collections might acquire lawful fortunes in the act of doing good to the Industrious Cultivators and Manufactures.

The imprudence of the Company in retrospective prosecutions relative to the provision of the Investment gave the alarm to the Servants in the Revenue line: My Successor did not compleat what I had begun; but what must in the end be completed to retain our Indian Empire. My endeavours were however crowned with another success. In seeing the interior of that beautiful revenue System, which the Virtuosu and great Ackbar had formally sanctioned, I saw and got the best insight into the Real Constitution of all India Government. I was accordingly enabled not only to create a new finance but to Hypothecate it on a general Reform of a Million & £200,000 in the Peace Establishment at Bengal. This arrangement united with the extraordinary resources acquired from Oude and the assignment of the revenues of the Carnatic enabled me to liquidate the arrears of all our armies and deliver over India in peace and reform to Earl Cornwallis in September 1786.

When you reflect that every measure I had pursued to discharge the duty I had undertaken to Lord North in 1781 was a measure that retrenched the profits of some Individual Servant or which in rectifying an abuse implicated those who had gone before me in office; When you recollect that those who had succeeded me had an Interest in displaying their own comparative Services and that those who had superceded me / irregularly could not be flattered by an exhibition of the merits of my administration. The Wonder with you, who knew so well the nature of Mankind will be that I have hitherto escaped from Enemies and not that I have been so little supported or rewarded. I have escaped I am Confident on two grounds 1st that I was not jealous of the Successes of others and 2dly because it would be found after every Attack or enquiry that I had sacrificed my own Interests to those of my Friends my Employers and the public.

I always took it for granted the India Scene would in the end develop itself. I believed that the Nabob would have repaid me if he had lived, and I afterwards hoped that his Successor would do me justice: He offered to name me his Minister here with a large Salary but I declined the Office and the Salary. The general situation of public affairs, from the Close of 1789 when I went abroad, till I was obliged to address the India Minister in April last gave me more anxiety than the state of my own fortune; and I was more solicitous to see this Country secured against the revolution than I was to realize my Claims. Hence my Travels and labours on the Continent which you so well know: and, after all, unless the revolution is repressed, and unless this Country is to escape from the revolution with less injury than surrounding states where is the disadvantage of a small fortune. My Farm will be my retreat and there I can find health and sufficient Occupation in making out a candid History of my India Administration and of my Travels upon the Continent unless the Ministers are disposed to do me justice. What can I say more?

Signed John Macpherson
I have acknowledge your last admirable Letter of the 1st December. This Letter was written as you will observe long before I received it.

Source: MSS EUR F291/97, ff. 78r–81v.

2. John Macpherson Ferguson to Sir John Macpherson

Hallyards 1st of July
[18]09
My Dear Sir John/

It was with the greatest satisfaction my Father and every body here heard of the happy Issue of your business after so much anxiety of mind.
My Father is as well as well can be and in high spirits about getting his St Andrews house which you have heard was procured by that most indefatigable of all Friends Cleghorn. We are just going to commence packing, and he is to sett off first. Him and old <u>Mary Cudry</u>. /
I am in hopes I shall be able to give some assistance particularly in getting all over the <u>Water</u>. I saw Colonel McCloed the other day in Edinburgh[.] Poor fellow he was not looking well. He told me he had had a severe fit of the Liver complaint but was getting better it

was just before he sett off for the North. My Brother Adam has at last gone off to see some service[.] He sett sail from Jersey 23rd of June for Lisbon going to join Sir A Wellesly. The 50t and two other Reg. I had a very kind letter from Captain Ussher the other day mentioning his having been ordered to fit out the Gun Boats again with all possible dispatch

Notwithstanding all my Philosophy / I can not avoid longing a little to have a share in all this service that is going on.

I have mentioned nothing to my Father of my Writing, as I suppose he will do it himself, I could not think of troubling you my Dear Sir John with any nonsense of mine before, I have to beg my kind remembrance to N[athaniel] Wraxall and all Friends in London.
I Remain my Dear Sir John
With sincere regard
Your most obe[dien]t
Humble servant
John M^{c}P Ferguson

Source: BL MSS EUR F291/97, ff. 86r–87v.

3. Hugh Cleghorn to Sir John Macpherson

St Andrews 24th Feby 1816
My Dear & Worthy Friend

The venerable Dr Adam Ferguson died here last night in the ninety third year of his age. It has fallen upon me to notify this event to his friends. In this numerous list you rank among the first. And I mean to give you the fullest detail of his last moments. His great age & feeble frame make his death more a subject of Regret than of Surprise. But it will be a consolation for you to know that he died without pain or a struggle, and in the perfect possession of his Mind. I feel a melancholy pleasure in being with him one Thursday last (the 22nd Inst) when he only slightly complained. I never left him, & I closed the Eyes of my friend & my Master. It was impossible to mark the moment of departing Life. It resembled sleep rather than Death, and being unaccustomed to such scenes, I had to send for a Physician before I could satisfy myself or his family that he was no more.

It is needless to look for a cause of dissolution at the age of ninety three. But Dr Ferguson was no / ordinary man, & ever the last feelings of such a life could be interesting to the world or at least to his friends. You will readily conceive, what those who enjoyed the Society of his last years known, that while he reasoned on Every passing Event with the sagacity of age, he embraced it with all the ardour & keenness of youth. The introducing the Jury Court in Civil Cases, with the Law of this Country, were to him a Subject of Constant & interesting Speculation & accorded with all his principles of Jurisprudence. The living to see that Court in actual progress; the appointment of Adam his friend, the son of his friend, to preside in that high department; together with very affectionate Letters which the Lord Chief Commissioner wrote to him on the subject, elevated his spirits to a degree which his worne out System would not support. A slight fever was the consequence. And I am honoured that the immediate cause of his death was an excess of joy. I do not believe that he has left any writings in a state for the publick. He dictated to me a year or two ago a few lines with the view / of being Inscribed on his Tomb. It was not a positive command which I should at all [?] have obeyed, It was a wish & that too rather implied than offered. I am therefore at liberty to consult mutual friends. These lines are among my papers in the Country; but my Impression is that they speak the language & breathe the sentiments of the Stoic school. That they will be understood by very few & that they might alarm the prejudices & raise against his memory the sleeping hypocracy of the Genius of the place. But though not appropriate to a Country Church yard, they might be inserted with safety & decorum into a memoir of his Life. And I have presumed in my letter of this day to his friends the Lord Chief Commissioner & Chief Baron to oppress my hope that the Royal Society of Edin^b will not allow one of its most distinguished ornaments to go without notice to his grave. Your old friend Mr Geo. Dempster resides almost constantly here. And until yesterday St Andrews might have been reckoned an antideluvian City. The accounts of Dr Fergusons situation the day before yesterday, exaggerated some what by the nurse / gave such a sudden pang to Mr Dempster, that he was taken ill in few hours after, is confined to his bed, and I understand that little hopes are entertained of his recovery. I always hear of you from my son; and after so long an Interuption of correspondence, it is melancholy to renew it by so dishappy a subject as the present. May I request you to communicate Dr Fergusons death to the humble Mr Greville. I remain my dear Sir John

Your most affectionate &

Obliged
Hugh Cleghorn

Source: BL MSS EUR F291/97, ff. 92r–93v.

4. Hugh Cleghorn to Sir John Macpherson

Wakefield, near St Andrews, 5th March 1816

My Dear Sir John

I had the pleasure of your kind letter of the [illegible] last night. A very heavy fall of snow prevents me from going to St Andrews this day, & mentioning your kind concern to the Fergusons; I shall however see them tomorrow; of your sympathy & friendship they have had long experience, & were confident how sensibly you would feel the loss they have sustained. The death of that excellent man Dr Ferguson has made a stronger impression than could well be imagined, considering his antediluvian Age, upon all of his friends. Lord Comm. Adam, from the circumstance which I mentioned, was in truth overwhelmed; and the letters which I have viewed from the Lord Chief Baron satisfy me that a worthier man does not exist. A memoir of Dr Ferguson must be written by some of his friends, & I have reason to hope that will be executed the Chaste & Elegant pen of Prof^r Playfair. I certainly may feel flattered that you, & some other Respectable friends, have suggested to me to become his historians. I have declined the honor with firmness & Concern. Writing is a trade, & I never practiced it and after sixty years of age a new calling cannot be acquired. To write the History of a Man of Letters, it is necessary to know the Literature of his age, and I am not a scholar. Altho' I / always revered him, & regarded him with a hereditary attachment yet for near thirty years we hardly saw, & were separated from each other by the distance of the globe. I am not therefore qualified in any respect for such an undertaking; Mr Playfair was his colleague during the active period of his life, & from a similarity of pursuits, will execute its History with great ability & con amore.

In a letter which I wrote two days ago to our friend Ld Commis^r Adam I suggested, that something more than a mere mortuary notification should appear in the newspapers and I left him to adopt, alter, or correct, as nearly as I can recollect, what follows: 'Died at St Andrews on Friday the 22 ult. In the ninety third year of his age Adam Ferguson Esqr L.L.D. formerly Professor of Moral Philosophy in the University of Edin^r.

He was the last of the great men of the Preceding Century. Whose writings did honor to their age and to this country. And none of them united, in a more distinguished degree, the acquirements of Ancient Learning to a perfect knowledge of the world in which he lived; or more Eminently added to the manners of a most accomplished gentleman the practice and principles of the Purest Virtue' – Something much better may, & probably will be said of him. But the above is short & true --- /

I am happy to hear that so many of his manuscripts are in your possession. I rather believe that few will be found among his Papers. He showed me some years ago, a Dialogue on <u>Beauty</u> in Imitation of Plato. It was unfinished. The Interlocutor, if I remember were himself, Robt Adam, Dr Wilkie, & My Uncle Wil^m then Prof^r of M. Philosophy Edin^r[.] To me, & those who may now know the character of the Speakers, it was extremely interesting.

I know very little of Dr Fergusons private affairs. He often talked to me about them. But it was a subject which could not be pushed further than he seemed perfectly inclined to go. His Pensions amounted to £600 a year, but of these £400 die with him. His daughters have the joint summary of his gov^t Pension £200 per annum, & his House in St And^r which cost him a £1000. I believe that he has left some other funds, but to no great extent. I once perused his will, but I cannot reveal particulars. To the Old Nurse for whom you do properly feel, he has left either £5 or 10 a year. He has appointed a <u>great</u> number of Executors. In doing this he probably meant, & it will be felt as a mark of Respect. But there can be nothing to do. The only on the spot are Colonel Macgill, for whom he had a very great love & esteem, Dr Robertson / Prof^r of Hebrew, St And^r, a very worthy & safe man, & myself. When Cap' Adam Ferguson either comes home, or sends authority the seals of Repositories will be removed; & his correspondence & papers arranged & examined. I am certain that you are one of the Executors; and as soon as every thing is known I shall write to you fully.

I am just dispatching a servant to Lord Kellie, 7 miles from house; and I hasten this letter to you, that I may avail myself of his Frank.

My son & I are perfectly sensible of your great kindness & attention to him. And I am perfectly confident that no good office on your part will ever be wanting either to him or to me. The plan of Peters going to India in the Line of his Profession was most strongly enforced by Ld Chief Commiss^r Adam, who had long been Council to the Comp[an]y at home. He represents the situation as affording not the hope only, but the certainty of a very decent competence by a few years practice. He could not have shown more zeal, or exerted more Interest had he been applying for his own Son. And he will furnish him with all the necessary Introductions to Judges, / Attorneys &c at Madras, almost all of whom owe their situation either to his sanction or interest. The prospects which this opens are mentioned to me even by Adam, as such that I am ashamed to state them. It is altogether a new time since you or I knew any thing of India. But any situation is preferable to living in Lincolns Inn like a monk in his cell, wasting the best part of life on idleness, & looking to the future of hopeless inaction. The great object now is, to get him if possible either named a Company Council before he goes or soon after his arrival at Madras.

I long very much to throw myself upon you at Fine Office of an Afternoon. I often in in imagination dine at the Grove. And if the farming trade does not amend I suspect that it will only be in Imagination that I can anywhere partake of a dinner. I do not despair & though I feel like other folk I am not a grumbler. I yet hope to be at Brompton, & till then god Bless you & believe me ever My Dear Friend

Most sincerely & affectionately
Hugh Cleghorn

Source: BL/MSS EUR F291/97, ff. 94r–95r.

5. Robert 'Bob' Ferguson to Sir John Macpherson

Bristol 10th March 1816

My dear Sir John

My Cousin John has communicated to me the melancholy news of his worthy Father's death. Among all of my late Uncles Friends, You deservedly stood the first in his affections, and I am certain that none regret his departure more than yourself. – Mr Cleghorn's

Letter to you is rightly interesting and consolatory: It does honor to his head & heart. He has proved himself a worthy Pupil of so great a Master. The absence of the two Brothers would have added poignancy to their Sisters Grief, had not Cleghorn performed e'ery kind office, that could be expected from an Affectionate Brother, or from a dutiful, affectionate, and pious Son. His interesting and affecting detail of my Uncle's easy and imperceptible death, brings most forcibly to our immediate recollection, this comfortable passage in the Scriptures – 'He is not dead, but Sleepeth' It would have been a subject of real regret had not such a faithful Friend as Cleghorn been present, to witness, and record, his last Feelings. – It is the lott of very few Men to live to so great an Age: to have such numerous and respectable Friends; and to possess those rare and amiable qualities, which will render Friendship sincere, permanent and Enthusiastic. Providence has rewarded a long, useful and virtuous life, by an easy and imperceptible Death. This is the greatest consolation that his Friends could receive or possibly wish for, on that not unexpected Event. It must be particularly comfortable to you, who knew him most, & loved him best. An ardent love of Country was his / predominant Passion. Mr Cleghorn informs us – 'That while he reasoned on every passing Event with the Sagacity of Age, he embraced it with all the ardour and ~~sagacity~~ keenness of Youth' More fortunate than the Immortal Mr Pitt he lived to see the consummation of his Patriotic Wishes, and kind Providence preserved his mind unimpaired that he might experience the full measure of Joy by knowing and also by comprehending that his Country was secure prosperous and happy. Such a death and under such circumstances is not only happy, but even enviable. I hope you enjoy good health. My son informed me that he called upon you the last Holy days. I was glad to hear he had paid due attention and respect to his Fathers best friend. I have most flattering account of him from Dr Crombie. A letter address'd at Bristol will find me whenever your inclination or leisure will permit you to write. Accept My dear Sir John my sincere good Wishes and believe me to be

Your Most Affectionate
And Obliged Friend
<u>Robert Ferguson</u>

Source: BL/MSS EUR F291/97, ff. 97r–v.

6. Adam Ferguson to Sir John Macpherson

St Andrews
19th March 1816

My Dear Sir John,

On my arrival here from my reg^t in Ireland, I found that my excellent friend Mr Cleghorn had communicated to you all the particulars relating to the last moments of your old & dear friend my late lamented father. Certainly never was there a transition from this to a better world attended with more enviable calm & perfect tranquility.

Yesterday his repositories were opened in presence of Mr Cleghorn and Drs Robertson and Lee of the University here. When all his papers were found in the most perfect order & arrangement. A Will was found leaving to my three sisters all he should die possessed of, ~~including~~ with the / house and garden here, and which including their pension of £200 will leave them a free income of £500 p^r annum – a sum perfectly sufficient to satisfy all their moderate wants.

The Will appoints yourself and nine other friends Trustees for the due execution of it. The names of the others are

Lord Chief Commissioner Adam	Co^l Macgill
Mr Campbell of Kailzie	Mr Cleghorn
Co^l Burnett	Dr Robertson of the
Prof^r Ja^s Rupell	University here
Ja^s Ferguson Advocate	& Cousin Robert Ferguson

Any three of these accepting to be a quoram – of course the business of the First Will be perfectly simple & can be easily managed by the three Trustees resident here viz Mr Cleghorn Co^l Mac Gill and Dr Robertson. But as the Lawyer cannot proceed to realise the funds till all the Trustees named have declared their intentions as to acceptance of the Trust. I will take it very kind if you will / as soon as convenient drop me a few lines to such effect.

I regret to say, that I find from my sisters that my Father previous to his leaving Peeblesshire committed to the flames a great Mass of Manuscript papers containing I have no doubt much valuable Correspondence with his early & celebrated friends of the

Poker Club. He used to say that he had a great dread of the Bookmakers of the present times, & such must have been his motive for this act certainly much to be regretted.

I am sorry to say that here is no change for the better in the state of my lame knee, & I am much afraid I shall be under the necessity of applying to the Commander in Chief to be invalided for a year or two to come.

My sisters join in most affectionate regards to you & we hope to hear that your health is improving daily with the Advance of the Spring.

I am my Dear Sir John
Always yours most sincerely
Adam Ferguson

Source: BL/MSS EUR F291/97, ff. 101r–102r.

Note

1. There are two versions of this letter differing slightly. This is MSS EUR F291/97, ff. 78r–81v, but the other is MSS EUR F291/97, ff. 72r–77v. Both are marked 'Copy' at different places. F. 78v reads: 'Confidential to my Preceptor & Friend Dr Ad^m Ferguson / 24 Novr. 1800 / on my memorial to the Board of Control & the <u>Secret History of India</u>.

Appendix B: The Correspondence of Adam Ferguson and Sir John Macpherson

The following is a list of the known correspondence between Adam Ferguson (AF) and John Macpherson (JM), ordered chronologically. We have given letter numbers in the Merolle correspondence and in ours (abbreviated here to 'S&S').

The list starts with Merolle no. 59, which is undated but which Merolle conjecturally dated to 1772. Based on internal evidence this letter can be dated to c. 1769. Between 1768 and 1770, John and James Macpherson worked as hack writers in favour of the Grafton administration, and in the letter Ferguson declines an invitation to join them. Given that John Macpherson only returned to Britain at the end of 1768, that Grafton fell in January 1770, and that John Macpherson departed for India in February 1772, it seems safe to date the letter to 1769. This was also the period during which the Macphersons were most prolific in their 'journalistic' work.[1]

One correction must be made: Merolle no. 265 (19 January 1790). If the endorsement is correct ('Doctor Ferguson, 19th Janry 1790 / By the Princess Amelia / Rec^d 4th August 1790') then this cannot have been sent to Macpherson. Macpherson had returned to Britain in 1787 and in 1790 was on the European continent, and therefore could not have been present to receive the letter from the EIC ship the Princess Amelia. Based on the content the date seems correct.

1. AF to JM, [Date unknown, c. 1769] (Merolle no. 59)
2. AF to JM, 3 Nov 1773 (Merolle no. 61)
3. AF to JM, 31 March 1774 (Merolle no. 66)
4. AF to JM, 9 April 1775 (Merolle no. 74)
5. AF to JM, 9 August 1777 (Merolle no. 97)
6. AF to JM, 27 Oct 1777 (Merolle no. 100)
7. AF to JM, 23 Dec 1777 (Merolle no. 103)

8. AF to JM, 15 Jan 1778 (Merolle no. 105)
9. AF to JM, 12 Feb 1778 (Merolle no. 108)
10. AF to JM, 18 June 1778 (Merolle no. 113)
11. AF to JM, 20 August 1778 (Merolle no. 117)
12. AF to JM, 22 Dec 1778 (Merolle no. 139)
13. AF to JM, 27 July 1779 (Merolle no. 166)
14. AF to JM, 25 Oct 1779 (Merolle no. 168)
15. AF to JM, 18 Dec 1779 (Merolle no. 169)
16. AF to JM, 10 Jan 1780 (Merolle, no. 171)
17. AF to JM, 12 June 1780 (Merolle no. 175)
18. AF to JM, 24 Aug 1780 (Merolle no. 186)
19. JM to AF, 13 Jan 1781 (Merolle no. 194)
20. AF to JM, 13 Sep 1784 (S&S no. 1)
21. AF to JM, 1 Feb 1785 (S&S no. 2)
22. AF to JM, 16 April 1785 (Merolle no. 235, II, 309–10 [partial]; S&S no. 3 [full copy])
23. JM to AF, 12 Jan 1786 (Merolle no. 241)
24. AF to JM, 16 Feb 1786 (S&S no. 4)
25. AF to JM, 15 Jan 1787 (S&S no. 5)
26. AF to JM, 31 March 1787 (S&S no. 6)
27. AF to JM, 22 August 1787 (S&S no. 7)
28. AF to JM, 27 Sep 1787 (S&S no. 8)
29. AF to JM, 1 Oct 1787 (S&S no. 9)
30. AF to JM, 7 Oct 1787 (S&S no. 10)
31. AF to JM, 26 Nov 1787 (S&S no. 11)
32. AF to JM, 13 April 1788 (S&S no. 12)
33. AF to JM, 26 April 1788 (S&S no. 13)
34. AF to JM, 18 May 1788 (S&S no. 14)
35. AF to JM, 21 June 1788 (S&S no. 15)
36. AF to JM, 6 Feb 1789 (S&S no. 16)
37. AF to JM, 7 April 1789 (S&S no. 17)
38. AF to JM, 18 May 1789 (S&S no. 18)
39. AF to JM, 31 May 1789 (S&S no. 19)
40. AF to JM, 31 July 1790 (Merolle no. 269, II, 340–2)
41. AF to JM, 12 August 1793 (S&S no. 20)
42. AF to JM, 11 Sep 1793 (S&S no. 21)
43. AF to JM, 25 Sep 1793 (Merolle no. 283)
44. AF to JM, 5 Oct 1793 (Merolle no. 285)
45. AF to JM, 19 Oct 1793 (Merolle no. 287)
46. AF to JM, 10 Dec 1793 (S&S no. 22)
47. AF to JM, 17 March 1794 (S&S no. 23)

48. AF to JM, 6 May 1794 (S&S no. 24)
49. AF to JM, 6 June 1794 (S&S no. 25)
50. AF to JM, 4 July 1794 (S&S no. 26)
51. AF to JM, 8 Sep 1794 (S&S no. 27)
52. AF to JM, 9 Jan 1795 (S&S no. 28)
53. AF to JM, 23 March 1795 (Merolle no. 289)
54. AF to JM, 20 May 1795 (Merolle no. 290)
55. AF to JM, 24 May 1795 (Merolle no. 291)
56. AF to JM, 1 June 1795 (Merolle no. 292)
57. AF to JM, 9 June 1795 (Merolle no. 293)
58. AF to JM, 3 Sep 1795 (Merolle no. 294)
59. AF to JM, 4 Sep 1795 (Merolle no. 295)
60. AF to JM, 17 Sep 1795 (Merolle no. 297)
61. AF to JM, 19 Sep 1795 (Merolle no. 298)
62. AF to JM, 10 Oct 1795 (Merolle no. 300)
63. AF to JM, 4 Dec 1795 (Merolle no. 302)
64. AF to JM, 9 Jan 1796 (Merolle no. 303)
65. AF to JM, 10 Jan 1796 (Merolle no. 304)
66. AF to JM, 25 Feb 1796 (Merolle no. 305)
67. AF to JM, 29 Feb 1796 (Merolle no. 306)
68. AF to JM, [March 1796, dated from contents] (Merolle no. 308)
69. AF to JM, 2 April 1796 (Merolle no. 309)
70. AF to JM, 7 May 1796 (Merolle no. 311)
71. AF to JM, 2 June 1796 (Merolle no. 313)
72. AF to JM, 20 June 1796 (Merolle no. 315)
73. AF to JM, 26 June 1796 (Merolle no. 316)
74. AF to JM, 7 July 1796 (Merolle no. 317)
75. AF to JM, 1 August 1796 (Merolle no. 318)
76. AF to JM, 1 September 1796 (Merolle no. 319)
77. AF to JM, 22 September 1796 (Merolle no. 321)
78. AF to JM, 23 December 1796 (Merolle no. 323)
79. AF to JM, 5 January 1797 (S&S no. 29)
80. AF to JM, 9 Feb 1797 (Merolle no. 324)
81. AF to JM, 2 March 1797 (Merolle no. 327)
82. AF to JM, 16 March 1797 (Merolle no. 328)
83. AF to JM, 14 April 1797 (S&S no. 30)
84. AF to JM, 17 April [1797] (S&S no. 31)
85. AF to JM, 30 June 1797 (S&S no. 32)
86. AF to JM, 26 Sep 1797 (Merolle no. 331)
87. AF to JM, 14 May 1798 (Merolle no. 339)
88. AF to JM, 3 July 1798 (Merolle no. 342)

89. AF to JM, 1 August 1798 (Merolle no. 343)
90. AF to JM, 31 Dec 1798 (Merolle, no. 348)
91. AF to JM, 21 Feb 1799 (Merolle no. 349)
92. AF to JM, 2 March 1799 (Merolle no. 350)
93. AF to JM, 4 March 1799 (Merolle no. 351)
94. AF to JM, 20 March 1799 (Merolle no. 352)
95. AF to JM, 15 July 1799 (Merolle no. 354)
96. AF to JM, 2 Sep 1799 (Merolle no. 355)
97. AF to JM, 27 Jan 1800 (S&S no. 33)
98. AF to JM, 14 Feb 1800 (Merolle no. 358)
99. AF to JM, 29 April 1800 (Merolle no. 360)
100. JM to AF, 24 November 1800 (S&S, Appendix A, no. 1)
101. AF to JM, 12 Oct 1801 (S&S no. 34)
102. AF to JM, 13 August 1802 (Merolle no. 370)
103. AF to JM, 26 Oct 1802 (Merolle no. 371)
104. AF to JM, 15 Dec 1802 (Merolle no. 373)
105. AF to JM, 12 Feb 1803 (Merolle no. 374)
106. AF to JM, 10 Nov 1804 (Merolle no. 378)
107. AF to JM, 13 May 1805 (Merolle no. 380)
108. AF to JM, 29 Aug 1805 (Merolle no. 381)
109. AF to JM, 7 June 1806 (Merolle no. 383)
110. AF to JM, 29 Dec 1806 (Merolle no. 387)
111. AF to JM, 16 Sep 1808 (Merolle no. 394)
112. AF to JM, 28 July 1809 (S&S no. 35)
113. AF to JM, 13 April 1811 (S&S no. 36)

Note

1. Maclean, 'Early Political Careers', 130–1.

Appendix C: Further Miscellaneous Anecdotes about Ferguson from Hugh Cleghorn

BL Add MS 39945: The Diary of William Erskine (1773–1852)

Monday 11. July 1836
 On Saty. I called on Mr. Cleghorn. He told me, what gives me no surprize, that Prof. Adam Ferguson, whom he knew well when he settled here some years before his death, was a thorough going & confirmed Unbeliever. Some instances of this he gave en passant. (f. 34r)
 Friday 9. Sept. 1836
 Breakfasted this morning at Mr. Cleghorn's . . . /He mentioned a curious fact regarding the successor to Prof. Ferguson, in the Moral Philosophy Chair. When P[rofessor] F[erguson] left Edin^r either to travel with Lord Chesterfield, or to attend the American Commissions, Dugald Stewart lectured for him. After one lesson as the prospect of a vacancy from his not returning was small Dugald Stewart wished to confine himself to his own Mathematical Chair. A new person was to be looked out for. As Ferguson was going to Lady Yester's Church, he happened to meet M^r. Cleghorn's mother whom he knew, & to whom he spoke. She ment^d the approaching change & spoke of her grandson. Mr Cleghorn was then at St Andrew where, the day he came of age (21), he had been rec^d as Professor of History. His uncle Dr Cleghorn had been Professor of Mor: Phil: (or Logic) in the Coll. Of Ed. and he was known to the Professors, having been a schoolfellow of Dug. Stewart . . . He soon after called on D.S. & told him he had found the man they wanted, naming Cleghorn. A letter was written to him and a Meeting fixed without loss of time at Kingdom. It took place Ferguson & I think Stewart going over. Cleghorn was a Prof. at 21, married at 22, and had an increasing family. He feared that if Ferguson returned, he w^d be thrown out of every thing, & had apprehensions too of succeeding such eminent Lecturers. He declined, & thus did

not remove to Edinr. & lost his connection with the Moral Phil. Class.- Ferguson was fond of him and his vicinity was one reason of the Doctor's moving to S^r. Andrews, where they saw much of one another. (I believe the arrangement was concluded by Playfair's becoming joint Prof. of Mathematics) / He spoke of Ferguson's having mentioned Mackintosh's having offered himself to Ferguson to succeed him in the Chair. (I think it must have been at the time when the Prof^r finally withdrew.) Ferguson said that Mackintosh waited upon him, addressing him in a set speech, telling him that he had lined <u>satis ad ertam, not satis ad gloriam:</u> and that he had shewn great talent. This agrees with what I have repeatedly heard Sir James mention; but I understood, though I do not distinctly recollect, that he had written to Ferguson from Aberdeen or immediately after coming to Edin^r. He may however have addressed him verbally. At all events I recollect distinctly that Sir J. said that Ferguson had behaved very kindly, and complemented & taken notice of him. D^r. John Thomson when I mentioned the incident, thought it impossible. I was therefore glad to have this confirmation from D^r. Cleghorn, who had the facts from Ferguson. Coming then from the two last quarters, I imagine there can be no doubt of the fact.

(ff. 34r–35r)

Bibliography

Primary Sources

Archives

British Library, London

MSS EUR F291/76/1: John Macpherson's letterbook to the Prince of Wales.
MSS EUR F291/83: John Macpherson correspondence with Hugh Blair.
MSS EUR F291/87: John Macpherson correspondence with Alexander Carlyle.
MSS EUR F291/97: Ferguson essay and correspondence with John Macpherson, and miscellaneous correspondence in relation to Ferguson.
MSS EUR F291/102: John Macpherson correspondence with Charles Greville.
MSS EUR F291/107: John Macpherson correspondence with various figures, including John Home.
MSS EUR F291/146: John Macpherson correspondence with various figures.
MSS EUR F291/172: John Macpherson miscellaneous correspondence.
MSS EUR F291/176: Various writings of John Macpherson.

Online Archives

'Memorandum of an Interview with Lieutenant Colonel James Paterson, 20 July 1776', *Founders Online*, National Archives. Accessed 25 October 2022. https://founders.archives.gov/documents/Washington/03-05-02-0295. [Original source: *The Papers of George Washington*, Revolutionary War Series, vol. 5, 16 June 1776 to 12 August 1776, ed. Philander D. Chase, 398–403. Charlottesville, 1993.]

Thomas Robertson (life dates unknown) commanded the *Busbridge* Indiaman from 1785 to 1793. Accessed 20 August 2021. https://threedecks.org/index.php?display_type=show_ship&id=29125.

Published Primary Sources

Anon. *Strictures on Lt. Col. Tarleton's History 'of the Campaigns of 1780 and 1781, in the Southern Provinces of North America'. Wherein Military Characters and Corps are Vindicated from Injurious Aspersions, and Several Important Transactions Placed in their Proper Point of View. In a Series of Letters to a Friend, by Roderick Mackenzie, Late Lieutenant in the 71st regiment. To which is Added, a Detail of the Siege of Ninety Six, and the Re-capture of the Island of New-Providence*. London, 1787.

Anon. *An Historical Journal of the American War. Extracted from the Publications of the Massachusetts Historical Society*. Boston, 1795.

Anon. [likely John Macpherson with input from friends]. *The Case of Sir John Macpherson, Baronet, Late Governor General of India; Containing a Summary Review of His Administration and Services*. London, 1808.

Black, Joseph. *Dissertatio medica inauguralis, de humore acido a cibis orto, et magnesia alba: Quam, annuente summo numine, ex auctoritate Reverendi admodum Viri, D. Joannis Gowdie, Academiæ Edinburgenæ Præfecti; nec non amplissimi senatus academici consensu, et nobilissimae facultatis medicae decreto; Pro Gradu Doctoratus, summisque in medicina Honoribus ac Privilegiis rite et legitime consequendis; eruditorum examini subjicit Josephus Black Gallus, Ad diem 11 Junii, horâ locoque solitis*. Edinburgh, 1754.

Black, Joseph. *Lectures on the Elements of Chemistry . . . by the Late Joseph Black, MD . . . Now Published From His Manuscripts*, 2 vols. Edinburgh, 1803.

Blackstone, William. *Commentaries on the Laws of England: Book the First*, 2nd ed. Oxford, 1766.

Burke, Edmund. *Speech on American Taxation*. London, 1774.

Burke, Edmund. *Mr. Edmund Burke's Speeches at His Arrival at Bristol, and at the Conclusion of the Poll*. London, 1775.

Burns, Robert. *Poems, Chiefly in the Scottish Dialect*. Kilmarnock, 1786.

Carlyle, Alexander. *The Question Relating to the Scots Militia Considered*. Edinburgh, 1760.

Carlyle, Alexander. *Autobiography of the Rev. Dr Alexander Carlyle; Containing Memorials of the Men and Events of His Time*. Edinburgh, 1861.

Carlyle, Alexander. *Anecdotes and Characters of the Times*, ed. James Kinsley. Oxford, 1973.
Cicero. *Tusculan Disputations*, trans. J. E. King. Cambridge, MA, 1927.
Clinton, Henry. *The American Rebellion: Sir Henry Clinton's Narrative of His Campaigns, 1775–1782*, ed. W. B. Willcox. New Haven, CT, 1954.
Cobbett, William, ed. *The Parliamentary History of England*, vol. XXXIII. London, 1818.
Cockburn, Henry. *Memorials of His Time*. Edinburgh, 1856.
Ferguson, Adam. *Reflections Previous to the Establishment of a Militia*. London, 1756.
Ferguson, Adam. *Institutes of Moral Philosophy*. Edinburgh, 1769.
Ferguson, Adam. *An Essay on the History of Civil Society*, revised ed. London, 1773 [1767]).
Ferguson, Adam, *Remarks on a Pamphlet Lately Published by Dr. Price, Intitled, Observations on the Nature of Civil Liberty, the Principles of Government, and the Justice and Policy of the War with America, &c.* (London 1776).
Ferguson, Adam. *History of the Progress and the Termination of the Roman Republic*, 3 vols. London, 1783.
Ferguson, Adam. *Histoire des progrès et de la chute de la république romaine*, trans. Jean Nicholas Démeunier, 3 vols. Paris, 1784.
Ferguson, Adam. *Histoire des progrès et de la chute de la république romaine*, trans. Jean Jacques Gibelin, 4 vols. Paris, 1791.
Ferguson, Adam. *Principles of Moral and Political Science*, 2 vols. Edinburgh, 1792.
Ferguson, Adam. *An Essay on the History of Civil Society*, ed. Duncan Forbes. Edinburgh, 1966 [1767].
Ferguson, Adam. *The Correspondence of Adam Ferguson*, ed. Vincenzo Merolle, 2 vols. London, 1995.
Ferguson, Adam. *An Essay on the History of Civil Society*, ed. Fania Oz-Salzberger. Cambridge, 1997 [1767].
Ferguson, Adam. *The Manuscripts of Adam Ferguson*, ed. Vincenzo Merolle, Robin Dix and Eugene Heath. London, 2006.
Hamilton, William. *Observations on Mount Vesuvius, Mount Etna, and Other Volcanos* (1772); *Account of the Discoveries at Pompeii*. London, 1777.
Hamilton, William. *An Account of the Earthquakes which Happened in Italy, from February to May 1783*. London, 1783.
Home, John. *The History of the Rebellion in the Year 1745*. London, 1802.
Home, John. *The Works of John Home*, 3 vols. Edinburgh, 1822.

Horace. *The Works of Horace, Translated Literally into English Prose*, ed. C. Smart. Edinburgh, 1777.
Horace. *Satires, Epistles, Art of Poetry*, trans. H. R. Fairclough, revised ed. Cambridge, MA, 1929.
Hughes, W. E., ed. *Monumental Inscriptions and Extracts from Registers of Births, Marriages, and Deaths, at St. Anne's Church, Soho*. London, 1905.
Hume, David. *Enquiry Concerning the Principles of Morals*. Oxford, 1975 [1751].
Hume, David. *A Treatise of Human Nature*, ed. L. A. Selby-Bigge and P. H. Nidditch. Oxford, 1978 [1739–40].
Hume, David. *The History of England from the Invasion of Julius Caesar to the Revolution in 1688*, 6 vols. Indianapolis, 1983.
Hume, David. *Essays, Moral, Political and Literary*, ed. Eugene F. Miller. Indianapolis, 1985.
Hume, David. *The Letters of David Hume*, ed. J. Y. T. Greig, 2 vols. Oxford, 2011 [1932].
Hutcheson, Francis. *A System of Moral Philosophy*, 2 vols. London, 1755.
Jones, William. *The Letters of Sir William Jones*, ed. Garland Cannon, 2 vols. Oxford, 1970.
Lavoisier, Antoine. *Opuscules Physiques et Chimiques*. Paris, 1774.
Lock, F. P. 'An Unpublished Letter from Adam Smith to Sir John Macpherson'. *Scottish Historical Review* 85 (2006): 135–7.
Locke, John. *The Second Treatise of Government*, in *Two Treatises of Government*, ed. Peter Laslett. Cambridge, 1988.
Macaulay, Catharine. *Political Writings*, ed. Max Skjönsberg. Cambridge, 2023.
[Macpherson, James]. *The Rights of Great Britain Asserted Against the Claims of America*. [London, 1776].
Macpherson, John. *Critical Dissertation on the Origin, Antiquities, Language, Government, Manners, and Religion, of the Ancient Caledonians, Their Posterity the Picts, and the British and Irish Scots*. London, 1768.
[Macpherson, John]. *First and Second Letter to a Noble Earl*. London, 1797.
Macpherson, John. *Mémoire sur le projet de l'Empereur Léopold avec une analyse de l'histoire politique de l'Europe depuis 1756*. N.d. [1797].
Mandredini, Marquis Federico and John Macpherson. *Correspondance entre un voyageur et un ministre, en octobre, et novembre 1792*. Place of publication unknown, [1796?].

Mémoires de l'Académie royale des sciences et belles-lettres. Berlin, 1798 [1792–3].

Montesquieu. *De l'Esprit des Loix*, 3 vols. Geneva, 1748.

Montesquieu. *The Spirit of the Laws*, ed. Anne M. Cohler et al. Cambridge, 1989 [1748].

Orme, Robert. *A History of the Military Transactions of the British Nation in Indostan, From the Year MDCCXLV.* London, 1763.

Otis, James. *The Rights of the British Colonies Asserted and Proved.* London, 1764.

Polybius. *The General History of Polybius. In Five Books. Translated from the Greek by Mr. Hampton.* London, 1756.

Price, Richard. *Observations on the Expectations of Lives, the Increase of Mankind, the Influence of Great Towns on Population, and Particularly the State of London, with Respect to Healthfulness and Number of Inhabitants.* London, 1769. And *Observations on Reversionary Payments; On Schemes for Providing Annuities for Widows, and for Persons in Old Age; On the Method of Calculating the Values of Assurances on Lives; and On the National Debt.* London, 1772.

Price, Richard, *Observations on the Nature of Civil Liberty, the Principles of Government, and the Justice and Policy of the War with America.* London, 1776.

Price, Richard. *Political Writings*, ed. D. O. Thomas. Cambridge, 1992.

Pufendorf, Samuel. *Law of Nature and Nations.* 1672, translated into English in 1703.

Ramsay, David. *History of the American Revolution*, 2 vols. Philadelphia, 1789.

Ramsay, David. *The History of South-Carolina: From Its First Settlement in 1670, to the Year 1808*, 2 vols. Charleston, 1809.

Sallust. *The War with Catiline*, trans. John C. Rolfe. Cambridge, MA, 1921.

Seton-Karr, W., ed. *Selections from Calcutta Gazettes of the Years 1784, 1785, 1786, 1787, and 1788, Showing the Political and Social Condition of the English in India Eighty Years Ago.* Calcutta, 1864.

Sherman, William Thomas. *Calendar and Record of the Revolutionary War in the South: 1780–1781*, 10th ed. Seattle, 2018.

Smith, Adam. *The Correspondence of Adam Smith*, ed. E. C. Mossner and I. S. Ross. Oxford, 1977.

Smith, Adam. *Inquiry into the Nature and Causes of the Wealth of Nations*, 2 vols. Indianapolis, 1982 [1776].

Smith, Adam. *The Theory of Moral Sentiments.* Indianapolis, 1982 [1759].

Stuart, Andrew. *A Genealogical History of the Stewarts*. London, 1798.
Transactions of the Royal Society of Edinburgh. Edinburgh, 1805.
Virgil. *Aeneid*, trans. H. R. Fairclough and G. P. Goold, 2 vols. Cambridge, MA, 1918.
Walker, Adam. *Ideas, Suggested on the Spot in a Late Excursion through Flanders, Germany, France, and Italy, by A. Walker, Lecturer on Experimental Philosophy*. London, 1790.
Wraxall, N. W. *Posthumous Memoirs of His Own Time*, 3 vols. London, 1836.

Secondary Sources

Published Secondary Sources

Allan, David. *Adam Ferguson*. Edinburgh, 2006.
Almack, Edward. *The History of the Second Dragoons: The Scots Greys*. London, 1908.
Baumstark, Moritz. 'The End of Empire and the Death of Religion'. In *Philosophy and Religion in Enlightenment Britain*, ed. Ruth Savage, 231–57. Oxford, 2012.
Castiglione, Dario. 'The Origin of Government'. In *The Oxford Handbook of British Philosophy in the Eighteenth Century*, ed. James Harris, 491–529. Oxford, 2013.
Berry, Christopher. *Social Theory of the Scottish Enlightenment*. Edinburgh, 1997.
Berry, Christopher. *The Idea of Commercial Society in the Scottish Enlightenment*. Edinburgh, 2013.
Berry, Christopher. *Hume, Smith and the Scottish Enlightenment*. Edinburgh, 2018.
Bolton, G. C. and B. E. Kennedy. 'William Eden and the Treaty of Mauritius, 1786–7'. *Historical Journal* 16 (1973): 681–96.
Brewer, Anthony. 'Adam Ferguson, Adam Smith, and the Concept of Economic Growth'. *History of Political Economy* 31 (1999): 237–54.
Bryson, Gladys. *Man and Society: The Scottish Inquiry of the Eighteenth Century*. Princeton, 1945.
DeGategno, Paul J. 'Macpherson, Sir John, first baronet'. In *Oxford Dictionary of National Biography*. Accessed 26 July 2021. https://o-www-oxforddnb-com.catalogue.libraries.london.ac.uk/view/10.1093/

ref:odnb/9780198614128.001.0001/odnb-9780198614128-e-17730?rskey=APGIYT&result=5.
Dirks, Nicholas B. *The Scandal of Empire: India and the Creation of Imperial Britain*. Cambridge, MA, 2008.
Ehrlich, Joshua. 'Empire and Enlightenment in Three Letters from Sir William Jones to Governor-General John Macpherson'. *Historical Journal* 62 (2019): 541–51.
Ehrlich, Joshua. *The East India Company and the Politics of Knowledge*. Cambridge University Press, 2023.
Elazar, Yiftah. 'Adam Ferguson on Modern Liberty and the Absurdity of Democracy'. *History of Political Thought* 35 (2014): 768–87.
Fagg, Jane B. 'Biographical Introduction'. In *The Correspondence of Adam Ferguson*, ed. Vincenzo Merolle, 2 vols. London, 1995.
Fagg, Jane B. 'Ferguson's Use of the Edinburgh University Library: 1764–1806'. In *Adam Ferguson: History, Progress and Human Nature*, ed. Eugene Heath and Vincenzo Merolle, 57–64. London and New York, 2008.
Ferguson, J. and R. M. Fergusson. *Records of the Clan and Name of Fergusson, Ferguson, and Fergus*. Edinburgh, 1895.
Forbes, Duncan. *Hume's Philosophical Politics*. Cambridge, 1975.
Guena, Marco. 'Republicanism and Commercial Society in the Scottish Enlightenment: The Case of Adam Ferguson'. In *Republicanism: A Shared European Heritage*, ed. Martin van Gelderen and Quentin Skinner, 2 vols, 177–96. Cambridge, 2002.
Haakonssen, Knud. *Natural Law and Moral Philosophy: From Grotius to the Scottish Enlightenment*. Cambridge, 1996.
Hamowy, Ronald. 'Adam Smith, Adam Ferguson, and the Division of Labour'. *Economica* 35 (1968): 249–59.
Hamowy, Ronald. *The Scottish Enlightenment and the Theory of Spontaneous Order*. Carbondale, 1987.
Hamowy, Ronald. 'Scottish Thought and the American Revolution: Adam Ferguson's Response to Richard Price', *Liberty and American Experience in the Eighteenth Century*, ed. David Womersley, 348–87. Indianapolis, 2006.
Heath, Eugene and Vincenzo Merolle, ed. *Adam Ferguson: History, Progress and Human Nature*. London, 2008.
Heath, Eugene and Vincenzo Merolle, ed. *Adam Ferguson: Philosophy, Politics and Society*. London, 2009.
Hill, Lisa. *The Passionate Society: The Social, Political, and Moral Thought of Adam Ferguson*. Dordrecht, 2006.

Hont, Istvan. *Jealousy of Trade: International Competition and the Nation-State in Historical Perspective*. Cambridge, MA, 2005.

Kettler, David. *The Social and Political Thought of Adam Ferguson*. Columbus, 1965.

Kettler, David. 'Political Education for Empire and Revolution'. In *Adam Ferguson: History, Progress and Human Nature*, ed. Eugene Heath and Vincenzo Merolle, 87–114. London, 2008.

McDaniel, Iain. *Adam Ferguson in the Scottish Enlightenment: The Roman Past and Europe's Future*. Cambridge, MA, 2013.

McDaniel, Iain. 'Unsocial Sociability in the Scottish Enlightenment: Ferguson and Kames on War, Sociability and the Foundations of Patriotism'. *History of European Ideas* 41 (2015): 662–82.

Marx, Karl. *Capital: A Critique of Political Economy*. Vol I: *The Process of Capitalist Production*. Chicago, 1909 [1867].

Meek, Ronald L. *Social Science and the Ignoble Savage*. Cambridge, 1976.

Moore, James. 'Natural Rights in the Scottish Enlightenment'. In *The Cambridge History of Eighteenth-Century Political Thought*, ed. Mark Goldie and Robert Wokler, 291–316. Cambridge, 2006.

Moore, James and Michael Silverthorne. 'Gershom Carmichael and the Natural Jurisprudence Tradition in Eighteenth-Century Scotland'. In *Wealth and Virtue: The Shaping of Political Economy in the Scottish Enlightenment*, ed. Istvan Hont and Michael Ignatieff, 73–87. Cambridge, 1983.

Mossner, E. C. *The Life of David Hume*, 2nd ed. Oxford, 1980 [1954].

Olsthoorn, Johan and Laurens Van Apeldoorn. '"This man is my property": Slavery and Political Absolutism in Locke and the Classical Social Contract Tradition'. *European Journal of Political Theory* 21 (2022): 253–75.

Oz-Salzberger, Fania. *Translating the Enlightenment: Scottish Civic Discourse in Eighteenth-Century Germany*. Oxford, 1995.

Oz-Salzberger, Fania. 'Ferguson, Adam, 1723–1816'. In *Oxford Dictionary of National Biography*. Accessed 6 October 2021. https://www.oxforddnb.com/view/10.1093/ref:odnb/9780198614128.001.0001/odnb-9780198614128-e-9315?rskey=rc4R7d&result=2.

Philp, Mark, ed. *Resisting Napoleon: The British Response to the Threat of Invasion, 1797–1815*. London, 2006.

Plassart, Anna. *The Scottish Enlightenment and the French Revolution*. Cambridge, 2015.

Pocock, J. G. A. 'Burke and the Ancient Constitution: A Problem in the History of Ideas'. *Historical Journal* 3 (1960): 125–43.

Pocock, J. G. A. *Virtue, Commerce and History: Essays on Political Thought and History, Chiefly in the Eighteenth Century*. Cambridge, 1985.

Pocock, J. G. A. *The Machiavellian Moment: Florentine Political Thought and the Atlantic Republican Tradition*. Princeton, 2016 [1975].

Port, M. H. and R. G. Thorne. 'Macpherson, Sir John, 1st Bt. (1774–1821), of Bromton Grove, Mdx'. In R. G. Thorne, *The History of Parliament: The House of Commons 1790–1820*. Woodbridge, 1986. Accessed 8 October 2021. https://www.historyofparliamentonline.org/volume/1790-1820/member/macpherson-sir-john-1744-1821.

Purvis, Randy A. 'Major James Wemyss: Second Most Hated British Officer in the South'. *Journal of the American Revolution*, 27 November 2018. https://allthingsliberty.com/2018/11/major-james-wemyss-second-most-hated-british-officer-in-the-south/.

Robertson, John. *The Scottish Enlightenment and the Militia Issue*. Edinburgh, 1985.

Sagar, Paul. *Adam Smith Reconsidered: History, Liberty, and the Foundations of Modern Politics*. Princeton, 2022.

Sebastiani, Silvia. *The Scottish Enlightenment: Race, Gender, and the Limits of Progress*. Basingstoke, 2013.

Selinger, William. *Parliamentarism: From Burke to Weber*. Cambridge, 2019.

Sher, Richard B. *Church and University in the Scottish Enlightenment: The Moderate Literati of Edinburgh*. Edinburgh, 1985.

Sher, Richard B. 'Adam Ferguson, Adam Smith, and the Problem of National Defense'. *Journal of Modern History* 61 (1989): 240–68.

Skjönsberg, Max. 'Adam Ferguson on Partisanship, Party Conflict, and Popular Participation'. *Modern Intellectual History* 16 (2019): 1–28.

Skjönsberg, Max. 'Adam Ferguson on the Perils of Popular Factions and Demagogues in a Roman Mirror'. *History of European Ideas* 45 (2019): 842–65.

Skjönsberg, Max. *The Persistence of Party: Ideas of Harmonious Discord in Eighteenth-Century Britain*. Cambridge, 2021.

Smith, Craig. 'The Scottish Enlightenment, Unintended Consequences and the Science of Man'. *Journal of Scottish Philosophy* 7 (2009): 9–28.

Smith, Craig. *Adam Ferguson and the Idea of Civil Society: Moral Science in the Scottish Enlightenment*. Edinburgh, 2018.

Stewart, Ian. 'Adam Ferguson, Sir John Macpherson, and the French Revolution: New Evidence and Perspectives'. *Scottish Historical Review* (December, 2023).

Towsey, Mark. *Reading History in Britain and America, c. 1750–1840*. Cambridge, 2019.

Trevor-Roper, Hugh. *The Invention of Scotland: Myth and History*. New Haven, 2008.
Vile, M. J. C. *Constitutionalism and the Separation of Powers*. Indianapolis, 1998 [1967].

Unpublished Secondary Sources

Maclean, James Noel Mackenzie. 'The Early Political Careers of James "Fingal" Macpherson (1736–1796) and Sir John Macpherson, Bart. (1744–1821)'. PhD thesis, University of Edinburgh, 1967.
Valmori, Niccolò. 'Private Interest and the Public Sphere: Finance and Politics in France, Britain and The Netherlands during the Age of Revolution, 1789–1812'. PhD thesis, European University Institute, 2016.

Index

Amiens, Treaty of (1802), 17, 20, 39

Barclay, Robert, 97, 124n
Beccaria, Cesare, 29
Black, Joseph, 109, 110, 173–86
   character, 183–6
   Ferguson's links to, 173
   fixed air, 177–8
   friendships, 183–4
   latent heat, 178–80
   publications, 182
   science of nature, 182
Blackstone, William, 171n
Blair, Hugh, 3, 13, 16, 21, 22–3, 24, 48, 77, 78, 80, 85, 88, 89, 91, 92, 102, 104
Burke, Edmund, 7, 21, 22, 48, 122n, 126n, 170n
Burnett, Joseph, 70, 92, 116n, 122n
Burns, Robert, 12, 76, 118n
   'The Cottar's Saturday Night', 76

Cadell, Thomas, 72, 116n40
[Cameron, John], 68
Campbell, Archibald, third Duke of Argyll, 82, 120n
Carlisle Commission, 4, 137, 153, 231

Carlyle, Alexander, 3, 10–11, 21–4, 66, 67, 77, 78, 88, 92, 94, 95, 114n, 122n, 174
Carmichael, Gershom, 28
Catilina, Lucius Sergius, 127n
Châtelet, Gabrielle Émilie Le Tonnelier de Breteuil, Marquise du, 73, 117n
Cicero (tags), 98, 103, 124n, 189n
Cleghorn, Hugh, 112, 218, 129n, 219–21, 221–3, 223–4, 225, 231–2
Cleghorn, William, 6
Clerk, Robert, 72, 108, 116n
Cornwallis, Earl of, Charles, 15, 20, 75–6, 116n, 118n, 217
Cullen, Peter John, 66, 113n
Cullen, William, 66, 67, 176–7, 180, 181

Dalrymple, John, 29–30, 73, 118n
Démeunier, Jean Nicholas, 86–7, 120n
Dempster, George, 220
Douglas, James, fourteenth Earl of Morton, 92, 122n
Dundas, Henry, 39, 66, 67, 71–2, 80, 81, 86, 87, 93–4, 6114n, 121n, 125n, 213

243

Dunkirk (1793 siege) 96, 123n, 124n
Dupré, Josais, 14
Durham, James, 72, 117n

East India Company, 7–8, 13–15, 16, 17, 20, 214–17
  East India Company servants, 20
Eden, William, 8, 46, 90, 119n
Eden-Rayneval Commercial Treaty, 8, 46, 81, 82, 119n
Erksine, Charles, 97, 101, 124n
Erksine, William, 5–6, 231–2

Ferdinand III, Grand Duke of Tuscany, 99, 125n
Ferguson, Adam, 3–5
  accommodation arrangements, 100–1, 112, 218
  acquisition by contract, 148
  affairs at death, 222, 225–6
  American Revolution, 4, 22, 28, 32, 36–8, 137–8, 139–72; conduct of British officers, 193; legitimacy of, 159–60, 162; likely outcome, 163–4
  ancient constitution, 157, 170n
  aristocracy, 142, 143
  Bankhead farm, 8, 52, 73, 77, 83, 84, 87–8
  Berlin Academy membership, 11, 98, 124n
  Board of Education (Ferguson's proposed), 111–12
  British constitution, 144, 145–6, 156–7
  British Empire, 7; American colonies, 147, 148, 149–50, 151, 152, 155, 157–8
  commerce, 8, 18, 19, 24, 39, 41–43, 45, 46, 47, 49, 51, 136

commercial society *see* commerce
crown charters, 149, 150–1, 152, 155–6, 162
death, 219–21
democracy, 9, 33, 38, 45, 47, 49–50, 142–3, 149
'Dialogue of Beauty in Imitation of Plato', 222
diet and health, 68, 77, 91, 115n
domestic political unrest, 100
'Dr Ferguson's Opinion [on the French Revolution]', 48–51, 134–6
empire, 32
English Revolution, 149
Essay on the History of Civil Society (1767), 17, 22–3, 26, 30, 49–50
European Union (Ferguson's proposed), 10, 45, 51, 136
family life, 68, 69, 70–1, 79
French Revolution, 8–10, 44–52, 99–100, 104; French Revolutionary Wars, 46–8, 96–7, 98, 99, 102, 104, 105–6, 106–8, 108–9, 109–10, 110–11
'Gentoo' religion, 72
government intervention (economy), 42–4
Grand Tour, 10–12, 95–6, 97–8
heroic poetry, 76
history of mankind, 164–5, 166
History of the Progress and the Termination of the Roman Republic (1783), 22–3, 72, 86–7, 89, 94, 96, 103, 120n, 138, 169n
human nature, 25, 138
India (civil budgets), 88, 89

Institutes of Moral Philosophy (1769), 4, 28, 29, 40, 41, 121n
liberty (civil and political), 27, 32–8, 41, 43, 107–8, 138, 139–50, 155, 156–7, 158–9
liberty (moral), 139, 141
militia, 38–9, 39–40, 105, 106, 107, 111
mixed constitutions, 143, 145–6
moral philosophy (purpose of), 112
moral science, 25–7
natural law, 28–9, 32, 147, 148, 167n
natural rights, 30–2
origin of government, 28–30
party politics, 26–7, 85–6, 93–4, 120n, 135, 146, 153
political authority, 145, 150–1
Principles of Moral and Political Science, Being Chiefly a Retrospect of Lectures Delivered in the College of Edinburgh (1792), 4, 12, 28, 30–1, 34, 35 38, 40, 41, 42, 44, 91, 95, 121n
public debt, 41–2, 48, 161
Remarks on a Pamphlet Lately Published by Dr. Price (1776), 137–72
representation, 33–4, 35, 37, 143–4, 146–7
security *see* liberty (civil and political)
slavery, 31, 32, 33, 35, 37, 139–40, 150, 151
sovereignty, 155–6, 158
stadial history, 29–30
taxation, 142, 149, 152, 153, 156; income tax, 44, 111, 129n

trade with America, 159–60
unintended consequences, 30
voting qualifications, 88–9
Ferguson, Adam and Macpherson, John (friendship), 17–21, 76–7
Efforts to secure Macpherson public favour, 93–4
Ferguson's pedagogical influence on Macpherson, 17–19
Ferguson proffering advice, 68, 70–1, 86, 89, 90, 92
Macpherson gifting money, 74–5, 78
Ferguson, Adam (son), 225–6
Ferguson, John Macpherson, 67, 80, 109, 112, 113, 115n, 218–19
Ferguson, Joseph, 71, 116n
Ferguson, Katharine, née Burnet, 67, 69, 70, 71–2, 81, 85, 87, 102–3
Ferguson, Patrick, 190–209
'Ferguson's Scottish corps', 190, 195
new rifle, 195–7, 206n
Ferguson, Robert, 69, 91–2, 223–4, 225
Forbes, Sir William, 102, 126n
Formey, Johann Heinrich Samuel, 11, 98, 124n
Fox, Charles James, 16, 21, 22, 120n, 122n, 126n

[Gibelin, Jacques,] 94, 120n
Gibbon, Edward, 11, 138
Goddard, Thomas Wyndham, 66, 114
Gordon, Alexander, Duke of, 81, 82, 119n
Grafton, Lord, Augustus FitzRoy, 14, 227

Greville, Charles Francis, 13, 66, 108, 114n
Greville, Francis, Earl of Warwick, 13
Greville, Robert Fulke, 13

Hamilton, Sir William, 67, 114n
Hastings, Warren 7, 14, 15, 214–15
Henri IV (France), 10, 51, 136
[Hertzberg, Ewald Friedrich Graf von], 98, 124n
Hobbes, Thomas, 26, 28, 29, 31, 61n, 168n
Home, John, 3, 10, 11, 16, 21–2, 23, 24, 67, 73, 77, 78–9, 80, 82, 88, 89–90, 92, 96, 102, 115n, 122n, 126n
Horace, 70, 71, 107, 111, 184
Howell, John Zepaniah, 72, 117n
Hume, David, 25, 27, 29, 30, 33, 35, 40–1, 42, 168n, 170n, 183, 190
Hutcheson, Francis, 26, 28–9
Hutton, James, 183–4, 188n

d'Ivernois, François, 48

Jenkins, Thomas, 97, 124n
Johnstone, George, 69, 83–4, 116n
Johnstone, John, 82, 119n
Jones, Sir William, 12, 23–5, 58n, 72, 117n

Lavoisier, Antoine Laurent, 178
Leopold II (Holy Roman Emperor), 9, 16
Locke, John, 25, 28–9, 37, 168n

McDaniel, Iain, 45, 50, 51
[Macdonald, Sir Archibald], 88, 121n

Macleod, Alexander, 66, 91, 95, 114n, 121n
McLeod, Hugh, 95, 123n
Macleod, Roderick, 95, 123n
Macpherson, James, 13, 14, 17, 21, 67, 74, 115n, 227
Macpherson, Sir John, 12–17
  campaign for financial restitution, 17, 79, 81, 93, 112, 119n 129n
  EIC finances (Macpherson's attempted reform), 13–21, 214–15
  EIC officials' peculation, 215–17
  Moderate literati, 21–4
  history of papers, 6–7
  tenure as governor general (Bengal), 8, 15, 16, 18, 19, 46, 56n
  translation of *Correspondance entre un voyageur et un ministre, en octobre, et novembre* (1792), 104, 126n
  speech in parliament (1797), 106–7, 127n
  Supreme Council (EIC), 14–15
Macpherson, Martin, 95, 123n
Mandredini, Marquis Federico, 99, 124n
Marx, Karl, 3, 63n
Merolle, Vincenzo (edition of Ferguson's correspondence), 3, 5, 9, 11, 22, 48, 56n, 64n, 133, 227
Moderate literati, 3–4, 10–11, 21–4
Montesquieu, 19, 26, 35, 37, 138, 140, 142, 173, 175–6
Morison, Colin, 103, 126n
Murray, John, Fourth Duke of Atholl, 80, 119n

Murray, Patrick, fifth Lord
    Elibank, 190, 205n
Myrton, Sir Robert, 92, 122n

Napoleon Bonaparte, 111, 129n
Nawab of Arcot, Muhammad Ali
    Khan, 13–14, 17, 115n
  First Anglo-Mysore War, 14
North, Frederick, Lord (ministry),
    4, 14, 28, 170n, 217
Nugent, Deborah Charlotte, 108,
    128n

Otto, Louis-Guillaume, 111, 129n

Paris, 89
Pigot, George, 14
Plassart, Anna, 45, 50, 51
Poker Club, 174, 188n, 225–6
Pope Pius VI, 99, 101
Pitt the Elder, William, 38
Pitt the Younger, William, 16,
    44, 72, 120n, 126n, 127n,
    129n, 224
[Playfair, John], 221
Plutarch, 103
Pocock, J. G. A., 8
Pollen, George, 107, 127n
Price, Richard, 36–7, 137–8
  *Observations on the Nature of
    Civil Liberty, the Principles
    of Government, and the
    Justice and Policy of the
    War with America* (1776),
    137–72
Prince of Wales, 16, 17, 19, 85,
    113, 120n
Pufendorf, Samuel, 168n, 169n
Pulteney, William Johnstone, 28,
    72, 87, 93, 107–8, 117n

Robertson, Daniel, 222, 225
Robertson, Thomas, 73, 117n
Robertson, William, 3, 13, 23,
    24, 77, 78, 81, 92, 96, 118n
Rockingham Whigs, 22, 151,
    153, 170n
Roman Republic, 138, 148, 150,
    163, 165
Rousseau, Jean-Jacques, 26, 29, 32
Russell, Alexander, 72, 117n
Russell, James, 74, 177, 186n
Russell, John, 72, 117n

Sallust (tag), 107
Shakespeare (allusions), 96, 97
Shelburne, second Earl of,
    William Petty, 172
Sinclair, Sir John, 16
Sloper, Robert, 93, 122n
Smith, Adam, 7, 8, 10, 19, 21–2,
    30, 31, 32, 39–41, 42, 43–4,
    63n, 111, 129n
Smith, Craig, 44
snuff, 109
[Stewart, Andrew], 80, 118n
Stewart, Dugald, 45, 71, 73, 85,
    87, 94, 116n, 231
Stirling, Sir James, 100, 126n
Strabo, 103, 126n
Strahan, William, 72, 116n

Virgil (tags), 79, 83, 200
Voltaire, François-Marie Arouet,
    73, 117n3

Walker, Adam, 99, 125n
Washington, George, 4, 137, 197
'Wilkes and Liberty', 27–8, 45
Wraxall, Sir Nathaniel, 16, 219
Wyvill, Christopher, 35

EU representative:
Easy Access System Europe
Mustamäe tee 50, 10621 Tallinn, Estonia
Gpsr.requests@easproject.com

www.ingramcontent.com/pod-product-compliance
Lightning Source LLC
Chambersburg PA
CBHW070816250426
43671CB00037B/2349